AMERICAN ENTERPRISE
IN
JAPAN

SUNY Series in the Anthropology of Work
June C. Nash, editor

AMERICAN ENTERPRISE

IN

JAPAN

BY TOMOKO HAMADA

Published by
State University of New York Press, Albany

For information, address State University of New York Press,
State University Plaza, Albany, N.Y. 12246

Production by Marilyn Semerad
Marketing by Fran Keneston

Library of Congress Cataloging-in-Publication Data

Hamada, Tomoko.
    American enterprise in Japan / Tomoko Hamada.
        p.   cm. — (SUNY series in the anthropology of work)
    Includes bibliographical references and index.
    ISBN 0-7914-0638-5. — ISBN 0-7914-0639-3 (paper)
        1. Industrial management—Japan.   2. Corporate culture—
Japan.   3. Corporations, American—Japan.   4. Comparative management.
    5. Industrial management—Cross-cultural studies.   I. Title.
    II. Series.
    HD70.J3H233   1991
    338.8'8973052—dc20
                                                                            90-38186
                                                                                CIP

10   9   8   7   6   5   4   3   2

TO MY FAMILY

CONTENTS

ACKNOWLEDGMENTS

This book was made possible by the generous assistance of a great many individuals both in Japan and the United States. My deep gratitude is given to those in Nippon Kaisha and United America, both of which are pseudonyms. Because I promised to keep identities anonymous, I cannot name individual managers or companies to express my gratitude, but without their support, my study would never have been realized.

I am grateful to Professors Chalmers Johnson, Bernard Karsh, June Nash, Roger Sanjek, Hideo Ishida, Akihiko Okumura, and Yoshiyasu Uno, and many others who read part or all of my early drafts and helped me through many sloughs of despondency in early work. I am particularly grateful to my mentors and friends, Professors Nelson Graburn and Jack Potter, for their consistent and continuous support and encouragement. Professor Craig Canning was generous in spending time with me for a detailed editing and critique of my work.

Much of the present manuscript was written while I was Director of Asian Studies at the Rose-Hulman Institute of Technology. I woulk like to thank President Samuel Hulburt, Professors Barbara Ito, Peter Parshall, Bill Picket, and Thad Smith, and others, who helped me sharpen my perspective on cross-cultural communication.

At the final stage of manuscript writing, Professor Stanley R. Mumford made a special contribution to the theoretical development of my work. Rosalie M. Robertson, Marilyn P. Semerad and staff of the State University of New York Press have provided me with outstanding editorial support.

My field work was supported by the Northeast Asia Council of the Association for Asian Studies, the Subvention Fund of the University of California, Berkeley, and the Rose-Hulman Institute of Technology. Additional financial support came from the Faculty Summer Fellowship of the College of William and Mary.

Finally I would like to thank my Japanese parents, who have believed in international education for their daughter, and my American parents, Mr. and Mrs. John F. Hall, who have loved me as if I were their own daughter throughout my training as an anthropologist.

I am also deeply grateful to my loving husband, and my bilingual daughter, Shannon Yumiko, who have always been my source of inspiration for cross-cultural understanding, and to whom this book is dedicated.

LIST OF ILLUSTRATIONS

TABLES

CHAPTER ONE

CULTURAL ENCOUNTERS

INTRODUCTION

This book is about managing cultural differences. Using examples of American direct investments in Japan, I will examine the issue of cross-cultural management from an anthropological perspective in order to demonstrate what an ethnographer can contribute to the field of comparative management studies. It is based upon fieldwork conducted in Japan and the United States between 1977 and 1981, and the summers of 1985, 1986, 1987, and 1988.

I will state major issues concerning foreign direct investment in Japan in this chapter and discuss my ethnographic approach to organizational culture. I will then describe my fieldwork on a United States-Japanese joint-venture company in chapter two. This is the first ethnographic study dealing with the experience of an American firm in Japan, and I would like to describe how I became involved in this study and how I collected the data.

Chapter three will concern the trends of American direct investment in Japan. The discussion on the general trends will provide a macro-view of American direct investment in Japan, illustrating operational problems that American businessmen are likely to encounter in Japan. In addition, a brief history of foreign direct investment will be given in the appendix to provide a more general and historical perspective.

The latter part of the book will focus on case studies. In chapters four and five, I will present case studies of one Japanese company and one U.S.-Japanese joint-venture company. I will describe a Japanese company, Nippon Kaisha, in chapter four. Using fictitious names to protect real persons and organizations, I will describe a Japanese company, Nippon Kaisha, and an American multinational, United America, that joined together to form a 50-50 joint venture (Nippon United Inc.) in Japan in the early 1970s.

Chapter five, the most important part of this book, gives a detailed ethnographic history of Nippon United leading to the manufacture of plastic wrappers at a plant in Kamiyama, Japan, using United America's technology. This account will trace chronologically joint decision making from the early 1970s to the late 1980s. Today the company is financially successful in the fiercely competitive Japanese plastics and resin industry, but the firm has traveled a rocky road to achieve this level of success.

The study of an international joint venture provides an opportunity for a direct and "close-up" comparison in cross-national frameworks. I hope that it is a good way for understanding better one's own culture in relation to that of the "other."

THE ISSUES

One of the fundamental and irreversible changes in American society in recent years is the globalization of its economic activities. The competitiveness of American business in international trade has become a common topic of discussion, and often a source of aggravation, among business leaders and policymakers. Today, foreign investors pour increasing amounts of money into this country. Public sentiment favoring protection against foreign direct investment in the United States has begun to emerge.[1]

Japan has often been the target of American criticism of foreign direct investment because of the general public's perception that the Japanese market is closed while the American market is open. The phenomenon of "Japan bashing" intensified during the late 1980s. Advocacy of using retaliatory measures against Japan carried an almost warlike tone in an article in the *Harvard Business Review:* "To hit the deficit where it hurts us most, we need a target rifle, not a shotgun."[2]

In examining the history of foreign direct investment in Japan as well as the present situation, on the other hand, we will see that: While the Japanese market was definitely closed in the past, it is no longer closed in *legal* terms; many American enterprises are extremely successful in Japan; and, most importantly, success in the Japanese market requires intelligent *cultural* strategies.

Given the fact that Japan is a culturally homogeneous unit with more than 2,000 years of tradition, one would expect American enterprises to encounter some cultural conflicts when they cross the Pacific to conduct business in Japan. On the one side is America, where the basic civic principles are individualism and freedom. On the other is Japan, where the governing principles are the acknowledgement of *bun*, or one's place in a group, filled with duties and obligations to parents, teachers, ancestors, co-workers, and employers. Underneath the modern glittering surface of downtown Tokyo with its skyscrapers, computers, and Western music, Japan is still very much an Asian nation, built on Confucian ethics, thought processes, and institutional arrangements. Japanese have never been, nor will they be, like Americans. That, I think, is often the root of frustration and anger with Japan among the American public. I believe that, by looking closely at interactions between American and Japanese businessmen, we will better recognize our cultural chauvinism, either Japanese or American. With such understanding, we will be able to see our differences not as a source of further conflict but of dynamic cooperation.

During much of modern United States history, American businessmen have moved around the world, investing in overseas ventures, exporting goods made in America, and dealing with host countries' politics. Yet, despite our use of sophisticated economic statistics and financial analyses, we often ignore basic cross-cultural issues such as American businessmen's relationships with their foreign customers, suppliers, associates, governments, and competitors.

More studies are necessary to reveal how the multinationalization of business occurs at the human level and what problems need to be solved in the process. We need to learn more about the "people" side of international business.

Ethnographic case studies, which reveal the process of cultural encounters, might benefit the Japanese. Today, more than ever, the Japanese need to critically reexamine their economic history and future direction as Japan assumes new international roles and responsibilities. During most of the postwar period, the Japanese focused their energy on rebuilding their economy. In this single-minded pursuit of economic goals, social, political, and institutional mechanisms were tailored to create an interlocking web, weaving new features into traditional patterns. These ingredients combined in a highly successful formula for economic prosperity.[3]

The current Japanese institutional arrangements, which seem to have worked well in achieving their economic success in the past, might pose serious difficulties for future globalization. Japan must try to balance policies, which pursue economic internationalism and trend toward free trade and investment, with economic nationalism and policies designed to protect Japan's national self-interests.

Kokusaika, or internationalization, has become a national preoccupation in Japan, and several books have appeared with a strong focus on this issue (c.f. Okimoto 1982; Inoguchi and Okimoto 1989). Not many Japanese realize, however, that kokusaika will compel fundamental changes in their society.[4] Kokusaika implies that the closely knit society of homogeneous population needs to respond to heterogeneous and often conflicting elements from outside. The problem of striking a balance between Japan's new drive for internationalism and her need to maintain internal homeostasis involves a paradigm shift in Japanese value orientation.

This study presents some insights into the issue by focusing on the problems of American enterprises in Japan. It dramatizes the amount of resistance the internal system generates when an alien entity attempts to enter the system. The problem of American direct investment in Japan is at the same time the problem of Japan's globalization.

Because the United States and Japan account for almost half of the free world's production, cultural encounters between two such different systems must be seriously examined.

CULTURAL ENCOUNTERS IN JOINT VENTURES

The joint venture is where two different institutions encounter each other in the most immediate way. A joint venture is a company where each of two or more firms has a nonmarginal equity position and where at least two parties in some way share the responsibility for managing the joint venture company. In the present study, the joint venture is 50-50, meaning that the two parent companies equally contribute the capital, and that they jointly manage the joint-venture company.

Firms form joint ventures for various reasons: better economy through larger scale of operations and risk spreading through sharing of technological, commercial, or financial risk are frequently mentioned. Multinationals enter into joint ventures principally for the following reasons: (1) need for local marketing know-how; (2) need to expand an integrated structure; and (3) need for resources (capital, etc.); (4) need for technological cooperation in research and development; and (5) need to circumvent economic nationalism of host countries (Shishido 1986). The parent firm could spread the risk by sharing the ownership of the joint venture.

In Japan until the liberalization of foreign direct investment in the 1970s, the joint venture was often the only form of entry into Japan for many American firms. Until the early 1970s, most direct investments were subject to the approval of the Japanese government, which discouraged 100 percent foreign ownership. In addition, because foreign companies typically found it difficult to operate in Japan, many preferred to form parternships with Japanese firms even when they had the option of forming a wholly owned subsidiary.

A joint venture, as a system, however, contains possibilities for schism, because it is by definition not under the control of a single management. Board directors of a joint venture represent the business interests of their respective parents. Joint ventures, if not managed properly, can exhibit many pathological symptoms.

In international joint ventures, two or more companies of different national origins commit people and resources to an organization, which will be influenced by the parent firms' corporate cultures, operational systems, communication processes, and power structures. The degree of their cultural differences affects the degree of conflict possibility. Thus, the international joint venture is the place where cultural collisions can be most vividly presented and analyzed.

Management scientists have begun to appreciate the case

study method in order to understand international business activities in different cultures under different ownership conditions. Many past studies on Japanese decision-making processes focused on the methods and styles, such as the analysis of the group decision making called *ringi* (c.f. Yoshino 1968; and Hazama 1973) and the studies of communication flows within the organization (c.f. Johnson and Ouchi 1974; Azumi et al. 1976; and Pascale 1978). Previous studies rarely discussed the content of decision making.

To American business negotiators, it is not very important what decision-making style the Japanese use; but it is crucial whether the Japanese agree with the American side. Difficulties in joint-venture operations arise when what the Japanese see as desirable differs from their partner's view.

This is where culture comes in to play: We need to recognize a fundamental fact that people cannot act or interact at all in any meaningful way except through the medium of culture. Lett suggests that this point is overlooked by most other social scientists, including psychologists, sociologists, and economists, "who uncritically base their investigations upon the foundations of their own cultural assumptions." (Lett 1987:59)

In contrast, anthropologists cannot avoid referring to the concept of culture when explaining the human condition. Culture may be defined as the learned, shared, interrelated, and symbol-mediated patterns of behavior, attitudes, and beliefs that are dynamically adaptive and that depend on human communication for their existence. This study takes a behavior-oriented approach to culture, although culture can include artifacts, objects, and products of symbolic human interactions.

An organizational culture with its shared assumptions enables its members to perceive, interpret, and evaluate events, people, and phenomena. Unless we understand the underlying system of meanings, we can not act effectively. In cross-cultural decision making, cultural strategies are needed to understand the basic objectives, management philosophy, value orientation, and communication codes that guide the other side's behavior. My ethnographic study is intended to address this area of inquiry, by bringing in "meanings" to corporate culture studies.

ETHNOGRAPHICAL APPROACH TO CORPORATE CULTURE

This is the first study directly dealing with the issue of acculturation of American firms in Japan.[5] An ethnographic history will examine in detail the company's adaptive strategies in a new environment and its organizational development. Such studies necessarily take many years, but studies with a historical perspective will help us understand complexities and intricacies of cross-cultural management. They will add a deeper knowledge to macro-level quantitative analyses.

For readers who are not familiar with anthropological methodology, I would like to explain how I approach industrial ethnography, and, more specifically, organizational culture.[6] My methods follow four governing principles of industrial ethnography: 1) participant observation; 2) emphasis upon cultural process; 3) cultural interpretation; and 4) comparative framework.

The first methodological principle requires that the investigator gains an intimate firsthand and direct familiarity with his or her subjects. An ethnographer should not be an observer outside the system of concern. He or she attempts to understand the inner workings of the office by an intensive process of observing the people over a long period of time and participating in their activities.

Anthropology attempts to explain social phenomena by placing them in local frames of awareness. Interpretative anthropology has always had a keen sense of the dependence of what is seen upon where it is seen from and what it is seen with (Geertz 1983:4).

My anthropological camera is set up within the organization, to take a feature film, not photography. I hope that the methodological advantage of operating an "internal movie camera" will become salient when you compare chapter four (The Japanese Company: Nippon Kaisha) and chapter five (The Joint-venture Company: Nippon United).

When I describe Nippon Kaisha in chapter four, I use the traditional "organizational behavior" approach based upon interviews, questionnaires, and written reports. Although I had access to key documents, and I conducted a number of open-ended interviews with Nippon Kaisha people, I was not directly in-

volved in the corporate operation of Nippon Kaisha. I was an outsider attempting to take many snapshots of organizational activities at different events. More of an ideal rather than actuality
seemed to be realized in this situation. Nippon Kaisha people
tended to tell their *tatemae* (formal side) of the organization. It was
more difficult to reach their *honne*, or true feelings, because I
could not participate in the internal organizational processes to
verify their views.

In the subsequent chapter on the joint venture, on the other
hand, I moved my anthropological lens inside the organization. I
was directly involved in the decision-making process of the joint-
venture company as an interpreter. I observed the actual operation of the company, recorded the process of organizational
adjustment, and noticed the people's sense of conflict and accommodation, which might not conform to an ideal. I hope that this
research method is effective in the sense that I could get behind
the façade of the organization to investigate the very real process
of managing a company.

Secondly, my research emphasizes cultural context. Nothing
has meaning except as seen in some context at a particular historical moment. Culture provides a context within which social
events, behavior, and institutions can be intelligibly described by
organizational members. This fact has been often ignored by organization researchers.

I view corporate culture as an 'unfinished' process of dialogue
between different social groups. In the joint-venture company
examined in this book, competing managerial ideologies, values,
and norms attempt to understand, digest, or sometimes even de-
vour, those of the others. It is a story of a meeting between two
contending consciousnesses. It is a story of the self versus the
others.

Today, we are constantly facing the other cultures in our existence. We realize more than ever that no culture is completely isolated or self-contained. Cultural meanings within a nation, a
group, or a person often become visible and significant in their
relationships to alternatives presented by others. Social phenomena, which include economic arrangements, become "real" to
the organizational members only through such cultural signification.

By replicating the voices of Japanese and American managers
in this book, I hope to penetrate the cultural deafness of many

past organizational studies. I take the view that organization can be analyzed from a comparative, relativistic, and historical angle, rather than from the steely monologue of scientific rationalism, economic reductionism, or Weberian positivism, which have their ideological roots in Western social sciences. The complexity of human life in an organization is, in my view, composed of "dialogues between partial truths" (Mumford 1990:11). My work is "a cry for breaking out of the information system/logical-positivist/quasi-experimental mold that has placed a mental and emotional straight jacket on organization theory and theorists for too many years" (Ott 1989:ix).

An international joint venture offers a good illustration for explicating this standpoint: To see ourselves as others see us can be eye-opening. To have our fundamental beliefs challenged or belittled is excruciating. To appreciate the others' views is the beginning of a cultural dialogue. But can we also see us among the others? Can we also see our chauvinism inside their chauvinism?

Thirdly, my inquiry is interpretive. Interpretive research would lead informants to describe the content and meaning of events in order to construct a sense of order in their organizational lives. As such stories are told, they often become internally persuasive to the storyteller.

An industrial ethnographer encounters numerous small events during his or her fieldwork. Among various events happening every day in an organization, only certain events are selected by organizational members as memorable, and stories begin to emerge. They are told, retold, modified, and reinvented. Only some stories of memorable events are recorded as texts.

An industrial ethnographer is interested in the dynamics of signification of events by organizational members in their constantly shifting relationships with the others. While historians may start their investigation by opening a recorded text, anthropologists create their own documents. Anthropologists are interested in the process of "texting": How and why a social group selects particular events as being worth remembering; how they narrate stories of their past; how they try to fit their past into their present world-view; and how they invent and reinvent their tradition in this creative process.

As we pass through history, we learn new ways of doing things and incorporate them into our cognitive and behavioral patterns. We constantly reinvent tradition in our manipulation of the past.[7]

An organization is full of half-told stories, remnants of past images, and traces of hidden paths that could have been taken if given the chance. These hidden memories may reemerge as historical consciousness at some future events, and may be written as text, perhaps as a metaphor to interpret newer events.

Unfortunately many social scientists are still blind to this notion of cultural dynamics and view it only as a frozen echo of past. It is vital for us to understand that organizational culture is not a dead object like an entity placed in a museum. Rather, culture is an ongoing dynamic process to create and re-create the meanings of social phenomena. Cultural communication is inherently emergent, with an ongoing dialogue over time between older and newer layers of tradition.

Last in my list of research methodology is an anthropological emphasis upon comparative framework. Concerning the principle of cross-cultural comparison, Dore's monumental work (1973) and the ethnographic works by Rohlen (1974) and Clark (1979) formed the foundation and inspiration for the present case study.

As an applied anthropological work, my study attempts to focus on a dynamic encounter of corporate cultures: what happens when one management system tries to cope with another system built upon a different managerial culture? What will happen in the process in order to create a cross-cultural synergy?

Only a few books have appeared discussing cross-cultural dimensions of managerial decisions in this respect: According to Adler, fewer than one-fifth (18.6 percent) of all cross-cultural management research articles have focused on interaction, in spite of the fact that when people from various cultures interact, the differences among them become salient.[8] Furthermore, the greater the cultural differences, the greater is the likelihood that barriers to communication will arise and that misunderstandings will occur.[9]

Graham (1984) showed that Japanese and American business people modify their "within culture styles" of behavior when engaged in intercultural negotiation. Yoshino discussed possible problems for Japanese enterprises in becoming multinational due to their particular organizational features (Yoshino 1976). White and Trevor (1985) surveyed six Japanese subsidiaries in England and analyzed the Japanese companies' cross-cultural adaptation, using questionnaires and interview techniques. They contended that further longitudinal investigations will be necessary to establish patterns of Japanese adaptation to the English soil.

Instead of listing differences and similarities of the two systems, I analyze a more intimate level of comparison in corporate cultures by observing the interactions between the two systems in an international setting. This approach will give this book something beyond what is found in earlier ethnographic studies of Japanese management.

CHAPTER TWO

WORKING IN JAPAN

INTRODUCTION

In most social science literature, the author is invisible to the reader. A glimpse of the author's life may be obtained in a short paragraph about his or her career and publication records, but usually no description is given as to what kind of individual the researcher is, and why he or she wanted to write the book.

This chapter is about this anthropologist and her fieldwork. One management scientist who kindly read a draft of this book has told me that I should not discuss myself in the text because it is irrelevant. The underlying theorem for the author's absence from the text in social sciences is that the researcher should be a person with an objective eye, aloof from the "reality" that he or she is observing.

On the other hand, as an interpretive anthropologist engaged in participant observation, I became acutely aware of my presence within the data. Every field note I write reminds me so vividly of where and how I took part in events with informants. This realization establishes a fundamental departure of interpretive anthropology from the premise for detached objectivity in other social sciences.

The recipient of anthropological inquiry is Man, or more precisely, the other men and women. While talking, eating, working, and sharing emotions with others, the anthropologist constantly uses his or her own self as a research tool. In the process of both external dialogue and internal dialogue our self identity vis-a-vis the "natives" emerges. The nature of anthropological fieldwork demands that the researcher takes his or her cultural orientation seriously when facing others.

I have mentioned in the previous chapter that anthropology has always had a keen sense of the dependence of what is seen upon where it is seen from and what it is seen with. Anthropology is also aware of the dependence of what is seen upon whom it is seen by.

In this study I used my personality, sensitivity, and intellectual capability to collect, interpret, and analyze data about other people. I was part of human interactions within the organization I was studying.

I believe that it is important for the reader to know this researcher's cultural bias, value orientation, and personal background. I would like to describe how I, as an individual, came to take up this study.

BETWEEN TWO CULTURES

Having been raised in the Tokyo area for nineteen years, I went to Vassar College, New York in 1969 as a transfer student from Keio University, Tokyo, Japan. The college at that time was experiencing an explosive student movement, and I was immediately thrown into hot debates over the 1960s civil rights movement, the Vietnam war, and the women's liberalization movement. There I encountered and overcame many cultural problems, which a non-Western foreign student from a conservative family background would be likely to face. After receiving a B.A. degree from Vassar College in American studies, I went back to Tokyo in 1971. In Tokyo I had to go through a different kind of cultural shock in order to readjust myself to my "primary culture."

Between 1971 and 1975, when I received a master's degree in sociology from Keio University, I worked as an interpreter in order to make my living. During this time, I met and interpreted for many American businessmen, journalists, union leaders, and politicians, who came to Japan to establish ties with Japanese people. Nippon Kaisha was one of many companies that hired me as an interpreter for their business negotiations during that time.[1]

In the course of my work experience in business negotiations, I became acquainted with Japanese and American executives, who often expressed their sense of frustration in attempting to understand the other side's viewpoints.

When I was working as a freelance interpreter, I usually received a call from an interpretation company's desk at the then Tokyo Hilton Hotel in Akasaka, downtown Tokyo district. They asked me to meet a client, usually, at a hotel lobby.

I often observed a sense of relief on the faces of my clients when they found that I spoke intelligible English and that I had some experience in business negotiations with Japanese. English signs are common on Tokyo streets today, but in the 1970s, public signs for most basic necessities were all in Japanese.

My first task usually was to arrange business appointments for my foreign clients and have their business name-cards printed in the Japanese language.[2] We usually took a taxi to the headquarters of the Japanese company where negotiations were held. As the Tokyo cab zipped through winding, back streets of Tokyo to avoid a traffic jam, narrowly missing cyclists and pedestrians on the way, the American businessmen and I would sway from left to right while talking about the meeting we would soon have with the Japanese. We would talk about individual businessmen and departments concerned. For an interpreter, there was much to learn about the firm's background and business, not to mention technical terms and product features.

CROSS-CULTURAL COMMUNICATION IN BUSINESS

On each interpretation assignment, I worked for one or two American visitors, but when we arrived at the headquarters of the Japanese company, we normally encountered five to eight Japanese in our meeting. The Japanese, mostly dressed in gray or blue business suits, would bow and shake hands with my clients and would lead us to a meeting room.

In the corporate meeting room, Americans and Japanese would often sit facing each other at a rectangular-shaped table, on which stood miniature American and Japanese flags as a symbol of friendship and cooperation.

A meeting with consecutive interpretation required twice as much time, because every sentence had to be repeated in the other language. Although many Japanese managers today understand English, they still prefer interpretation, partly for confirmation and partly for allowing them time to read the situation more closely.

While I was translating their words into Japanese, my American clients would survey the faces of the Japanese participants in their efforts to read their reaction, look into space, sometimes smile, cross their legs, or glance at the ceiling. When I was translating into English, my American clients would look at me, take notes, or occasionally glance at the Japanese, while the Japanese participants would look into space between them, nod repeatedly, sometimes cross arms in front, or simply sit still.

Very often, a "spokesman" for the entire Japanese group was prearranged, and a middle-level Japanese manager who assumed that kind of role did most of the talking. They sometimes had two spokesmen, one whose role was conciliatory and another who adopted a more aggressive or critical stance toward the American proposal. While these middle-level managers/spokesmen talked in Japanese, they nevertheless often glanced at senior Japanese participants for confirmation and assurance.

Meetings sometimes lasted a full day. We had lunch with top executives in an executive meeting room or in a private room at a nearby restaurant. If the luncheon was held at a corporate dining room, the Japanese would prearrange the seating, according to the corporate hierarchy of status.

In the corporate dining room of a Japanese company, one's seat assignment tells a lot about one's status, both formally and informally. In a traditional Japanese-style room, the most senior person always sits in front of the *tokonoma,* or an alcove where an ornamental hanging and *ikebana* flowers are placed. The lower one's status, the further away from the alcove, and closer to the exit door the person sits.

There is no *tokonoma* in a corporate dining room, but there is a carry-over of this tradition. The most senior person sits furthest from the exit door. The guest is considered as the most senior person, so my American clients would sit there. Usually the guests were seated facing the most senior Japanese executives.

Because I was their interpreter, I would sit next to the Americans, in spite of the fact that I was junior (in age, gender, and other social status).

When everyone was seated, the Japanese president or a Japanese senior executive would stand up, bow slightly, and give a formal speech of welcome, stressing his hope for a long and trustful friendship between the two firms. Then it was time for the American to give a speech. This was the moment when the interpreter became a little tense, because some Americans liked to crack a joke, one of the most difficult things to interpret.

Around this time, they would also toast for the success of the negotiation, standing up, and lifting the glass, saying *"kanpai"* (bottoms up!)[3]. Japanese businessmen still like to drink beer, but increasingly we see wine being served at such a luncheon.

Unlike a typical American business luncheon, not only dishes, but also drinks often would be determined in advance. You eat and drink what you are served. Nobody asks about one's preference for salad dressing, or for tea or coffee, for example.

Once one of my American clients asked for decaffeinated coffee at such a business luncheon. It created a commotion among Japanese, and finally acute embarrassment, because the Japanese dining room did not have decaffeinated coffee. In this instance, my American client did not realize the consequence of his "simple request." In Japan, the host is supposed to prepare everything for the guest so that everything is the way the guest would enjoy. Revealing the fact that they did not have decaffeinated coffee for the important American guest was the equivalent of pointing out the host's lack of attentiveness.

When Japanese businessmen took us to a nearby restaurant, it was not uncommon for all Japanese participants to follow the lead of the most senior person (i.e. the guest) in ordering dishes. My American client—who was asked by the Japanese "what will you have?"—often did not realize that his choice might have serious consequences for others. This responsibility could have been avoided if he had returned the same question to the Japanese host and had managed to be the last to choose. Likewise, when asked "what would you like to drink?" American businessmen should understand the possible consequence of their reply.

After lunch we would resume our negotiation, often in an improved, more amicable mood, if the lunch was successful. The

Japanese would not hesitate to ask very detailed, technical questions, on a certain specification of a product, for example.

They might ask the same questions twice for clarification and call in additional staff if their expertise was required to assess the situation. It was not unusual to have more than ten Japanese attending the meeting at the end, while the American side consisted of one American and myself.

In general, business meetings with the Japanese were conducted in a very polite and formal manner, following a certain protocol. There were times, however, when I interpreted very difficult negotiations, where both sides could not reach agreement. In such a meeting, the Japanese would sometimes start talking among themselves in the Japanese language, ignoring the fact that the American could not understand the language. They would even ask if they (the Japanese) could leave the room to consult among themselves. However, I have never seen Japanese businessmen curse, swear, or use derogatory words at business meetings. They usually behave as gentlemen, even when they are upset.

On giving negative personal feedback in communication, a Japanese might suck air through closed teeth, creating a hissing sound, tilt his head sideways, frown, or grunt. In giving a definite "no," he would shake his head and use some variation of *"komarimashita-nee"* (We are having a difficulty), followed by sucking air through closed teeth. Then he might sink deeply into his chair, crossing arms in front, saying nothing.

Japanese may not say "no" verbally like Americans, but behavioral variations on "no" are many in the Japanese code of communication. Such Japanese communication behaviors must be interpreted in the total context of conversation, beyond a simple Japanese-English translation.

For example, when the speaker says *"hai"* (yes) to your proposal but then gives a long explanation on how difficult it is, you should be aware that he is de facto saying "no." Or he may suddenly become vague, evasive, ambiguous, and does not clearly answer your question. The Japanese speaker may also use some variation of "I will consider it" as an escape hatch to save "face" on both sides.

Another common contextual signs for "no" are that the speaker abruptly changes the subject, that he suddenly assumes a highly apologetic tone, or that he starts criticizing someone who has little direct relevance to your present case. For example, when talking about the importation of an American product into Japan, a Japanese businessman might suddenly start criticizing Australian trade policies and their export practices. It is not wise to take Japanese "yes" or "no" by itself for an answer. American businessmen need to be sensitive to subtle word plays and games of tacit communication among actors, in order to read "between the lines."

In a rare occasion when the Japanese felt extremely aggressive in giving negative feedbacks, he may make sarcastic comments about the proposal, followed by a sudden laughter. It is not uncommon for Japanese to break into short laughter in order to break an uneasy atmosphere.

I also observed that Japanese businessmen, in general, asked many questions on factual data and kept good records of the meetings, which were distributed to a larger number of organizational members later.

Meetings with Japanese almost always started on time. If the meeting turned out to be successful, however, it could extend long beyond the scheduled time, sometimes for a few more hours, and often with an on-the-spot invitation for dinner afterwards.

At the end of the day's meeting, my American clients shook hands with every Japanese participant and picked up their brief cases now full of documents, reports, and forms related to the negotiation, both in Japanese and English. All the Japanese participants would go out to the elevator hall to bid farewell.

When we went back to the hotel, I would often sit with my clients to discuss and "interpret" what had happened that day. This was when the Americans asked intriguing questions as to the hidden meanings of certain Japanese behavior they had observed: Why did so many Japanese attend the meeting? What do they mean by saying that they will consider the proposal? Why didn't the president talk at all during the meeting? What was the role of a certain participant of the meeting?

Americans who were pressed for time and who had to go home without a firm reply from the Japanese were irritated by the slowness of Japanese decision making. Most American businessmen I met commented that it required far more patience and personal sensitivity to negotiate with the Japanese. Negotiations through an interpreter are difficult because many nonverbal communication clues can be lost in interpretation and because one does not share codes of communication.

In addition to the verbal aspects of cross-cultural communication I have discussed so far, I became aware of the fact that American clients often failed to notice or understand Japanese nonverbal signals such as the lack of eye contact, prolonged silence, smiles, or nodding. For instance, to a native Japanese, the lack of eye contact does not mean lack of confidence but rather a show of respect to the speaker. Prolonged silence in the middle of conversation is natural and common in Japanese conversation, but Americans usually tried to break such silence. Americans tended to talk a lot, forcing the Japanese to listen.

In Japanese communication, the use of nodding or *aizuchi* is much more frequent than in English.[4] Not using *aizuchi* implies that you are not listening carefully to the speaker. I observed that a Japanese speaker became increasingly nervous when his American listeners looked straight at him without nodding. The Americans were simply attentive to the Japanese speaker, who nevertheless took it as an expression of challenge to his statement.

On other occasions, Japanese negotiators smiled because they were embarrassed or felt uncomfortable. My American clients interpreted it as the sign of a positive attitude towards the issue at hand and became confused.

FIELDWORK: NIPPON KAISHA

I became increasingly interested in the problems of international communication, especially cultural conflicts between different management entities. I contacted top Japanese executives whom I had worked for, expressing my wish to investigate their organizations in contrast to American firms and to analyze their joint-venture operations with American firms.

Nippon Kaisha responded favorably to the proposed study. I visited Japan three times during the late 1970s to prepare myself for the fieldwork.

On one mid-July morning, through the introduction of the top management, I met a 55-year-old personnel director of Nippon

Kaisha, Mr. Yamashita, at the headquarters of Nippon Kaisha. Mr. Yamashita had a well-tanned face set off by a shock of black hair with silvery streaks. I later found out that his hobby was golf, a popular sport among Japanese executives. He was dressed handsomely in a well-tailored blue suit with thin white stripes. On his lapel shone a round emblem of Nippon Kaisha.

After a Nippon Kaisha receptionist announced my arrival at the Department of Personnel, Mr. Yamashita got up from his desk and said that we could talk in a conference room. He led me to a meeting room, located at a corner of a large open office. As Mr. Yamashita and I walked past the desks of personnel staff, some staff members gave a quick glance at me before turning their eyes back to their work. Everyone in the department could see Mr. Yamashita and me enter the glass-screened meeting room.

Once in the room, we first exchanged name cards, following the Japanese custom. "*Kōyū mono-desu, dōzo yoroshiku onegai-itashimasu* (I have this type of background. I humbly ask your favor, if you please. I trust it to your discretion)." I bowed deeply, knowing the age and status differences between the two of us and the formality of the occasion.

On the name card, Mr. Yamashita noticed my affiliation with the University of California. He said that he had been to the United States twice on business trips; he liked San Francisco. I took out a box of Japanese rice crackers to present to him. It was a small token of my respect for Mr. Yamashita, many years my senior.

The summer gift-giving season called *o-chūgen* had started. In Japan, there are two seasons for gift giving, one in summer (*o-chūgen*) and one in winter (*o-seibo*). Bonuses are paid in these traditional gift-giving seasons.[5] During these periods, those who are in a lower status send gifts to persons of senior or superior status. Banks and firms send gifts to their clients and business associates. The idea is that everyone thanks someone from whom special service or favor has been received, thus returning *on* or one's sense of indebtness to the person.

Mr. Yamashita smiled and said that I should not have worried about such a matter. He kindly accepted my gift and put it aside because in a formal occasion of gift giving a traditional Japanese does not open a gift immediately.

We started talking about my background and my intended research. We found out that both of us had attended the same Japanese university, Keio. Mr. Yamashita was an economics major. I told him that my elder brother was also an economics major at Keio. "So you are part of the Keio family," he said. It broke the ice, as we talked about Keio professors, campus life, and the recent Keio University-Waseda University baseball game.

Psychologically I moved into a position under his patronage in the *senpai-kōhai* (senior-junior) relations of the school clique. He told me that Nippon Kaisha has a large Keio-*batsu* (Keio university clique). "But there are many Waseda men here, too." he added. Waseda University is another prestigious private university, considered as a traditional rival of Keio.

At that time, a young woman dressed in a beige-colored Nippon Kaisha company uniform brought two cups of Japanese green tea. Although he invited me to drink the tea, because it is a custom to follow the lead of the senior in eating and drinking, I waited until he lifted his cup and started drinking.

We continued our general conversation. He asked about my father's occupation, my family, and my life in general. As I had expected, no specific question about my research paper came up. I knew that once I passed the initial screening by Mr. Yamashita, someone junior to him would handle that matter. Mr. Yamashita's role was to evaluate me as a total person — my personality, general intelligence, and quality as a human being.

At the end of the meeting, Mr. Yamashita said that he would extend his personal cooperation to assist my research, and said, "*Dōzo ganbatte kudasai* (Please work hard at it)." I bowed deeply, thanked him, and left the office.

I stepped out of the Nippon Kaisha building, into the noise of the metropolis's midday traffic, and the hot, humid air of the approaching summer. Streams of people were moving towards a railway station, which accommodates about two million commuters a day.

People were also coming out of office buildings for lunch breaks. Men were all well-dressed, tidy, and affluent-looking. Some young women who passed by me were dressed in the latest European fashion, carrying imported handbags. As I started to walk toward the station, I looked up at the patch of blue sky carved out by glassy skyscrapers high above our heads. The Nippon Kaisha building was one of them, rising high into the sky. Business Nippon was in full swing in this energetic metropolis of twelve million people.

Mr. Yamashita later helped me obtain access to many top managers and was extremely helpful throughout my fieldwork in Japan. I interviewed him about his life history and about his views on personnel management of Nippon Kaisha. Later I visited him at his home and met his wife and children. It meant a lot to me because the Japanese invite only close friends and relatives to their homes. The Japanese businessmen usually entertain guests at a restaurant, bar, or club. In Japanese society, an invitation to one's home means that one has finally achieved the status of an insider.

Mr. Yamashita and another senior manager who had been working for the joint venture since the beginning became the most valuable informants and advisors in my Japanese fieldwork.

FIELDWORK: UNITED AMERICA

While I was trying to establish rapport with the Japanese company, I wrote to the chairman of United America Inc. for whom I had worked on several of his visits to Japan.

Mr. Lang was a handsome, six-foot-tall man of European descent. He had a wide forehead with silvery hair and was always dressed in a three-piece suit. Because of his height and mannerism, this sixty-year-old executive had an impressive statesmanlike presence.

He also had a flair for oratory. He would come up with an inspiring speech to stir people's imagination, based on a short briefing and executive summary of the situation. He was well liked by many of my American informants, who said that Mr. Lang was good at creating a vision to motivate people.

I interpreted for Mr. Lang on his one-week trip to Asia by the company jet. Mr. Lang told me that he was the first non-WASP (white, Anglo-Saxon, Protestant), ever to assume presidency of United America Inc. "United America was a very conservative firm when I entered as a chemical engineer. Now it's changed. I believe that United America is open to everybody."

Mr. Lang had been very active in expanding the company's

businesses in the Pacific Rim. Diversification and internationalization were two sides of his management philosophy. He told me that he was determined to make United America a major player in Asia.

I sent a personal letter to Mr. Lang about my intended research, and he granted me permission without any difficulty. Mr. Lang suggested that I should meet the new area president of Asia, Mr. O'Leary, on his next business trip to Japan. I knew his predecessor, Mr. Franklin, well, but he took Mr. O'Leary's old job and moved to the European Division recently. In exchange, Mr. O'Leary became new Asia Division president.

I wrote to Mr. O'Leary about my research. He wrote back to me, granting permission. He also suggested that I should look into another joint venture that United America had had in Japan, Yamato-United, because they had "more cross-cultural communication problems." Yamato-United had been in operation for four years, but they had not produced operational income yet. The chairman of Yamato Kaisha was a gentleman in his late seventies. He had just stepped aside to give the presidency to his long-term *migiude* ("right arm") man. Through the assistance of United America managers, I met Mr. Matsukawa, ex-sales manager of Yamato-United.

When I explained my research objective, his initial response was rather negative. Mr. Matsukawa said that Yamato Kaisha was very conservative and would not like such research. He doubted that I would have much success in obtaining permission.

Nevertheless, I tried to contact various levels of Yamato people through personal connections and through United America's connections. I even used an introduction from the president of an industrial association of which the president of Yamato was an important member. However, such a top-down approach backfired on me. Yamato's responses were all negative, and after three months I had to give up the inquiry because I received a letter from the president of Yamato Kaisha, who formally refused my request. The letter warned that I should not disclose any sensitive information on the joint venture that I might have gained through my past interpretation work.

I wrote to Mr. O'Leary about the outcome of my efforts. Mr. O'Leary wrote back to me: "I am sorry that the Yamato organization did not grant you permission to conduct your research since I think the Yamato group is more old line Japanese than the Nippon group, and an investigation of Yamato-United would have revealed significant cultural and philosophical differences which may not exist in the Nippon-United relationship."

Shortly after this incident, on an October afternoon, I went to Hotel Okura to meet Mr. O'Leary. He stopped in Tokyo for a few days on his way from New York to Singapore. Mr. O'Leary, a big 47-year-old Irish American with a broad smile, had been involved in the chemical field within United America for fourteen years. His previous assignment was in Europe, and he had traveled extensively in Asia. Mr. O'Leary would travel out of the United States for at least one week every month. He said that people were the key to business success, and that it was important to keep in constant touch with his operators in the field. Mr. O'Leary said that I might want to expand my study to include some joint ventures that had been unsuccessful.

He knew a great deal about unsuccessful joint ventures and cited the recent breakup of Kraft-Morinaga, in which Kraft's loss amounted to almost $10 million. Mr. O'Leary said that many American companies felt frustrated by both regulatory and non-regulatory barriers in Japan and were annoyed by the closed nature of the Japanese market. Throughout my research Mr. O'Leary performed an advisory function and gave me many insightful comments on American businessmen's viewpoints.

After I talked with Mr. O'Leary, I visited the office of United America in Japan to discuss my work with Mr. Martin, vice president for Asia and general manager of the Japan operation. Mr. Martin had worked for Mr. Franklin before the personnel change, and currently he worked under Mr. O'Leary. These three men became my key informants on the United America side.

United America had just moved its office to a prestigious downtown Tokyo address. United America shared a ten-story white marble building with several other companies, most of which were European-based firms. The elevator stopped at the floor of United America, the door opened, and one would step onto thick-piled soft-colored carpet filling a spacious entry hall. (Spaciousness is a luxury in Tokyo). Beyond the hall was a glass French door with a United America logo in golden inscription; a receptionist sat at an Italian-designed modern desk.

Mr. Martin's office had wide windows on two sides overlooking streets below. The windows were covered with *shoji* (Japanese paper screen) to soften the sunlight. Oriental *objets d'art* adorned a shelf. Underneath was a mini-wet bar, and a small refrigerator. The office had an elegant and rich ambiance, quite a contrast to the functional utilitarianism of the Nippon Kaisha offices.

Mr. Martin was a quiet man in his early fifties with a gentlemanly manner. He had worked his way up the corporate ladder, first through the machinery division and then through the international division. Starting out his career as an accountant, Mr. Martin had a wide range of experience in everything from production analysis to sales and labor negotiation. His previous assignment was in the international sales of machinery, involving extensive overseas trips.

Under Mr. Martin was a Japanese vice president, Mr. Ōbayashi, another Keio graduate. Mr. Ōbayashi started his career in a large Japanese trading company, just when Japan's export economy began to accelerate. While still in his thirties, he was transferred to a branch office in Los Angeles. This was where he met Mr. Martin for the first time.

They worked together on the sale of certain United America machinery to a Japanese manufacturer. Later, United America recruited him to start their Japan operation. Mr. Ōbayashi had five years of residency in the United States.

Mr. Ōbayashi, now in his early forties, represented a new and increasingly common type of internationalized Japanese businessmen. He was very outspoken (unusual for a middle-aged Japanese businessman) and did not hesitate to make straightforward remarks. He said that he had some enemies in Japanese society because they consider him "arrogant." He was also concerned about maintaining a high-level urban lifestyle, as well as his individualism in his relations with the company. After several years working as a vice president, Mr. Ōbayashi left United America's Japan office because he was recruited by another joint-venture company in Japan to head their operation. After three years working there as president, Mr. Ōbayashi again moved to a larger foreign-related company.

While conducting my field research, I interviewed all the managers, both Japanese and American, who were involved in the joint venture. I went to the Nippon United factory and Nippon

Kaisha's factories, observed their plant operations, and talked with foremen and workers.

Mr. Yamashita of Nippon Kaisha arranged for me to attend Nippon Kaisha's seminars for managers. I visited Nippon Kaisha's three-story seminar house in a suburb of Tokyo, where *kachō* (section chief) from different departments attended the annual human resource development seminar. I sat at a corner of the seminar room as *kachō-san* listened to lectures, and talked about quality control, new recruits, production methods, and computer applications. They knew each other and the atmosphere was open and relaxed. I was struck by the fact that *kachō-san* talked very freely with senior executives, sometimes openly criticizing the company's policies. For five days, I ate lunches and dinners with them in the seminar house dining room and stayed in a Japanese room at night. In the evening, I chatted with *kachō-san* about their families and hobbies.

When I visited the United States, I interviewed all the managers in the International Division. Unlike Nippon Kaisha, every American manager had his own office. A 45-year-old marketing manager in charge of Asian operations for United America International, Mr. Seymour, talked extensively about how he had tried to teach the Japanese basic concepts of marketing, such as how to establish direct communication with end-users of the product. He thought that the Japanese distribution network was archaic, and that television commercials in Japan were too vague and often lacked specific messages, although the artistic quality of commercials was superb.

By the time I met Mr. Seymour, he had already been transferred from Asia to the Europe Division, due to the personnel changes at a higher level, involving Mr. O'Leary and Mr. Franklin. Mr. Seymour said that it was a new challenge for him to deal with Europeans.

A few years later, while I was in Japan, I was surprised to learn that Mr. Seymour was fired due to the poor profit results of his European operation. Mr. Seymour had been working for the company for twelve years. I contacted Mr. Seymour, but he did not want to discuss the issue at all.

I had an extensive interview with United America's lawyers who had been involved in developing the joint-venture contract and technical agreement. I conducted open-ended interviews with financial managers, sales managers of different product lines, and the personnel manager of the International Division.

Overall, the American managers were open and frank with me. I had a clearly negative response on only one occasion, from an individual who asked about my motives and wanted to tape the conversation for his record. He was concerned about how I would use the findings of his interview. I explained that the purpose of my interview was to understand cross-cultural decision making and that no real name would be used so that individual sources of information would be protected. His attitude throughout the interview was that of suspicion, and I could not get much data out of this particular interview.

After I finished with the International Division, I moved to the production side. I visited domestic divisions, which handled similar products and plants in other states. I drove through the interstate highway system to United America's plant in Hammond.

INVESTIGATION ON THE PRODUCTION UNIT

In contrast to the Japanese Kamiyama plant, located near the city of Kamiyama, the sprawling Hammond plant lies in the middle of green fields. Mr. Nicholson, the general manager, told me that everyone lived within fifteen minutes drive from the plant. Everyone in the Hammond plant, including Mr. Nicholson, was referred to and addressed on a first-name basis. "We work hard and play hard," commented Mr. Nicholson, when I asked him to describe the organizational climate of the Hammond plant.

I interviewed two American technical experts in the Hammond plastic resin operation. Mr. Weaver, a chemical engineer, recalled the time when he and his colleagues visited Japan to solve a series of technical difficulties in the Kamiyama plant. He considered cultural and language differences to be significant enough barriers and believed that one should never take things for granted when transferring technology cross-culturally.

I observed production methods employed at the Hammond plant for two weeks and interviewed plant engineers, foremen, and workers. Mr. Cox, a foreman, said that he would never like to work as hard as the Japanese. His work was important, but his family came first, he said. This ethos was clearly observable at closing time. A bell rang for the end of a shift, and in five minutes workers had all gone home.

As I became closely involved in the Nippon United company, they allowed me to participate in business decision making as an interpreter/observer. When Japanese managers from Nippon Kaisha visited United America in the summer of 1979 to discuss technological issues, I was there as their interpreter.

I also interpreted for Mr. Aono, a new chief engineer of the Nippon United's Kamiyama plant on his trip to the United States in 1980. Mr. Aono was a thin, tall man, who actually spoke good English. Upon graduating from the Engineering Faculty of Chiba University, he entered Nippon Kaisha. During the previous year Mr. Aono was transferred from Nippon Kaisha to become the new chief engineer of Nippon United's Kamiyama plant.

As part of his job training, Mr. Aono spent several days in the Hammond plant discussing chemical formulae and extruder problems with Mr. Weaver and other technical people through my interpretation.

At the end of Mr. Aono's stay in the United States, we left Hammond and went back to New York. Mr. Aono and I went to a sushi restaurant together. He thanked me for my interpretation service and gave me *sumie* calligraphy as a gift. He said that calligraphy was his hobby and that the words written on the handmade rice paper symbolized his life philosophy. It said, "Like the Water, Reflecting the Full Moon."

The meaning was, Mr. Aono explained, that our mind should be flexible and adaptable like the water capable of fitting into any shape of container. We should be like the water, never rigid. Our spirit should reflect an image of the shining truth, just like the water reflects an image of the moon in the sky. No matter what shape the container is, the water can always reflect a moon image. No matter what your current environment is, you should always see the truth.

Mr. Aono had been recently transferred from Nippon Kaisha to this smaller, less prestigious affiliate, Nippon-United. This transfer was possibly the first major downturn of his career. His chance of going back to Nippon Kaisha was slim, although not zero. Yet, he still wanted to reflect an image of the moon. At the sushi counter of a small restaurant in New York, Mr. Aono sipped sake (rice wine) quietly.

✳   ✳   ✳

As I met the same people over many years, I could ask questions that I had earlier omitted but later found important. It was possible to continuously expand my data, which would not have been possible had they been seen only in the context of a single interview appointment.

A correct historical reconstruction of the events posed a problem, because of changes in perception of past events and the loss of memory of informants. I surveyed available documents and records written at the time of the events in order to correct possible distortions. During the 1970s and early 1980s, I was also present at many business meetings between the two parties as a participant observer.

While I interpreted, I always took notes, mixtures of speed writing, symbols, arrows, and numbers. Over the years, I accumulated these memos with the dates and places of meetings, names of participants and agendas. I cross-checked my memos, with the official minutes of the meetings and other written reports by managers to correct discrepancies between the actual event and the interpretation by the managers.

I promised to report to their respective departments regularly on my progress, and to present the draft of my paper to receive their feedback.

After completing the initial research in the 1980s, I visited Japan annually to update the data, although my marriage to an American, and subsequent personal circumstances moved me to various parts of the world, including the Republic of South Africa, where my daughter was born. During the summers of 1987 and 1988, I went back to Japan and conducted intensive fieldwork with my old friends in Japan to prepare for this publication.

✳   ✳   ✳

I have discussed how I became personally involved in the study of a U.S.-Japanese joint-venture company in Japan. During the time I was working for Japanese and American firms and later while I was doing my fieldwork, the world of business was undergoing many changes. In Japan, the legal and regulatory environment of foreign direct investment went through many drastic changes. In order to provide background information on the adaptation problem of American enterprises in Japan, I will discuss the trends of foreign direct investment and the corporate environment in the next chapter. Our discussion in chapter three will give an overview of foreign firms in the 1980s.

I will also briefly describe the Japanese business environment in order to assist those who might not be familiar with the Japanese institutional arrangements during this period. In addition, a brief history of the Japanese government's foreign direct investment policies is given in the appendix as background information.

CHAPTER THREE

FOREIGN ENTERPRISES AND JAPANESE CORPORATE ENVIRONMENT

INTRODUCTION

Direct foreign investment increased rapidly in Japan during the 1980s, and in recent years there have been noticeable signs of a strong commitment to Japan by American multinationals. In this chapter the trends of foreign direct investment in Japan will be discussed.

Although the reader will recognize that many American firms are doing extraordinarily well in Japan, direct foreign investment in Japan is still very low and pales in comparison with the Japanese direct investment overseas, particularly in the United States. This chapter will explore causes for the current low level of foreign investment. We will look closely into the following issues of concern: How profitable is American direct investment in Japan?; and what are major operational problems facing American enterprises in Japan?[1]

EXTENT OF DIRECT INVESTMENT IN JAPAN

According to the Ministry of Finance, the surge of direct investment in Japan during the 1980s reached a cumulative total of $7.4 billion.[2] Japanese government statistics do not distinguish American investments from those by other nationalities. They do, however, supply a breakdown of American firms across in-

31

dustries in Japan, and it is possible, through independent analyses, to get a general picture of American direct investment in Japan.

Throughout the 1980s, Americans were the largest foreign investors in Japan, accounting for about half of total foreign investments in Japan (48.5 percent, or $3.4 billion). During the late 1980s, U.S. investments grew at a 15 percent annual growth rate. Overall, American companies invested more in Japan in the last five years of the 1980s than they did in the previous thirty years combined. The Ministry of International Trade and Industry (MITI) has annually surveyed foreign affiliates' business trends in Japan since 1967 (*gaishi-kei kigyō no dō kō chōsa* Vol. 1–19). In its 1987 report, 2,094 firms were officially considered as foreign affiliates.[3]

Concerning the new investment, in the first half of 1987, new foreign investments marked a record high $1.4 billion, and again Americans made about a half of these new investments (JETRO 1988:42). It should be also noted that 16.0 percent of such investments were done by foreign affiliates in Japan, indicating healthy growth of those firms already in Japan.

More than a half of these American firms were in manufacturing industries. Chemical companies (including pharmaceutical firms) were the single largest investors in Japan, accounting for a quarter of cumulative direct foreign investment.[4] Again, the American presence was strong here: fifty-one American chemical manufacturers accounted for 22.7 percent of total foreign chemical firms present in Japan.

Another group of large investors was found in the machinery business. Machinery manufactures demonstrated a fast pace of investment, particularly in the late 1980s.

The petroleum industry also comprised a significant portion of foreign direct investment (8 percent), although its growth rate stabilized in the late 1980s.

Many American multinationals are operating in Japan: By 1987, 114 firms out of the Fortune 200 corporations had made capital investments in Japan. All the twelve giant pharmaceutical companies and the five precision machine makers in the Fortune list were in Japan. Fifteen out of nineteen large machinery manufacturers and twenty-one out of twenty-three chemical companies had established operations in Japan.

The areas where American presence was negligible were textiles (none of the four giants) and steel industries (one out of nine).

Americans had invested a cumulative total of $3.4 billion, or 48.5 percent of total foreign direct investment, in Japan by 1987. About half of such investments were in the manufacturing sector, although investments in the service and commerce sectors also increased rapidly. The chemical industry, the general machinery industry, the electric industry, and the petroleum industry were major areas of American manufacturers' direct investment.

PROFITABILITY OF AMERICAN ENTERPRISES IN JAPAN

How were they performing financially? Let us examine how profitable they were in the Japanese market in the last few decades.

Japanese government statistics, which do not separate American enterprises from other foreign investors, indicate that foreign-related firms consistently maintained a higher level of profitability than Japanese corporations except during the 1974–75 energy crisis and the 1980–1981 recession periods.

In spite of the Japanese government's restrictions, American firms in Japan in the early 1970s reported a *higher* level of profitability than American firms in Europe. According to the American Chamber of Commerce, the average return on equity for foreign-related firms in the 1970s exceeded 20 percent (The American Chamber of Commerce in Japan and the Council of the European Business Community: ACCJ & EBC 1987). This contradicts the popular belief that the Japanese government's restrictions hurt American firms. American firms in fact did very well financially in Japan during the non-liberalization period.

The situation in the 1980s was not as profitable as before, in spite of liberalization, but was still very positive. A 1987 MITI report indicated that foreign manufacturers showed a slightly better profitability than the average Japanese firm in terms of the operation profit as a percentage of sales: 3.7 percent compared to 3.6 percent of all the manufacturers in Japan.

There was a substantial variation in profitability among industries. In the electric industry, for example, foreign firms' operating profits were indeed very impressive: Their profits as a percentage of sales were twice as high as that of all firms in this industry in Japan (12.8 percent vs. 6.0 percent).

In the manufacturing industry, excluding the oil industry, foreign manufacturers were also doing very well. They reported a 6.8 percent profit/sales ratio, three times higher than that of all firms in Japan (2.1 percent). Likewise, in the petroleum industry, the foreign firms' operating profits as a percentage of their sales was more than double that of all the oil manufacturers (1.7 percent vs. 0.6 percent).

In the chemical and general machinery industries, on the other hand, the profit/sales ratio of foreign firms was lower than the industrial average. Foreign chemical firms reported 4.4 percent profit/sales ratio, compared to all manufactures' 5.2 percent. The profit/sales ratio of foreign general machinery manufactures was 3.4 percent, lower than the industry's average of 3.8 percent.

It is difficult to generalize on the overall profitability of foreign firms because of a large variation across industries. It is important, however, to note the two facts: (1) those that were in Japan before and during the liberalization period reported impressive levels of profitability, in spite of the fact that governmental restrictions were far more numerous at that time, and (2) many foreign firms did well in highly competitive fields such as the semiconductor, pharmaceutical, and computer industries.

At another point of comparison, U.S. government statistics indicated that the returns on investments (ROI) in Japan were comparable to the returns that could be expected in Europe. During the late 1970s, the ROI for American investments in Japan consistently exceeded the ROI for American investments in Europe and other parts of the world. Except for 1977, the ROI for investment in Japan was in the twenties, around 23–24 percent, compared to 14–16 percent in Europe. In the 1980s, the differential narrowed between investments in Japan and investments in Europe. In 1985, for example, the ROI for investment in Japan was 17 percent compared to 19 percent for investment in Europe (ACCJ & EBC 1987).

The preceding evidence verifies that American corporate investments in Japan in the 1980s were, in general, profitable, and that the profitability of investments in Japan was comparable to the levels of profitability in Europe. A widespread perception that foreign companies have not been profitable in Japan should be dismissed.

Today, American companies have many options for establishing a presence in Japan. They can establish 100 percent subsidiaries, open branch offices, or form joint ventures.[5] They can invest in existing Japanese enterprises or merely keep representative offices in Tokyo.

As foreign firms strengthened their operational bases in Japan, the number of cases of expanding local manufacturing by constructing new plants increased. Between 1978 and 1982, there were, on the average, twelve annual cases of plant construction by foreign firms. From 1983 through 1987, the number doubled to 22 cases annually.

Together with plant construction, the number of foreign firms that established research centers in Japan increased, especially in high technology areas such as electronics, computers, pharmaceutical, bioengineering, and chemistry. More than one-third of the manufacturing companies in the survey by the American Chamber of Commerce in Japan and the Council of the European Business Community conduct research and development (R&D) activities in Japan.

The listed reasons for establishing research and development centers in Japan were (1) to develop products that would suit local needs, (2) to meet the needs of Asian countries and to supply new products to the region, and (3) to engage in basic research in certain technological fields where Japan leads the world. For example, most of the world's semiconductor makers have production and research and development in Japan.

Another important area of growth in American investment in Japan is pharmaceuticals. Major foreign drug companies together command a 20 percent share of the Japanese pharmaceutical market and are aggressively expanding their businesses. Most of these companies established their own research centers and manufacturing plants during the 1980s.

For the world's pharmaceutical companies, no market holds as promising a future as that of Japan. In 1985, a scale of pharmaceutical markets showed $26.5 billion for the United States, $14 billion for Japan, $6 billion for West Germany, $4.5 billion for France, and $3.7 billion for Italy.

The strengthened value of the Japanese yen and the unprecedented rate at which the Japanese population was aging greatly increased the importance of the Japanese market in the 1980s.[6]

In the early 1980s, common complaints heard from foreign drug manufacturers concerned the governmental regulations and the complicated Japanese pharmaceutical distribution system. Governmental regulations were improved dramatically in the late 1980s. Because of the strong Americans demand for liberalization of Japan's pharmaceutical markets through Market Oriented Sector Selective (MOSS) talks, the Ministry of Health and Welfare agreed to reduce paperwork for approval of the use of new drugs. A schedule was also set to consider eligibility and pricing of drugs within health insurance regulations.

The new drug approval and pricing system for the National Health System, under the guidance of the Ministry of Health and Welfare, streamlined time-consuming application procedures and aided large drug manufacturers with capabilities for new drug research and development. Foreign companies, which were large multinationals, as well as large Japanese pharmaceutical firms, benefitted from the Japanese government's policy change to reduce the length of time required for the authorization of new pharmaceuticals.

By the early 1990s Japan's pharmaceutical industry became more oligopolistic: Giant Japanese firms such as Shionogi, Fujisawa, Takeda, Chūgai, and Tanabe, together with foreign multinationals pushed out smaller firms with less research and development capabilities.

Foreign pharmaceutical firms also became accustomed to the Japanese system because of past partnerships with Japanese firms. They moved to set up their own market research and sales operations, minimizing their dependence on Japanese firms. Foreign drug makers such as Essex Nippon, Japan Upjohn, Squibb Japan, Nippon Roche, Smithkline, and Beckman Corporation took up their own independent sales networks. Together with the new sales strategies, they built new research centers and plant facilities, such as in the case of Ciba-Geigy, Bayer Yakuhin, Rhone Poulenc Agro Co., Nippon Glaxo, and Eli Lilly Japan.

Overall, the Japanese pharmaceutical industry became markedly internationalized as giant Japanese firms strengthened basic research capabilities, meeting the challenge of world drug makers. As a consequence, U.S.-Japan competition in the pharmaceutical field intensified.

According to the "Report on the Survey of Research and Development," published by the Management and Coordination Agency, fiscal 1986 was a watershed for the import/export balance of pharmaceutical technology. For the first time, Japanese exports in pharmaceutical technology (17.3 billion yen) exceeded imports (12.6 billion yen). In 1986 Japan and the United States were tied for first place for the development of new pharmaceuticals, with each country claiming fifteen of the forty-seven new drugs developed that year. American and Japanese pharmaceutical manufacturers were riding a wave of internationalization that was sweeping the two countries.

Reflecting such a trend, the technology of Japanese companies became a more important reason for joint-venture tie-ups, although foreign companies still were the major sources of technology in joint-venture arrangements with Japanese companies in the 1980s and early 1990s. Forty-five percent of the respondents in the American Chamber of Commerce survey listed technology as the number one contribution of the foreign partner to a joint-venture. However, in 11 percent of the cases, technology was the number one contribution of the Japanese partner, and in 14 percent of the cases sales and distribution was the number one contribution of the foreign partner. Overall, these trends point to the worldwide competitiveness, and advancement of Japanese technology in selected industries.

In summary, one observes the following trends of foreign investment during the 1970s and 1980s:

1. Foreign direct investment grew, very rapidly, and Americans were key players in this expansion;
2. Direct investment in Japan, in general, was very profitable in the 1970s, before the complete capital liberalization. In the 1980s, it was still profitable in general, and extremely profitable in selected industries such as the electronic industry; and
3. More firms established production facilities and research and development centers in Japan. Monitoring and accessing Japanese technology became an important element of foreign companies' strategy in Japan.

In the late 1980s a dozen or so foreign affiliates appeared among the top 300 Japanese companies in terms of declared corporate income. They included IBM Japan, Coca-Cola, Fuji-Xerox, Nestle, Seven-Eleven Japan, NCR Japan, and Mobil Sekiyu.[7]

Already, quite a number of American products commanded a major share of the Japanese market. For example, Schick safety razors enjoyed 70 percent market share, Coca Cola, 60 percent, Pampers, 50 percent, Pyrex heat resistant cooking ware, 30 percent, Xerox, 23 percent of the photocopier field, and Kodak, 11 percent of the photographic film (JETRO 1986:22).

The shares of the large-scale computers in Japan in use/value base were divided into IBM Japan (25.0 percent), Fujitsu (23.1 percent), Hitachi (17.6 percent), NEC (17.0 percent) and Univac (9.0 percent) in 1986. In the personal computer market, NEC dominated the market with 51.3 percent market share, followed by Fujitsu (15.2 percent), IBM Japan (7.0 percent), Toshiba (6.5 percent) and Seiko Epson (6.2 percent). (Nikkei Sangyo Shinbun, June 10, 1987)

There are many success stories of American enterprises in Japan. Surprisingly, Coca Cola Company, whose main soft drink product is often associated with the American popular culture, sells more coke in Japan than in the United States. In 1988 the company dominated 64 percent of the Japanese soft drink market. It introduced a special coffee-based soft drink, "Georgia," catered particularly to the Japanese consumer taste. The product was not sold in the United States.

The manufacturing capacity of a giant pharmaceutical firm, Johnson & Johnson is larger in Japan than in the United States. All Life Insurance in 1988 controlled 18.4 percent of the Japanese insurance market, with its "cancer insurance" again aimed specifically at the aging Japanese society.

Today, with 120 million affluent consumers, Japan is fast becoming a battle ground where intense international competition takes place in technology, market, and product development. Both Japanese and American multinationals are spreading corporate wings to seek resources and markets in every corner of the globe. In the process, some Japanese firms have emerged as awesome competitors to Americans. Today the Tokyo Office of an American multinational is not only a base for penetrating the Japanese market, but also, and perhaps more importantly, a radar post for gathering the latest technological, scientific, and market information.

According to the previously mentioned survey by the American Chamber of Commerce in Japan and the Council of the European Business Community, 82 percent of foreign executives in Japan cited the importance of Japan in global business as a major factor of their investment in Japan. Understandably, large American multinationals have been the leaders in expanding their investment in Japan.

PROBLEMS OF FOREIGN DIRECT INVESTMENT

In spite of recent growth in foreign investment, the total foreign direct investment in Japan remains extremely low, especially compared with Japan's overseas investment, particularly in the United States. The overall foreign investment in Japan accounted for less than one-tenth of Japan's overseas investment in the 1980s. In contrast to the European market where American multinationals played a significant role, American investment in Japan accounted for only 4.4 percent of the total U.S. investment abroad, less than in the much smaller economies of Italy, Mexico, and the Netherlands.

Foreign firms as a group accounted for only 3.2 percent of total corporate sales in Japan, and employed only 0.4 percent of the total Japanese work force (Japanese Government: Tsūshō-sangyō-shō 1987).

The very low level of foreign direct investment is often regarded as resulting from past restrictive government regulations. The present study disputes this position, by saying that governmental restrictions have been largely removed, and yet there has not been a rush of foreign direct investment into Japan. Japan placed many restrictions on foreign investment until the mid-1970s, and in some cases until the early 1980s.

Studies show, however, that legal and regulatory barriers that once kept foreign investors out of Japan no longer have any pervasive impact on direct investment decisions. In a survey by the American Chamber of Commerce in Japan and the Council of European Business Community (ACCJ & EBC), two-thirds of the 398 top foreign executives in Japan (of whom 202 are Americans) claim that no investment restrictions exist in their industry.

Secondly, as we have observed, some foreign firms have

achieved an exceptional level of presence in the industries that are presumably the most strategic, and were well guarded with legal restrictions by the Japanese government in the past.

For example, the Japanese government strategically assisted the development of domestic firms in the computer and electronics industries in the 1960s and early 1970s, while delaying the entry of foreign firms. In spite of past regulatory barriers, foreign electric machinery firms enjoyed a high level of profitability in the late 1980s as presented in this study. Companies like IBM, Texas Instruments, Burroughs, NCR, and Honeywell have achieved a major position in this fiercely competitive field. If the problems were simply governmental restrictions, either past or present, these firms could not have achieved such levels of success.

What are the current causes for the low level of investment in Japan? It must be that the limits on foreign investment are not simply the result of Japanese government's past resistance, but also the reluctance of foreign investors. Why are they reluctant? We need to look into the issue of perception: How do foreign investors perceive the Japanese market?

There is an overall consistency across foreign affiliates on major factors that are inhibiting investment, according to the American Chamber of Commerce in Japan survey.

1. The perception that a long time period is required to reach corporate average profit levels in Japan (38 percent of all respondents, and 42 percent of the American respondents).
2. Difficulties and complexities of doing business in Japan. (38 percent of the respondents, and 39 percent of the Americans).
3. Difficulties in hiring good personnel (36 percent, 36 percent).

The respondents say that it takes roughly four years to reach breakeven for a new affiliate in Japan, and seven years to reach corporate average profit levels. However, one must be careful in interpreting such data because only those who are still present in Japan answered the questionnaire. Firms that have withdrawn from Japan might have a more negative view on the time frame needed to reach profitability.

The difficulty and complexity of doing business in Japan was the second major reason listed as an inhibiting factor (38 percent of the respondents, and 39 percent of the Americans). This factor is also closely related to the third major inhibitor, "difficulty in hiring good personnel." Hiring good personnel in an environment where few managers switch companies is a serious problem, particularly for firms that require many specialists, professionals, and managers. Seventy percent of foreign medical equipment firms, for example, cite this factor as a very significant inhibiting factor.

Problems of hiring good personnel are largely due to the lifelong employment system of big Japanese corporations, which will be discussed later. A further handicap in personnel recruiting is a rather negative public perception of foreign companies in terms of employment stability and opportunities for career development. These institutional obstacles often relate to prevailing social norms, values, and perceptions of the Japanese people.

Investing in an alien environment requires serious studies of local conditions and cultural variables. A potential foreign investor must start by putting aside most of his culturally based instincts and preconceived notions about how to do business. He needs to see situations through the eye of the local businessman. In the next few sections, let us examine aspects of Japanese corporate environment that are particularly relevant to American enterprises in Japan.

JAPANESE CORPORATE ENVIRONMENT

The way in which a particular group of people develop a certain kind of organizational culture and create certain organizational features is closely related to their perception of the evolving competitive environment.

Certain organizational characteristics have been developed in a particular task environment because the people involved have attached significance to particular events, have interpreted them in certain ways, have believed that certain behavioral responses would be effective at that time and place, and have implemented them. In this process, they have reconstructed their past experiences and have incorporated them into their present.

I agree with Okimoto and Rohlen (1988) that Japan's organizational principles are deeply embedded in the structure of Japanese labor and capital market. They mention:

> The emphasis on organizational networks and human relationships, based on structural interdependence, is so strong that Japanese capitalism might perhaps be called 'relational capitalism,' in contrast to the American model of 'transactional capitalism,' which gives greater weight to the 'invisible hand' of the market. (Okimoto and Rohlen 1988:16)

Although a number of books discuss Japanese corporate environment in the 1980s (c.f. Johnson 1989; Koike 1988; Okimoto & Rohlen 1988; Yamamura and Yasuba 1987), it is still beneficial to summarize some of the basic factors of Japanese "relational capitalism." A brief discussion of the Japanese business environment is given here as background information.

First, when discussing the corporate environment, we cannot neglect the importance of the Japanese political structure, where the conservative Liberal Democratic Party has been in power for most of the postwar era and where relatively young and able bureaucrats in the economic ministries have created long-term economic policies for industrial development. The interrelationship between the Japanese government and industry is an important area of concern (Okimoto 1989).

Besides the structure of the Japanese political economy, there are important institutional arrangements of Japanese firms in the 1980s. The include the following areas: (1) the capital market, (2) the interorganizational network, and (3) the labor market. Each of the above interrelated institutional arrangements directly affected a firm's strategies on capital formation, day-to-day business transactions, and human resource development.

The first important characteristic that has distinguished the Japanese corporate environment concerns the formation of capital. Imai and Itami suggest that differences in capital and labor allocation patterns led to entirely different corporate systems in Japan and the United States.[8] There are well-recognized historical characteristics of Japanese corporate finance that differ in comparison to practices in the U.S.: (1) a heavier reliance on bank loans, (2) less internal financing, and (3) less dependence on the equity market.

Historically speaking, the long-term bank-industrial complex was an important environmental factor, which supported the expansion of Japanese business and influenced inner workings of the Japanese firm. We know that the high Japanese savings ratio, encouraged by the government's tax policies, created large capital funds in Japanese commercial banks.[9] These funds were then channeled in the form of bank loans to Japanese companies for industrial expansion. In general, Japanese firms relied less on the equity market to generate funds and had a higher debt ratio, when compared to American firms.

During the early 1970s, big Japanese firms depended on banks and other financial institutions for almost half their funds, but in the 1980s firms were increasingly able to finance their activities using retained earnings and depreciation charges.[10] Net short- and long-term borrowing by large firms as a percentage of total funds decreased from 46.7 percent in the fiscal year 1974 to 11.1 percent in 1988 (Japan Economic Institute 1990:11)

This is where the second characteristic of the Japanese corporate environment, namely the interorganizational network (*keiretsu*), comes into play.

INTERORGANIZATIONAL NETWORK: KEIRETSU

The Japanese market is usually dominated by four to eight large firms, partly because of the Japanese government's past industrial policies and partly because of the past fierce competition and high-volume/low-cost strategies of Japanese firms. As Abegglen and Stalk described, different firms in the same market compete fiercely to increase their market share and to raise their ranking (Abegglen and Stalk 1985). These firms at the same time have strong connections in other business fields. It is important to understand the nature of this cross-industrial, interlocking relationship and cohesion among the group members called *keiretsu*, which have evolved into permanent ties between buyers and sellers, subcontractors and their parent firms, or suppliers of service and receivers of service.

One needs to understand this institutional arrangement from an overall political and economic viewpoint. The main feature of the Japanese business hierarchy is the stratification of firms according to size. In general, the bigger a company, the better its quality in terms of technological advancement, productivity, financial strength, labor relations, and other conditions of competitiveness. Although there are some very successful middle-sized firms, especially in emerging high technology industries, big firms still dominate the Japanese market.

The top 100 Japanese industrial firms are especially impressive. They are powerful national-level institutions, closely affiliated with giant firms in other industrial sectors, and together they form an energy center of Japanese business and push themselves to achieve international competitiveness and technological advancement. In terms of capital these top 100 companies control another 3,000 firms because of the *keiretsu* (literally "alignment") system of industrial groupism, which we will discuss shortly. The parent firms, their subsidiaries and affiliated firms altogether account for nearly 40 percent of Japan's total industrial capital.

Because of the long-term business relationships among member firms, a Japanese company may prefer to buy from another member of its *keiretsu* group even when a foreign firm can offer a better price or more favorable conditions.

A study conducted by *The Economist*, described this particular cultural barrier as follows:

> Groups are an obstacle. Six groups — Mitsubishi, Mitsui, Sumitomo, Fuyo, Sanwa and Dai-Ichi Kangyo (Furukawa) — link together batches of firms, banks and trading houses with small cross-shareholdings: another ten combine suppliers and subsidiaries of a big firm (for example, Matsushita or Toyota) or a bank. The 16 account for a quarter of all Japanese firms' sales. As long as prices are not exorbitant, component members of the group feel obliged to buy from each other.[11]

This system, which was created for ensuring high quality, speedy delivery, and cost effectiveness based upon long-term intercorporate relationships, often blocks outsiders, both Japanese and foreign. Foreign salesmen who have tried to sell industrial equipment or components to a large Japanese firm complain about this type of nontariff barrier.

Japanese buyers would rather use their own suppliers or subcontractors, from whom they are reasonably confident of receiving quality products, meeting their specifications, personalized and efficient after-service and technical support, not to mention prompt delivery without problems relating to long distance shipping. Competition among suppliers and subcontractors is fierce, and they all strive for better quality and pricing, especially in the high-value-added product and high-technology fields. Foreign salesmen, unless their companies are firmly committed to wage economic combat in this intensely competitive Japanese market, will have a very difficult time overcoming the structural obstacles and convincing Japanese buyers to switch to foreign products. Some have argued that this *keiretsu* arrangement is against newcomers that have not established credibility in the market, either Japanese or foreign.

Rodney Clark (1979) described three major patterns in which Japanese industrial groups are organized. According to him, the three main types of *keiretsu* in Japan are: (1) descendants of prewar *zaibatsu* (financial cliques), (2) banking groups, and (3) manufacturing groups. In fact, the ex-*zaibatsu* groups can be considered as banking groups because their institutional arrangements also involve powerful banks. However, they are categorized separately because of their historical origin and of their strong cohesiveness.

[1] Ex-Zaibatsu *Group*

The first major group is the descendants of the prewar *zaibatsu* (financial clique), namely Mitsui, Mitsubishi and Sumitomo. These modern *keiretsu* firms are not *zaibatsu*, which were abolished after the war. Unlike the prewar *zaibatsu*, where the family holding company alone controlled a vast majority or near majority of the shares of most member companies, *keiretsu* firms, as most modern Japanese companies, are public corporations with professional management without significant individual or family shareholders. Big businesses in Japan today are almost completely under control by managers, or "management workers" (Nishiyama 1984:133). The control by capital ownership has collapsed in contemporary Japanese big firms.

Modern day *keiretsu* group members do not hold more than a small percentage of each others' share. The emphasis is on the sharing of a common past, the close personal connections, and an in-group mentality. The most prominent *zaibatsu*-derived

groups are Mitsubishi, Mitsui, and Sumitomo groups. Each group has its bank and trading company and has close personal connections among top management, and each group enjoys varying degrees of business liaison and cooperation.

They jointly use the name and trademarks of the group, conduct joint funding of new research and ventures, and pursue the goal of strengthening the position of member firms and diminishing competition in a variety of industries.

Of the three former *zaibatsu* groups of Mitsubishi, Mitsui and Sumitomo, Mitsubishi is considered as the most goal-directed and having strong leadership (Japan Economic Institute 1990; Okumura 1981a and 1981b).

The Mitsubishi group, with 29 main members in its Mitsubishi presidents' club, includes such giants as Mitsubishi Bank, Mitsubishi Heavy Industries, Mitsubishi Electric Corp, Mitsubishi Motors Corp., Tokyo Marine and Fire Insurance, Asahi Glass, Mitsubishi Oil, Mitsubishi Trading, Kirin Brewery, Nikon, and Mitsubishi Chemical Industries.[12] The more obscure Mitsubishi Estate Co. Ltd. became famous in the United States when it bought a majority interest in the Rockefeller Center in New York City.

Likewise, the Mitsui Group includes the world's second largest Mitsui-Taiyo Bank, Japan Steel Works, Toshiba, Toray Industries, Mitsui Trading, Mitsui Marine and Fire Insurance, Mitsui Toatsu Chemical, Mitsui Real Estate Development, and Mitsui O.S.K. Lines. All these members in turn have their own vertical groups of manufacturing or enterprise *keiretsu*, which will be discussed shortly.

[2] Bank Group

The second major *keiretsu* group is the bank group, which consists of a dozen or more major companies to which a central bank lends money and in which it owns shares. It is sometimes difficult to distinguish the bank-centered *keiretsu* groups from the ex-*zaibatsu* groups. For example, the successors of the former Yasuda *zaibatsu* have formed a confederation with the Fuji Bank Group to establish the Fuyo Group with twenty-nine companies.

The most important *keiretsu* bank groups are centered on the Daiichi-Kangyo Bank, the Fuji Bank and the Sanwa Bank, although Japanese banks of major economic significance such as Mitsui, Sumitomo, Mitsubishi, Tōkai, Kyowa, and Daiwa also have their string of major client companies.

The Daiichi-Kangyo Bank group has more than forty-five members, including both former Daiichi Bank and Kangyo Bank groups plus Daiichi-Kangyo Bank-affiliated trading companies such as C. Itoh, Nissho Iwai, and Kanematsu Gosho. The Daiichi-Kangyo Bank is the world's largest bank.

In the past, scholars stressed that the member firms benefit from interfirm business, interlocking personnel management, borrowing from the same banks, use of the same service firms and interindustrial information exchange, and, to a lesser degree, mutual shareholding. Using the case of the semiconductor industry, Flaherty and Itami described the banking-industrial (*keiretsu*) complex:

> In terms of modern organizational economics, the banking-industrial complex is a governance system shaping the actions of companies and banks. The Japanese banks are willing to lend and the Japanese firms are willing to borrow so much money, not because of Japan, Inc., and government loan guarantees, but because they have consistent, long-term, mutual interests, large amounts of bank-controlled capital, and the power and information to protect them.[13]

Japan's "economic miracle" was heavily dependent upon the combination of a very high use of debt for business expansion and very low profit margins for the sake of market share expansion and eventual financial return in the future.

The Japanese have had remarkably high savings, at a rate of 17–18 percent of disposable income throughout the postwar period. These savings flew into time and savings deposits and, in turn, through aggressive loan policies of commercial banks, personal savings have helped finance the production and technological expansion of Japanese corporations. Ninety-seven to 98 percent of the deposits in commercial banks were extended as loans, and large Japanese firms usually received favorable loan terms with low interest rates.

The number of banks from which a company received loans was usually greater than in other industrial nations, which reduced the risk to each individual bank and increases the availability of capital to each company.

From the bank's viewpoint, the grouping of unrelated companies into *keiretsu* minimized the loan risk factor, while from the standpoint of member firms, the *keiretsu* grouping put the member company in a position to enjoy higher debt capacity due to the security portfolio of the bank.

In the early 1980s, however, capital market liberalization led large Japanese firms away from banks for their financing needs as the companies moved more directly to capital markets, selling bonds and other securities in Japan and abroad. In fiscal 1986 large corporations' dependence on borrowed funds became negative. In 1988 and 1989, however, with a capital spending boom of unprecedented proportions, large firms again made themselves significant borrowers from the bank.

In the 1990s, we have begun to see more flexible bank-industry relationship, away from heavy dependence of firms upon borrowed capital. During the past decade, the mutual shareholding between *keiretsu* members remained below 30 percent, and the main banks held less than 4 percent (or below the maximum legal limit of 5 percent) of the stock of any member firm.

From a strictly economic viewpoint, the preceding facts seem to confirm the looseness of *keiretsu* integration and control because, according to economic theories, a capitalist society is a system in which control is based on ownership. However, the classic economic principle based upon capital ownership does not seem to sit comfortably in the case of Japan.

Nishiyama (1984) proved that corporate control in Japan is not based on ownership: The key stockholders of Japanese firms are banks and life insurance companies; and the major owners of the banks are life insurance companies and member firms of their respective *keiretsu* groups. Thus, Japanese major life insurance companies seem to hold ultimate control over banks and *keiretsu* member companies as their owners.

However, major life insurance companies in Japan are not joint stock companies but mutual insurance companies. A mutual insurance company is an association of insurance holders, and its fund is entirely an accumulation of premiums paid by insurance holders, i.e. the general public, not the capital owned by capitalists. Thus the control by ownership almost disappears into the clouds in Japanese businesses.

In the case of the United States, the separation of ownership and management has reference to the fact that ownership is held by stockholders while professional managers are responsible for corporate operation. If this is not the case, the very idea of separation between ownership and management becomes meaningless. Nishiyama notes:

> The large businesses in today's Japan are controlled via the position and dominance of the management workers. . . . It exists to supply workers with the means of daily living, to satisfy their common interest, and further, to provide for their common destiny. . . . Their management objective is the perpetuation of the firm as a communal body, and the pursuit of profits is merely a means for achieving this objective. (Nishiyama 1984:125)

If we accept the classical economic concept of capitalism based upon a Western model and apply it to the Japanese condition, where corporate control is based not on ownership but on position and dominance, it follows that Japanese society, which is the world class economy, cannot be called a capitalist society! Or, the definition of control by capital in Western economic theories needs to be reexamined.

An interesting trend related to this issue was observed during the 1980s on the question of personnel transfer from the main bank to its member companies. This practice refers to the Japanese institutional arrangement where a bank officer moves out of the main bank to take up a new managerial position in its *keiretsu* member company. They are called *shukko* (short-term transfer) and *tenzoku* (permanent transfer). It has been said that this function of bank personnel helps the bank obtain firsthand, detailed information about the operations of a member company and enables the bank to provide better financial guidance. However, it is also a relationship of control and subordination because the flow of the personnel is always one-way, from the main bank to a member company.

Between 1981 and 1989 Mitsui and Dai-Ichi Kangyo banks sent a roughly constant number of high-ranking officers and directors to other member firms, while Mitsubishi, Fuji and Sumitomo banks gradually increased their numbers by a cumulative 10 to 20 percent. Sanwa had a cumulative increase of 50 percent over the eight years (Japan Economic Institute 1990:12). The increases for

Mitsubishi, Fuji, Sumitomo, and Sanwa suggest a rise in personnel dispatch greater than expected from economic factor alone.

While a demographic factor in the labor force (i.e. aging)has an important impact on the system of personnel transfer, I consider that this phenomenon is another indication of control not by ownership but by managerial position. It is a manifestation of the "relational capitalism" based upon human communication and interpersonal relationship that Okimoto and Rohlen suggested earlier.

In both ex-*zaibatsu* and bank groups, the members are all independent firms in their respective industries, and their relationships are more lateral. Member firms in such fields as banking, trading, insurance, and shipping perform special functions for industrial member firms, sometimes with preferential treatment, but not usually to the absolute exclusion of competitors.

The Fair Trade Commission's study on the top 200 nonfinancial firms (1987) and other research suggested that the financial group membership was not decisive in guiding individual member firms' business activities.[14]

In looking at specific products or services, the Fair Trade Commission found divergent patterns among large Japanese nonfinancial firms. With mainframe computers, 10 percent of the respondents claimed to choose their suppliers on the basis of group membership. Also on the list of the *keiretsu* influence were the purchase of pension fund management services, where 95.9 percent chose a member firm, and the purchase of fire and marine insurance, where 75.3 percent selected a member supplier.

In general, however, most companies dealt with more than one supplier, and only 2.3 percent of the responding firms cited membership in a horizontal *keiretsu* as a factor in selecting their suppliers.

The cohesiveness of the bank group, when compared with the ex-*zaibatsu* group, tends to be less clear. The major bank typically holds less than the maximum of 5 percent of the shares of any company allowed by law, and the insurance company can legally hold the stock of a nonfinancial company up to 10 percent. (While antitrust laws in the United States prohibit commercial banks from holding stock in other companies, Japan's Anti-monopoly Law does not outlaw it altogether).

Members have several financial companies and life insurance companies as shareholders whose *keiretsu* companies typically borrow from a half dozen banks, while the *keiretsu* bank is the primary source of loans and often with managerial participation. In terms of ownership, the banking *keiretsu* have much less lateral liaison among members than ex-*zaibatsu* groups, and the influence of the primary bank over managerial decisions of member companies varies too much to make any generalizations.

[3] Enterprise Group

The third important *keiretsu* is the enterprise or manufacturing group formed around a large company such as Toyota, Nissan, Hitachi, Sony, or Matsushita. This *keiretsu* is most relevant to the present study, and this is where the most cohesive interorganizational relationship is observed.

The enterprise *keiretsu* is a constellation of subsidiaries, affiliates and subcontractors owned or dominated by a major manufacturing or trading corporation. The major characteristic of this *keiretsu* is its vertical relationship, which symbolizes the commercial and financial dependence of the smaller firms for business, credit, and other services. A large manufacturer that belongs to one of the previously mentioned ex-*zaibatsu* or bank groups has its own manufacturing *keiretsu* and functions as the core of their vertical association in a particular industry. Together these enterprise groups are engaged in fierce competition with other enterprise groups, which operate in the same industry. These enterprise *keiretsu* have important strategic effects on the way firms in Japan operate, particularly member firms.

Okumura identifies five forms of enterprise affiliation: (1) vertical affiliation in production, (2) horizontal affiliation for the purpose of market share expansion, (3) sales network expansion, (4) diversification, and (5) overseas advance (Okumura 1984:175).

Historically, industrial groups of this kind have been formed by entering into the group of smaller firms; the spinning off of specialized divisions from the large companies at the center of the group; or establishing a new wholly owned subsidiary or joint venture. Like the ex-*zaibatsu* firms, many of the "spin-off" firms use the name and logo of the major firm and continue to identify themselves with the parent firm.

The manufacturers' *keiretsu* is overall a much more controlled unit than the loosely affiliated bank *keiretsu*. While financial group members are laterally positioned and mutual shareholding between them rarely exceeds 30 percent, in enterprise *keiretsu* much larger blocks of stock are in one company's hands. Major Japanese companies have a large number of subsidiaries (which are 51 percent owned), and affiliates (less than 50 percent owned), as well as subcontractors. It is in this group where one can clearly observe the so-called industrial gradation.[15]

Big Japanese manufacturers rely on subcontracting to a great extent. The famous *kanban* system of quality and inventory control of Toyota would not have been possible without this nexus of the "Toyota family of companies," where subcontractors, who range from a small family business to a thoroughly automated assembly plant, produce and deliver on a daily base the exact amount of manufacturing parts required by Toyota.

Smaller firms are dependent on the major company for business and credit, and the larger firm benefits at the expense of smaller firms, including both entrepreneurs and workers. When business is bad, the principal firm cuts down on its orders to subcontractors and pays them lower prices. Larger subcontractors in turn impose harsher conditions on their subcontractors. Industrial gradation implies that the smaller the firm is, the more unstable it is.

The dual wage structure between large and small firms was considered as the primary reason for the vertical *keiretsu* formation in the 1950s and 1960s. Although a subsequent shortage of young workers led to a rise in starting pay in smaller enterprises, the wages difference is still noticeable between large and small firms, particularly for marginal workers such as the older workers and female workers.

Another important motivation for the vertical formation of *keiretsu* concerns risk shifting. Okumura noted that it is "a very common practice for the parent company to farm out pollution-causing projects to affiliated companies and accident-prone jobs to sub-contractors" (Okumura 1981:176).

More attention should be paid to this issue of risk shifting, especially in the light of Japan's globalization: *Keiretsu* is expanding beyond the Japanese archipelago, and Japanese firms are operating overseas manufacturing operations in developing countries with less stringent environment protection laws.[16]

The purpose of this overview of the *keiretsu* system is to illustrate the mechanism of industrial gradation where Japanese large firms depend for their highly praised performance on the squeezing of smaller firms, especially in the lower tier of the industrial hierarchy. Large firms have developed not only a simple user-supplier relationship with subcontractors but also a vertical relationship of paternalism through credit control, personnel management, training, and education.

Subcontractors understand the fine details of operational requirements, product specification, business strategies, and inventory control of the large firm, and they adjust their production and business schedules to such a degree that they operate as if they were production units within the large firm.

The large firm, while expecting prompt and efficient performance from smaller companies, assists them financially, often guaranteeing the subcontractor's bank loans from city banks. The large firm also leases or sells equipment at favorable conditions, provides labor by arranging for its retired employees to be hired by the subcontractors, often at about half the preretirement salary.

For example, Matsushita Electric, which is known for its Panasonic products, has almost 600 subsidiaries and affiliates in which it holds at least 10 percent of the shares. It has some 200 subsidiaries and affiliates of which Matsushita holds over 50 percent of the shares. Around each of these important affiliates and subsidiaries in the Matsushita group are dozens to 100 smaller suppliers and sales companies in which one or another of the Matsushita companies may have a shareholding interest. Nearly every member company will be engaged in a narrow range of activities so that each will be dependent on the rest. Each firm has its place in the industrial hierarchy with the largest company at the top and firms of decreasing size and stability placed underneath it to form the pyramid of the "Matsushita family." The vertical order is maintained by subcontracting, the extension of credit, and the parachuting of employees from large corporations to smaller ones.

This hierarchical cohesion of Japanese firms is a distinct environmental factor, particularly in the manufacturing sector, and it has affected the formation and development of a corporate culture such as that of Nippon Kaisha. Irrespective of the actual ownership share, the *oya-gaisha* (parent firm) - *ko-gaisha* (child firm) mentality creates a strong Confucian-type hierarchical relationship.[17] One important offshoot of this mentality is that a *ko-gaisha* is expected to subordinate its personnel policies to the needs of the parent company.

An important feature of Japanese enterprise groups is that one cannot belong to two *keiretsu* groups simultaneously. Intragroup stockholding is active but intergroup stockholding is virtually nil among the enterprise *keiretsu* and the ex-*zaibatsu* groups. If there is any intergroup stockholding, it is a unilateral ownership by financial institutions.

Only in the bank *keiretsu* where the member relationship is lateral and where the control is less rigid, some instances of multiple membership are observed. Thus, one can conclude that the enterprise group, which involved vertical relationships, tends to be self-contained, and avoids interchanges with other enterprise groups.

JAPANESE LABOR MARKET

The third important environmental factor is found in the labor market. The Japanese labor market has been characterized by its (1) low labor mobility, (2) limited ports of entry for new employees, and (3) enterprise unions. Because of the low labor turnover in Japan, until the early 1980s the norm in personnel policies was to recruit recent graduates once a year and promote them internally according to a seniority-based wage and promotion system. The lifelong employment system means that an employee enters a firm after leaving school and stays in one firm until retirement. The seniority rule implies that the wage/salary and position that an individual enjoys in the corporate hierarchy correspond to his age and years of service.

Until very recently the port of entry for new employees was extremely limited because of the "lifelong employment system," where an employee works for one company until retirement. We will look at this issue in detail later.

Thirdly, Japanese labor unions are usually enterprise unions rather than industry or trade unions, where workers of one firm join the same union regardless of their occupational specialization. One of the important difference between American and Japanese system is that both blue-collar and white-collar workers join the same union in Japan. Moreover, union officers are elected from among the regular employees of the enterprise. Both blue-collar and white-collar workers' concerns and loyalty are directed toward the local enterprise union and their representatives, who handle labor negotiations for their colleagues.

This system of enterprise unions enhances close ties between blue-collar and white-collar workers, and between workers and management, who often were previously union members who have been promoted into managerial positions internally. The system reduces the differences between groups of workers and helps create an ambiance of egalitarianism in the corporate community.

Another aspect of the enterprise union is that union-company relations tend to develop according to the realities of the enterprise. By having union leaders within the company, union demands are more likely to be "pragmatic," based upon factual data of the company performance. The participation of salaried employees, in particular, increases union knowledge about the financial situation of the firm.

Enterprise unionism does not mean that management and workers do not experience conflicts. In fact, labor disputes are plentiful in Japan, but Japanese strikes are in general much shorter than those in America. For example, in 1983 there were 893 strikes and lockouts in Japan, compared to only 62 strikes in this country. However, Japanese strikes averaged 2.3 days, compared to the U.S. average of 22.6 days.

Almost 30 percent of wage and salary workers in Japan belong to unions, compared with 19 percent in the United States, and enterprise unions play an important role in forming the characteristics of Japanese labor management.

The three characteristics of the labor force — low labor mobility, limited port of entry, and enterprise unionism — inevitably influence the Japanese corporate culture. For example, low labor mobility and limited entry of mid-career personnel imply that internal labor allocation and reallocation must be done more actively in Japan so that the firm can cope with changing demands and technology. Because of this need, the development of internal labor markets is more extensive in the Japanese firm, as we will see in Nippon Kaisha, and the personnel department takes an active role in overall corporate strategies toward/for the internal labor market. The existence of the enterprise union enhances rather than inhibits labor-management cooperation (for metabolizing such internal labor market).

Historically speaking, the organizational features of the Japanese firm such as the lifelong employment system and the seniority-based wage and promotion system were created during the first round of Japan's industrialization when the market was characterized by a skilled labor shortage and difficulty in holding workers. Within the rules of the labor market, the firm tried to trade off the cost of labor turnover and lost production due to the lack of manpower against the cost of the lifelong employment. (Taira 1970:119).

Koike proved that the so-called lifelong employment system and the "seniority rule of wage and promotion" are not unique to Japan but are held in common with white-collar groups in Western Europe, and to a lesser degree in the United States (Koike 1988). According to Koike, the white-collarization of Japanese blue-collar workers means that workers' on-the-job experience extends to related workshops. Because of the wide-ranging skill formation, Japanese blue-collar workers at large firms gain a good understanding of their department's production process.

Because the range of skills widens and becomes more sophisticated for a worker employed for a long time, his long length of service synchronizes with the seniority curve for wages, which usually applies to white-collar workers.

As a buffer for business fluctuations, many large firms have relied on subcontractors and workers who are at the periphery of the system: When a recession begins, the company can cut back on subcontract work instead of laying off its core workers. If the recession becomes very severe, the company then cuts out part-time and temporary workers.

Thus, the maintenance of the labor relations by large Japanese firms in the past few decades was based upon the sacrifice of those who were temporary or part-time, or those who worked for smaller, less financially secure subcontractors. The system largely excluded female workers who tended to fall into the above category of the "adjustable" labor force. The system tended to benefit those who were male, university graduates, and working for large companies. They consisted of less than a quarter of the Japanese labor force.

WINDS OF CHANGE

The task environment of a Japanese firm has been changing rapidly. I predicted that both the lifelong employment system and seniority system would have to change due to changing demography and other environmental requirements.[18] Environmental factors that would force changes in corporate labor management include the aging of the Japanese labor force, the shortage of high-tech professionals, and increasing global competition. Among them perhaps the most important environmental change is demographic.

The seniority-based wage and promotion system was based upon the economic rationale that a large number of younger and inexpensive workers at the bottom of a corporate pyramid support a smaller number of older and more expensive workers. This system worked well when corporations were expanding rapidly during the economic boom of the 1960s and when new managerial positions were opening within the corporation.

However, the corporate environment has changed drastically since then. In the mid-1970s Japan entered into a period of much slower economic growth. Increased life expectancy and lower birth rates created fundamental demographic changes. Among the most important are that the Japanese labor force is aging and that the percentage of youth in the corporate hierarchy is shrinking. The Japanese life expectancy is now the world's longest. By the year 2045, 25 percent of Japanese will be older than 60 years old.

Currently, among large firms modifications in the lifetime employment system and drastic changes in and sometimes elimination of the seniority-based wage and promotion system are underway. Japanese employment practices are shifting toward a more performance-oriented wage and salary scale and more diversified paths of promotion. In general, Japanese companies are trying to maintain the system of long years of service among core employees but their promotion is no longer automatic. Firms would like to eliminate incompetent or redundant employees, although they try to avoid direct dismissal. Instead, more moderate forms of rationalization are used, such as voluntary resignation and transfer to affiliates and subsidiaries.

An important feature of the Japanese labor relations in the 1990s is that personnel redundancies are concentrated among middle-aged and older workers, while Japan is experiencing an overall shortage of skilled labor. Those older workers possess company-specific, wide-ranging skills, which are no longer needed. It is difficult for these workers to find employment in other companies which also utilize their wide-ranging and enterprise-specific skill. Today, the social stress of redundancies is concentrated among the older workers, who strived to build up Japan's postwar prosperity.

Ironically, with rapid technological and economic advancement, Japan in the 1990s is being plagued with shortages of technical personnel. Many companies, desperate for trained professionals, are hiring people away from their competition. Large firms are hiring a very selected group of mid-career managers, whose skills are needed for immediate use, especially in high-technology areas. Because of this trend, we observe a higher turnover in a very selective segment of the labor force — those who are in their thirties or early forties with professional expertise of one kind or another.

Speaking of the Japanese labor market in general, however, it still exhibits lower labor mobility and more limited ports of entry for new employees. In 1987 only about 2.7 million people or 4.4 percent of the work force changed jobs. Although the number of job shifts is increasing, it is still limited in scope. The Japanese union system continues to be based upon enterprise unions. Therefore, it is safe to say that the system is changing, but it is not becoming a highly market-oriented system, as is the case in the United States.

ORGANIZATION CULTURE

In three major areas of environmental requirements—capital, intercorporate groupings, and labor—there are still very notable differences between Japan and the United States, which affect corporate behavior.

With this overview of corporate environment at an interorganizational level, we will look next at how one company's organizational culture and its structural features have been created, modified, and developed.

We understand that organizational culture does not exist in a vacuum. Attitudes, values, principles, and patterns of social relations found in the workplace are likely to have a certain congruence with institutional arrangements outside the firm because they are interrelated. At the same time, the firm's values, attitudes, and norms relate to the rest of corporate environment because what happens in one area directly and indirectly influences what happens in other areas of the company community.

Organizational culture in this sense is a web of interactive systems with multiple directions of causes and effects. We will explore some of these connections, focusing particularly on Nippon Kaisha's human resource management. We will look at how the corporate culture of Nippon Kaisha in terms of its people policies works, and how corporate norms are expressed and supported by its members.

As I mentioned in my discussion on methodology, my research here utilizes an authentic Organization Behavior approach, composed of questionnaires, interviews, observation, and documentation. The organization analysis of Nippon Kaisha in chapter four will be contrasted to a more process-oriented, interpretive, ethnographic approach I will present for their joint venture, Nippon United, in chapter five.

During my fieldwork on Nippon Kaisha, I tried to reach Nippon Kaisha people's value orientation by soliciting individual stories from several managers about their careers in Nippon Kaisha. Out of many pieces of such personal data on personnel management, a first approximation of the management structure emerged as I started to notice the overlapping of individual experiences. It was like putting many pieces of a jigsaw puzzle together to create an image of an organization. Metaphorically speaking, I collected many snapshots of the organization and tried to combine them in order to present Nippon Kaisha in an intelligible way to outsiders.

I encouraged Nippon Kaisha managers to talk about past crisis because they seemed to notice most of a distinct existence of the corporate culture when routines were broken. People notice how they have always done things when some events force them to do things differently. When they are forced to change their habits, they realized more clearly the existence and often resistance of the Nippon Kaisha culture.

Besides the recording of the "oral tradition" of Nippon Kaisha management, I participated in and observed their recruitment procedures, training, and education programs. I recorded and interpreted recurring remarks and events underlining the socialization processes of Nippon Kaisha employees and attempted to present the cultural legacy of Nippon Kaisha, as perceived and validated by insiders.

CHAPTER FOUR

NIPPON KAISHA

INTRODUCTION: NIPPON KAISHA IN TOKYO, JAPAN

Urban Tokyo represents kaleidoscopic and energetic construction activities of over forty postwar years: buildings sprang up throughout the city without architectural unity or integrative city planning.

At a "scramble"pedestrian crossing, the light turns green. Computer-simulated music of a Japanese folk song *tōryanse* or "you may pass" starts to alert the visually handicapped that the light has changed. The multilane traffic temporarily stops in all directions. Before the light turns yellow, a computerized female voice politely urges pedestrians to rush to the other end. Above the traffic light is an electric board indicating today's noise and air pollution levels at this particular spot. On top of a nearby bank building is an electronic newsboard, announcing today's major stock prices.

Although Tokyoites have voiced grave concerns about many of their city's ills, Tokyo still functions with an amazing efficiency. It stands as the world's largest financial center, consuming and emitting enormous amounts of information and services.

More than fifteen subways and railways, which crisscross the city, provide twelve million Tokyoites with mass transportation. Along the Yamate Railway loop line, which circles the inner city, major urban hubs have been created at Shibuya, Shinjuku, Ikebukuro, Roppongi, Akasaka, Harajuku, and Ginza. Every day each hub linked by multiple railway/subway connections, handles millions of commuters and shoppers. More than two million people pass through Shinjuku Station every day. Trains run every few minutes, on time to the second. Immaculately clean buses and taxies flood already crowded city streets in front of the station. In one of these urban centers, we find the headquarters of Nippon Kaisha.

Nippon Kaisha occupies several floors of an ultramodern building, which, from the outside, resembles the Sears Tower in Chicago. The first-floor lobby with twenty-feet-high marble walls is spacious, airy, and aesthetically pleasing. Elevators are located at the center behind a desk of security guards who watch multiple-screen television monitors. Businessmen stream to and from the elevators. Most of Nippon Kaisha departments are located on the twenty-seventh floor.

The atmosphere of Nippon Kaisha's entrance hall is quite different from the first-floor lobby: It is clean, functional, gray, and bare. Plastic plates on the wall indicate the names of departments along a long corridor lit by white fluorescent lights. It reminds one of a high-technology manufacturing plant.

At the end of the elevator hall, two young women sit at the reception desk, dressed in beige-colored uniforms with a name plate and company emblem. They bow to visitors and, with a smile, ask what they can do to help. This is the world of Nippon Kaisha.

STATUS HIERARCHY

Behind the reception area there are several rooms with leather sofas and coffee tables. One wall is all glassy windows from floor to ceiling, revealing a magnificent view of metropolitan Tokyo. These rooms are the front face of Nippon Kaisha, where most first-time visitors meet Nippon Kaisha businessmen.

Conversation usually begins with a ritualistic exchange of name cards so that all parties will know exactly where to place each other in the Japanese status hierarchy. It is the Japanese custom to examine the business cards very carefully and to put the cards in front on the table for quite a while (at least about a half of the meeting time) to show that ample time and due respect have been given to the person's position, background, and status.

A visitor would also notice that only senior executive officers of Nippon Kaisha have their own individual offices and meeting rooms, which are located on the top floor. Nippon Kaisha men often refer to the top management as *ue no kai* (upstairs) or simply *ue* (up) indicating both the physical and social location.[1] The rest of the managers and employees have their desks in a large open space, which occupies an entire floor for each department on the twenty-seventh and twenty-sixth floors.

Once a person becomes more familiar with Nippon Kaisha's business, he can bypass the receptionists to go directly to these departments. This is where you see the real face of Nippon Kaisha at work.

The department room looks like a newspaper editorial room where people, desks, filing cabinets, and telephones are spread out in a gymnasium-like space. Near the entrance door are gray metal lockers, filing cabinets, umbrella stands, and coat racks. From the entrance, you can see the entire staff of the department.

Men generally wear white shirts and ties, leaving jackets on the hangers near the door. Women, who are mostly in their twenties, wear beige-colored company jackets with little name plates on their chests. The subtle distinction in the code of clothing and the requirement of a name plate for women, but not for men, suggests a functional distinction between the sexes.

In this huge office space, a particular project/section/task force entity is defined by the island formation of desks. Each island represents a more or less independent functional unit within a particular division. A manager who is accountable for the unit sits at the end of attached desks of his subordinates.

A manager's desk is slightly bigger and his chair has arms while others do not. Compared to an average American office, in terms of size, quality, and location, the symbolic status distinction between managers and ranks is far less obvious. There is no separate manager's office, executive parking lot, or executive dining room. Nevertheless, status distinctions exist in different styles and forms.

For example, the status hierarchy is expressed in the order in which green tea is served and in linguistic rules and taboos. In the Personnel Department everyone has his or her own cup and every morning twenty-one-year-old Miss Nakamura or one of her female colleagues prepares green tea. Every morning Miss Nakamura places several tea cups on a tray and delivers it first to Mr. Yamashita, director of the department, then to his managers and to Miss Nakamura's male colleagues. She then makes more tea, this time for her female colleagues and herself. Although everyone gets tea, the order of the tea service is a part of the morning ritual of corporate life.

Status distinction is also apparent in the Japanese language and its forms of address and reference. When a subordinate addresses or refers to a manager, he or she uses the manager's position title, not his name. Mr. Matsuda, a section chief, is always addressed by his subordinates as *kachō* (section chief), not Mr. Matsuda. A subordinate would call him Mr. Matsuda only in defiance. If such an event occurred, everyone within earshot would be immediately aware that something unusual had taken place. They might stop working and try to overhear what the man and the section chief were saying. Juniors in the department are often called by personal names. The atmosphere of the Personnel Department is very casual and friendly. Most of the junior members are called by friendly short names, or nicknames, such as Torachan (Mr. Baby Tiger), and Doka-ben (Large lunch box, because he is newly married and his wife always prepares a nice box lunch for him).

Co-workers form informal groups mostly according to ages, and they get together for lunch and for drinks after work. Mr. Yamashita, the director, is always addressed as *buchō* (director) by the people of the department.[2] Mr. Yamashita occasionally takes his subordinates out for lunch or for a drink. On such occasions, he usually pays the bill for everyone.

To create a congenial atmosphere while at the same time completely acknowledging the status hierarchy, the linguistic rule is as follows: When addressing or referring to a subordinate or a colleague, one uses personal names, nicknames, or personal pronouns. When addressing a superior, one uses his position title. The position title defines a senior person's social identity and status within the organization. Its correct use acknowledges that the position and its occupant is appreciated and respected.

This rule breaks down only at the very top of the corporate hierarchy, where Nippon Kaisha president, Mr. Kubo, uses positional titles in addressing very senior executives, perhaps to confirm and sanction linguistically mutual respect for one another's senior status. Mr. Kubo is almost always addressed and referred to as *shachō* (president) by everyone else in the company.

Status distinction is also apparent between the sexes. In spite of recent improvements in the status of women, a majority of female employees have little chance for promotion to a managerial level. With a few exceptions, women in Nippon Kaisha provide clerical assistance to their male colleagues. Nippon Kaisha female employees are expected to, and many do, resign from the company after marriage or after having their first child. They are replaced by younger, less expensive female employees. In other words, female employees are still considered as largely expendable labor, excluded from the system of lifelong employment and seniority of Nippon Kaisha. Only in the last few years, has the use of female workers in Nippon Kaisha begun to change, a subject which will be discussed later.

CULTURAL LEGACY OF NIPPON KAISHA: DAI-NIPPON KEIRETSU

Interviews with managers of Nippon Kaisha led to the discovery that the most significant cultural legacy of the corporation derives from its historic relation to its parent company, Dai-Nippon Inc., a large Japanese multinational manufacturer of machinery, electric and electronic products, and consumer products. The general public as well as Nippon Kaisha employees perceive Nippon Kaisha's status relative to other member corporations of the Dai-Nippon industrial group, according to Nippon Kaisha officials. The Dai-Nippon group exemplifies the third type of *keiretsu* (manufacturing type) discussed before.

In the early 1960s Nippon Kaisha was established as a subsidiary of Dai-Nippon through a spin-off of the Dai-Nippon Chemical Division. Although the history of Nippon Kaisha is relatively short, the production of chemical products under Dai-Nippon Inc. goes back to the turn of the century when Dai-Nippon started the production of electric insulation materials and insulating varnish.

The independence of Nippon Kaisha in the early 1960s was part of the long-range program of Dai-Nippon Inc. to decentralize its activities and to strengthen the overall position of the Dai-

Nippon Group in the Japanese industrial structure. Prior to the inauguration of Nippon Kaisha, the management of Dai-Nippon announced:

> Nippon Kaisha will continue to maintain a close and inseparable relationship with our company, but at the same time will strive to develop its markets as an independent organization.

In the early 1960s, Nippon Kaisha was established with a capital of 2.5 billion yen ($6.9 million, at the exchange rate of $1 = 360 yen at that time) and about 2,000 employees. It also obtained five factories and nine sales offices in Japan, which were also spun off from Dai-Nippon Inc.

Nippon Kaisha's historical connection to Dai-Nippon is one of the most important legends of Nippon Kaisha. The pride in being a part of the Dai-Nippon group was expressed on numerous occasions by Nippon Kaisha managers. Nippon Kaisha inherited its name from Dai-Nippon and adopted the same company emblem. Nippon Kaisha is an important member of the Dai-Nippon Group, and ranks in the upper middle tier of the industrial hierarchy.

In the mid-1960s, Nippon Kaisha started to form its own *keiretsu* firms, separating its specialty products divisions into independent companies. The company also expanded its product lines as well as geographical distribution.

In the late 1960s, Dai-Nippon transferred its production of household products to Nippon Kaisha, which expanded and diversified its product lines to include solar panel systems, water pipes, bathroom units, kitchen units, and construction materials. Nippon Kaisha's new Division of Housing and Environmental Products grew rapidly, meeting the increasing demands of the Japanese "housing boom" in the late 1960s. In the chemical products field, Nippon Kaisha's Chemical Division entered into the field of fine chemical products, including pharmaceuticals, synthetic resin products, anticorrosion products, and plastic films and foams. It also entered the field of new ceramics, carbon products, and other inorganic chemical products, supplying materials to Dai-Nippon's manufacturing divisions and to the automobile industry.

The following chart shows the relationship between Dai-Nippon and Nippon Kaisha in terms of ownership.

Dai-Nippon owns 69 percent of Nippon Kaisha, one of Dai-Nippon's more than 100 *ko-gaisha,* or child companies. Nippon Kaisha, as a core member of the Dai-Nippon Group, in turn owns thirty-three companies, including a 50 – 50 joint-venture company with United America. Surrounding this network of subsidiaries and affiliates are a large number of independent subcontractors. Consequently, about 6,000 companies of various sizes make up the Dai-Nippon Group manufacturing *keiretsu.*

The vertical relationship between Dai-Nippon (parent) corporation, Nippon Kaisha (child), and Nippon-United (grandchild) becomes obvious when one looks at the flow of personnel between them. Because Japanese companies in an industrial group are part of a financial and social hierarchy, a subsidiary is positioned at a certain rank vis-à-vis other member companies (fig. 1).

The status hierarchy of the Dai-Nippon manufacturing group becomes more apparent when a retiring manager of Nippon Kaisha becomes a director or president of a subsidiary company. All the presidents and executives of Nippon Kaisha are *tenzoku* men. *Tenzoku,* which literally means "changing one's affiliation," is a type of personnel transfer where an employee is officially retired from the parent company and is moved to an affiliate or subsidiary. We will discuss this practice again when we examine the relationship between Nippon Kaisha and its subsidiaries, but basically the same relationship exists between any parent firm and its child firm.

Tenzoku men from Dai-Nippon Inc. were given senior managerial positions one or two ranks higher than their previous positions in the parent firm before their transfer to Nippon Kaisha. Mr. Kubo, current president of Nippon Kaisha, previously held a position as senior board director in Dai-Nippon, and the senior directors of Nippon Kaisha were junior directors of Dai-Nippon before their transfer.

Tenzoku represents a one-way flow of personnel, from the center to periphery: Dai-Nippon sends its junior directors to Nippon Kaisha, who become senior directors in Nippon Kaisha. Likewise, when Nippon Kaisha created its own subsidiary or affiliate such as Nippon-United, it sent their *tenzoku* junior directors to staff senior positions in the new company. The traffic flow of personnel is always from a higher status organization to a lower status one.

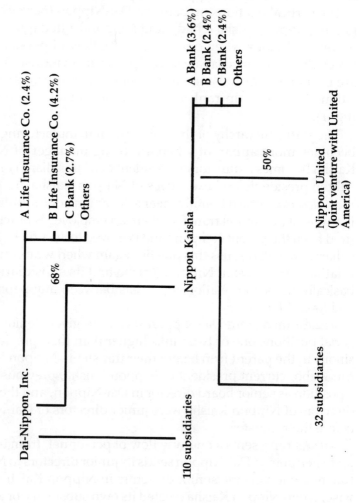

FIGURE 1: DAI NIPPON-NIPPON KAISHA INDUSTRIAL GROUP

Dai-Nippon, Inc.

A Life Insurance Co. (2.4%)
B Life Insurance Co. (4.2%)
C Bank (2.7%)
Others

68%

Nippon Kaisha

110 subsidiaries

32 subsidiaries

50%

Nippon United
(Joint venture with United America)

A Bank (3.6%)
B Bank (2.4%)
C Bank (2.4%)
Others

While Dai-Nippon managers are slightly better paid than Nippon Kaisha managers, salary is not the most important status differential. Power, authority, prestige, and other intangible rewards are important factors to stratify this interorganizational relationship (fig. 2).

Dai-Nippon managers enjoy higher social prestige than Nippon Kaisha managers, and they possess and sometimes exercise "informal" authority to influence Nippon Kaisha's internal decision making. When Mr. Yamashita, personnel director of Nippon Kaisha, needs to discuss personnel matters with someone in Dai-Nippon, he is more likely to place a call to Mr. Ayabe, section chief of Dai-Nippon's personnel department, rather than calling Mr. Sugiyama, personnel director of Dai-Nippon, directly, in spite of the fact that Mr. Yamashita has the same nominal title of personnel directorship. When Dai-Nippon section chief Mr. Ayabe visits Nippon Kaisha, he is treated almost as if he was a department head. In a black-colored company limousine, Mr. Ayabe would sit with Mr. Yamashita at the back while Mr. Matsuda (Nippon Kaisha's personnel section chief) would sit next to the chauffer.

Status stratification works not only at the individual level but also at the organizational level. Dai-Nippon *keiretsu* membership can be divided into two groups of different status. One group identifies the Nichi-wa kai (Sun and Peace Society) for some fifty affiliate (children) firms, many of which are owned more than 50 percent by Dai-Nippon. The other, the Nichi-mu kai (Sun and Friendship Society) has membership of some fifty firms.

Nichi-wa kai tends to include larger firms, which share an interlocking directorate. Many ex-Dai-Nippon executives serve in the top management of these firms. These executives socialize with one another frequently at the Nichi-wa kai monthly meetings, golf tournaments, and dinner parties. Nippon Kaisha has been a member of Nichi-wa kai from the beginning.

The second group, Nichi-mu kai, on the other hand, includes firms that have less personal and business ties with Dai-Nippon and with other Dai-Nippon member firms.

When a firm's business with Dai-Nippon has grown to be significant, the firm may switch membership from the second tier to the first tier (Nichi-mu kai to Nichi-wa kai). There have been seven cases of this kind. One firm was a member of Nichi-mu kai

FIGURE 2: ORGANIZATION OF DAI-NIPPON KEIRETSU: ONE-WAY FLOW OF TENZOKU TRANSFER

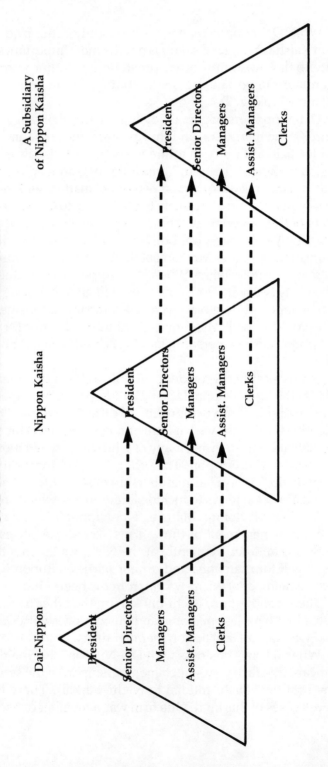

until a *jōmu* (junior director) of Dai-Nippon transferred as a *ten-zoku* man to become its new president. At that time Dai-Nippon increased its shareholding from 40 percent to 60 percent and invited the firm to join the Nichi-wa kai group.

The membership to these groups is, however, not only the matter of corporate ownership; firms with less than 10 percent of Dai-Nippon ownership are included as important *keiretsu* members in the Nichi-wa kai, while some firms with 50 percent ownership do not belong to either group.

Analyses of each *keiretsu* case revealed that a firm is considered as a *keiretsu* member when there is intended or actual "control" and "guidance" by the parent company. There is a tacit agreement between Dai-Nippon management and the child firm for such arrangements. Corporate guidance and control are given in terms of technical advice, quality control management, training programs, manpower supply, leadership by a board of directors, financial supports, material and parts procurement, and intercorporate businesses.

Most *keiretsu* members are in fact vendors or subcontractors for Dai-Nippon, and they are at least 10 percent owned by the parent company. To Nippon Kaisha managers, *keiretsu* membership is like being part of a prestigious club where members share a sense of belonging and common historical experiences. Unlike an ordinary social club, however, there is an identifiable hierarchy of membership status reflected in actual power and control within the *keiretsu*. It represents an interwoven nexus of business and personal relationships where a boundary is drawn between insiders and outsiders and between seniors and juniors.

Surprisingly, there are several firms with 50 percent or more Dai-Nippon ownership that do not belong to either of the two *keiretsu* groups. The reason for their nonmembership becomes clear when one looks at an important characteristic of Dai-Nippon *keiretsu*: each member firm belongs to a different industry, and members do not share the same market. *Keiretsu* is not a cartel where independent commercial enterprises design to limit competition in a particular industrial market. As a matter of fact, competition in each market is fierce among firms with different *keiretsu* connections.

Even when Dai-Nippon owns more than 50 percent of an affiliate firm that company is not considered a Dai-Nippon *keiretsu* member if it is involved in a joint venture with one of Dai-Nippon's competitors. Because of vast network of Dai-Nippon businesses, its competitors in one industrial field may be vendors/clients/partners to Dai-Nippon in other fields. For example, a nuclear-energy-related firm was formed between Dai-Nippon, two Japanese electric/electronics multinationals (competitors) and one American multinational. Another very successful electronics company was formed by Dai-Nippon and its major Japanese competitor in the field of large computers. These firms, in spite of Dai-Nippon's large share of ownership, are not considered as *keiretsu* (insider) firms by the Dai-Nippon group. They do not belong to the club.

In order to enhance the solidarity of the Dai-Nippon group further, Dai-Nippon Research Institute of Management Science was established in the early 1960s to provide various training programs for the management of group members, and the Central Research Laboratory of Dai-Nippon offers technical advice to affiliates and subsidiaries.

Like many other *keiretsu* members, a large percentage of Nippon Kaisha's business has been to provide parts and materials to Dai-Nippon and Dai-Nippon group members. To this end a Dai-Nippon department was established within the Sales Division of Nippon Kaisha to undertake just such business transactions. Ten percent of the total sales of Nippon Kaisha is to Dai-Nippon, while 24.7 percent is to Dai-Nippon member firms. In other words more than one-third of Nippon Kaisha's business is with firms in its own *keiretsu*.

Dai-Nippon *keiretsu* is like a multilayered pyramid: while Nippon Kaisha serves Dai-Nippon and group member companies by supplying parts and materials to them, the subsidiaries of Nippon Kaisha provide components and materials to Nippon Kaisha and Nippon Kaisha member firms. Forty-two and four-tenths percent of Nippon Kaisha's cost of sales is due to buying from its subsidiaries.

In sales brochures and annual reports, the close relationship of Nippon Kaisha with Dai-Nippon and the Dai-Nippon *keiretsu* group is stressed. Sales managers of Nippon Kaisha say that the prestige of being a member of the Dai-Nippon Group helps Nippon Kaisha greatly in dealing with its clients.

Nippon Kaisha's emblem, which combines two *kanji* (Chinese characters) meaning Dai-Nippon, symbolizes its close tie with Dai-Nippon.

ORGANIZATION

Because of Nippon Kaisha's clear identification with Dai-Nippon, Nippon Kaisha tends to follow Dai-Nippon as its role model. Historically many organizational structural changes were made copying those of Dai-Nippon.

The product lines of Nippon Kaisha are divided into the following four categories: electronics, electrical equipment, chemical products, and housing materials. The Chemical Division, the oldest division and the largest source of income, accounts for 34 percent of the total company's annual sales. In 1965 Nippon Kaisha, following the organizational structure of Dai-Nippon Inc., adopted the "operation center" system. Each operation center, or *jigyō-bu*, handles particular product lines and is responsible for the overall results of the products, supervising respective plant operations. Currently there are seven *jigyō-bu* in the manufacturing sector: chemical products, electronic material, electronic parts, consumer products, inorganic chemical products, housing and environmental products, and the international division.

The sales division is organized according to geographical areas and handles products manufactured by the operation centers. Under each operation center there are many subdivisions or sections (*ka*). Nippon Kaisha grew rapidly in the late 1960s when more than forty sections were added within the organization.

In the late 1960s, the company abolished sections within the operation centers in order to decrease the number of levels in the organizational hierarchy. The objective was to create a system of larger groupings so that the communication flow would improve both horizontally and vertically.

The late 1960s was also a time when the company started seriously reconsidering the merits of the seniority rule of promotion. The number of newly hired workers (school graduates recruited once a year) was increasing. Nippon Kaisha annually hired almost 100 university graduates up to the late 1960s. Management realized that if they continued the seniority-based promotion system, they would have to increase the number of managerial positions accordingly. The abolition of the section system and the title of section chief was the company's first move in the direction of modifying the seniority system.

Another characteristic of Nippon Kaisha's corporate culture is the relative power of production people. In the current organizational structure, the director of an operation center is responsible for production, delivery, and sales of the company's products with the cooperation of the sales people. In the case of critical decisions, in general the operation center director has a stronger position than do sales people. All of the operation center directors have technical backgrounds; most have B.S. degrees in engineering or science.

The Executive Committee or *yōmu-kai*, the supreme decision-making organ of the company, regularly meets to discuss the company's overall policies. All but one *yōmu-kai* member have technical backgrounds. The dominance of engineers and scientists at the top echelon of Nippon Kaisha contrasts sharply to the predominantly finance-oriented United America management.[3]

Nippon Kaisha's emphasis upon engineers and scientists is reflected on its personnel policies, which we will examine shortly. The following chart indicates the official organization chart of Nippon Kaisha. Although all *jigyō-bu* are listed equally in the official chart, managers of Nippon Kaisha told me that the chemical and electronics-related divisions are considered as power centers of corporate decision making. The Chemical Division is one of the oldest and most traditional division, while the Electronics Material Division and the Electronics Parts Division are where the top management wish to grow business in the future (fig. 3).

RECRUITMENT

An important characteristic of Nippon Kaisha is found in its labor management. I have mentioned that among the Japanese task environment's main characteristics are low labor turnover and limited ports of entry. Because of these constraints, a tremendous amount of corporate energy is put into recruiting, training, and developing Nippon Kaisha employees. While Nippon Kaisha recruits, trains, and enculturates individuals, these individuals in turn create, modify, and develop the Nippon Kaisha culture.

An examination of Nippon Kaisha's recruitment procedure reveals that the company qualifies the application criteria extremely rigidly so as to ensure the selection of certain type of employee. As for the male employee, i.e. management trainees, who are to work for many years at Nippon Kaisha, the criteria are very strictly applied. The first criterion is that only male university graduates between age 22 and 25 can apply for the job of management trainee. Although there are exceptional cases of mid-career recruitment, the prevailing norm is that Nippon Kaisha annually recruits only recent university graduates.

As for engineers, Nippon Kaisha continues to recruit only among graduates of Japan's top ten universities. In spite of the recent Japanese government policy for open recruitment, which makes it illegal to limit the pool of candidates, Nippon Kaisha continues to concentrate its recruiting efforts on the campuses of the top ten universities. Nippon Kaisha prefers not to hire those with less formal educational accomplishment, older men, or women to join the cadres of management.

Another characteristic is that recruitment is often through personal connections between Nippon Kaisha and university professors.

All these criteria indicate that Nippon Kaisha's freshmen employees are to be highly homogeneous in terms of sex, age, and educational background. Let us examine in detail the recruitment procedure.

Most large companies in Japan recruit recent university or high school graduates every fall, new employees who start working the following April. All Japanese students graduate in March.

Nippon Kaisha's personnel policy involves discussions among various departments and commitment by the top-level management. The policy, which can be called "company-wide human resource management," is similar to company-wide quality management involving quality circles.

Nippon Kaisha does not recruit as the need arises in each section or department. Rather it approaches the issue with a long-term perspective as an overall corporate strategy.

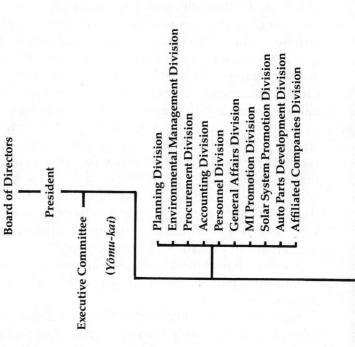

FIGURE 3: ORGANIZATIONAL CHART OF NIPPON KAISHA

Board of Directors

President

Executive Committee
(*Yōmu-kai*)

Planning Division
Environmental Management Division
Procurement Division
Accounting Division
Personnel Division
General Affairs Division
MI Promotion Division
Solar System Promotion Division
Auto Parts Development Division
Affiliated Companies Division

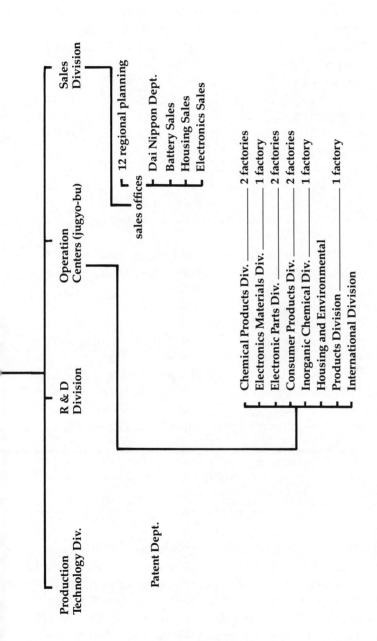

Production
Technology Div.

Patent Dept.

R & D
Division

Operation
Centers (jugyo-bu)

Sales
Division

12 regional planning
sales offices

Dai Nippon Dept.
Battery Sales
Housing Sales
Electronics Sales

Chemical Products Div. —————— 2 factories
Electronics Materials Div. ————— 1 factory
Electronic Parts Div. ——————— 2 factories
Consumer Products Div. —————— 2 factories
Inorganic Chemical Div. —————— 1 factory
Housing and Environmental
Products Division ——————————— 1 factory
International Division

In April or early May the number of new employees required by each operation center for the next year is reported to the personnel department. Each division's needs and the company's long-range policies are discussed in detail. Personnel directors, such as Mr. Yamashita and later Mr. Higashi, act as coordinators of various demands and needs of those concerned and facilitate much discussion on the future direction of the firm and its human resource strategies. Consequently personnel directors have considerable authority and decision-making power on overall corporate policy making—another Japanese characteristic different from usual American practices. The final decision on manpower requirement comes from the members of the executive committee (*yōmu-kai*) and President Kubo, who often personally interview job candidates/college seniors. By the end of May, the personnel department has a clear idea how many new graduates they will recruit for the next year.

There are two tracks of recruitment, one through personal connections, or *kone*, especially with professors, and the other through public announcement. Core members of the firms are usually recruited through personal connections.

The staff of the personnel department visits a handful of leading Japanese universities where they have long personal associations with individual professors. The professors recommend capable students to the company. Through personal negotiations with the students and professors, the personnel staff decides which students will be accepted by the company next April. They informally notify the students of their private decisions (*naitei:* internal decision); the students get an almost certain guarantee from the company for jobs, although they may formally take the company's entrance examinations together with other candidates. According to Mr. Higashi, successor to Personnel Director Mr. Yamashita, a half of the recruitment of university graduates was done this way in 1987.

Nippon Kaisha is attractive to senior university students specializing in chemistry and chemical engineering because of its well-known name and its connection to the Dai-Nippon Group. In this field, Nippon Kaisha has little difficulty in recruiting top-level graduates through personal connections with professors of chemistry and chemical engineering at the leading Japanese universities. All the chemical engineers who entered the firm in the early 1980s were recruited through such personal connections. None joined the firm as a result of public announcements.

Throughout the 1980s Nippon Kaisha was expanding its business into the electronics field. A large part of its electronics business is to supply materials and parts to Dai-Nippon Inc., which has a leading computer and semiconductor operation. As a result, Nippon Kaisha's need for competent electronic and mechanical engineers has increased. Competition among major Japanese manufacturers for top-level electronics engineering majors is increasingly fierce, as Japan shifts toward a high-technology and information-oriented society.

An important function of the personnel director is to visit professors of electronic and mechanical engineering at university campuses, take them out for lunch, invite them occasionally as guest speakers for company seminars, and write to them frequently to keep the positive relationship between the firm and the university. University professors have considerable influence in recommending students for *naitei* selection. It is important for Nippon Kaisha to secure the high-quality graduates recommended by university professors.

In 1982 the company started to offer scholarships to engineering students enrolled in master's degree programs at top-ranking universities with the hope that the students would join the firm after graduation. Currently, six students are receiving full scholarships of about $3,000 a year from Nippon Kaisha.

Most staff members in the personnel department are busy throughout the year visiting leading universities, establishing personal relationships with professors, and identifying promising young men. Once they have selected a potential candidate, the personnel staff starts what they call *ippon-zuri* or the "catching one fish at a time" method: they visit the student's family regularly, invite the student to the company headquarters, put him up at the best hotel in town, organize elaborate dinners and drinking sessions, and try to persuade him to join the company. A Nippon Kaisha employee who is a graduate from the same university as the job candidate joins the personnel team to persuade a candidate from his alma mater. Although the official examination date for the job is not until November 1, recruitment activities for top candidates start early in February of that year. For electronics and electrical engineering jobs, potential candidates are identified while still in their junior year at college or at the time they enter a master's degree program. *Ippon-zuri* is particularly important for recruiting engineers who receive offers from competing firms.

Personnel people obtain high school alumni lists in the areas where Nippon Kaisha's manufacturing plants are located. Among the alumni of local high schools, some may be graduating from top universities with engineering degrees in Tokyo and may prefer to go back to the countryside instead of staying in the metropolitan area.

The examination of the company's recruitment procedures reveals that Nippon Kaisha has developed a strict standard for membership of the organization, and spends considerable amount of energy in obtaining such manpower. They prefer candidates who are recent graduates of top universities, with strong engineering backgrounds. The idea is to acquire human resources of high quality who could enhance the production/manufacturing side of the firm. Nippon Kaisha spends far less energy in recruiting other types of management candidates, namely those with finance, marketing, accounting, economics, and other social science backgrounds. The firm's emphasis on engineers/scientists contrasts sharply to the great attention often paid to the recruitment of MBAs in this country.

PUBLIC RECRUITMENT

So far I have discussed the recruitment of the elite core of Nippon Kaisha, i.e. science and engineering majors who are expected to be company managers someday. For white-collar jobs for managerial cadres, clerical positions, factory jobs, and manual labor, Nippon Kaisha uses a different method: public recruitment.

Every summer or early fall, Nippon Kaisha sends announcements of job openings to universities and high schools. Announcements also appear in major newspapers. The form of the announcement is usually as follows:

Nippon Kaisha, like many other Japanese companies, does not specify the skills required for the job, partly because the company believes in attracting young people of high intelligence and

FIGURE 4: ANNOUNCEMENT OF JOB OPENING

Company: Nippon Kaisha.
Address: 1–2 xxxx, Tokyo
Tel: xxxxxxx
Job Openings For: 63 recent graduates
Company Visit: The personnel department
                will provide an orientation
                seminar on October 2, Heisei 3.
Date of Examination: November 1, Heisei 3.[4]

appropriate personality to be trained and educated over many years within the company.

Nippon Kaisha is very much committed to the internal education and training of their employees, particularly university graduates. According to Mr. Higashi, Japanese universities serve as a screening device of the young, rather than as a provider of skills and specific knowledge. He said, "We would like to get good intelligent young men, but much of the technical knowledge they need to learn is company specific. It is better that the company trains them on the job."

Graduating college seniors, especially those applying for white-collar jobs, do not know what specific job assignment they will get when they are accepted by the company. They usually state the jobs they would like at the time of the interview, but it is very possible that a person will be assigned to a department that has nothing to do with his academic specialization. The underlying principle for this practice is that a person is recruited to become part of the company community not just to function in a specific assignment.

CONCEPT OF PERSONAL ABILITY

Because most of the newly hired workers will work for the firm for a long time, and the company intends to provide various training programs, the most important consideration in recruitment is the potential ability and personality of the candidate rather than the skills that can be put to use immediately. As for job interviews, Mr. Yamashita says:

We ask such questions as what extra-curricular activities they have had at schools, what books or persons have influenced them, and what kind of families they come from. We also ask the reasons for choosing our company and their general opinions about our industry.

The purpose of such questions is to evaluate the overall quality of the candidate, whether the person has a balanced viewpoint, whether he has a cooperative spirit, and whether he has a sound family background. In short, they evaluate a person as to whether he has enough potential to make a good Nippon Kaisha man through long years of service.

A distinction must be made in analyzing the Japanese concept of capability, which forms the basis for this practice. Iwata distinguishes two types of human capability[5]: *jitsu-ryoku* or actual ability and *nō-ryoku* or potentiality. *Jitsu-ryoku* is an ability that can be achieved by training or experiences and can be immediately put into effect. For example, a competent marketing manager who has been in the field for a long period demonstrates his *jitsu-ryoku*. *Nō-ryoku*, on the other hand, is a potentiality that is latent and has not been put into use yet. The marketing manager may have great talent as a financial analyst although he has never tried his hand at it.

Iwata says:

In American society, there is a tendency to pay more attention to *jitsu-ryoku*, which is clearly reflected in American management practices, especially in its recruitment procedures. In contrast, the Japanese concept of human ability has two implications: (a) it is the general capacity of an individual, and (b) it is the potentiality or *nō-ryoku* which can be further developed through training and experiences, rather than that which the man has already acquired. (Iwata 1978:107–8)

THE CONCEPT OF THE JOB

An important characteristic of Nippon Kaisha's labor management concerns the concept of the job. Americans tend to consider that the organization is composed of functions directly related to positions. An individual is hired to fulfill the functions of a specific position so that the organization as a whole operates as the result of interaction among functional individuals. The human resource is a dispensable and flexible asset contingent on the structural and functional requirements of the organization.

Until recently, human resources in Japan have been considered far less flexibly. In the past, there was a socially accepted norm that white-collar male employees, in particular, stayed in the company until retirement. Nippon Kaisha's management legitimized the long-term development of human resources and utilized its human assets as the primary base for the organization. Consequently, jobs and functions, but not people, became flexible. Depending upon a person's actual and potential abilities, management created or changed the functions attached to the position the person held. This perceived mechanism of human dynamics has been a key factor in understanding Nippon Kaisha's organizational development and decision making.

This is one reason why Nippon Kaisha selects an elite group of their management cadres from leading Japanese universities. The Japanese education system is highly competitive and only a small percentage of students can enter top-level universities. In highly meritocratic Japanese society, a degree from one of these universities serves as a powerful credential attesting to a person's overall competence. The company feels it is "safe" to recruit students of top universities who are already labeled as intelligent by the general public. The number of employees from top-ranking universities is in turn used by the public as an index of the company's social prestige. Large and successful companies attract "intelligent" students, which further increases the prestige of the company.

As for the rest of job candidates, Nippon Kaisha examines the candidate's intellectual and skills potentiality, or *nō-ryoku*. His willingness to serve the company community and spirit for teamwork are also considered important.

Compared to ten years ago, attitudes of young people towards the company have changed considerably, the so-called Me-ism is apparent among job candidates. However, Personnel Director Higashi states that young workers are not egotistically pursuing their individual goals relating to monetary gains or increase in leisure time. He says, "They actually enjoy work which gives them personal satisfaction, and they work hard, perhaps harder than those senior to them. But they are not company men."

Partly reflecting a different expectation concerning the company and the job by younger employees, the company's expectations of employees have also changed.

In the late 1970s Personnel Director Yamashita stressed the importance of selecting those who could cooperate with fellow workers, stating that:

> The Nippon Kaisha man must be hard-working and loyal to the company. We prefer a man who can cooperate with his colleagues and develop a team spirit, since we are operating in an organized manner. Even when a man is proven to be genius, we will hesitate to hire him if he can not develop smooth human relationships with his co-workers.

In the late 1980s, however, Personnel Director Higashi emphasized the importance of individual spirit, saying:

> Nippon Kaisha has a tradition of pioneer spirit. There is a distinct corporate atmosphere where a person who expresses himself loudly and openly, and produces results is highly respected. A man of no talk and all deeds (*fugen-jikko*) is not praised here. We want a person of challenging spirit.

The top management of Nippon Kaisha is aware of fundamental social changes and is trying to present Nippon Kaisha as a dynamic, high-tech company, rather than a traditional chemical company. In recent years, "The Pioneer Spirit," a company motto Nippon Kaisha has inherited from Dai-Nippon, an originator of many technological innovations, is frequently used in speeches by company executives. Mr. Takahashi, a new employee who joined Nippon Kaisha in 1986 as a result of *ippon-zuri*, found the company's atmosphere very open.

> My bosses encourage me to speak up. We tend to argue a lot at meetings. If I think my idea is better than my superior's, I can and should tell it straight to him, even when he is director or President. I think that Nippon Kaisha has that type of open atmosphere.

STARTING SALARY

Another salient aspect of Nippon Kaisha's corporate culture is its conscious efforts to create egalitarian ideology within the entering group of organizational elites (male graduates with engineering or science degrees from top universities).

Unlike the United States, where salary is determined by individual negotiation, starting salaries at Nippon Kaisha are exactly the same amount for newcomers of the same age, sex, and educational degree. Whether one is a computer science major or a chemistry major, one gets the same amount for joining Nippon Kaisha. Likewise, no matter how competent he is or how prestigious his university is, a job entrant receives the same starting salary as another newcomer with a similar educational qualifications.

Nippon Kaisha constantly monitors the level of starting salaries offered by its competitors and matches its own salary to the current industrial standard. There are no wide differences in starting salaries among major competing firms in the same industry, although there are considerable variations between industries.

Young college graduates are well aware of this practice, and they approach the issue of employment with a holistic view beyond their immediate financial goals: They look at the overall performance of the firm, its potentiality in the industry, the opportunity for promotion and salary increases over the years, fringe benefits, job security, and the chance for self-development and achievement within the company.

NEW FEMALE PROFESSIONALS

The new wave of female participation in career-oriented jobs affected Nippon Kaisha in the 1980s. In 1983 the company for the first time recruited female researchers for its pharmaceutical products and for laboratory research. Since then, every year three to four female graduates from top pharmaceutical universities have been recruited to strengthen Nippon Kaisha's research and development laboratory. A few women were also hired in 1983 to design home and kitchen products. Nippon Kaisha intends to increase the number of female product designers because they possess qualified skills and the "aesthetical senses of women." As in the case of the recruitment of male engineers, Nippon Kaisha selects candidates from a handful of leading women's colleges that offer such degrees. This practice is again based on the company's wish to secure a certain level of competence and homogeneity among job candidates.

The recent recruitment of a small group of female professionals created a two-tier status system among Nippon Kaisha female
employees. The vast majority of female employees at Nippon
Kaisha are high school graduates who are hired for clerical help
or for factory jobs; these women have little or no chance for promotion to managerial ranks.

High school graduates usually work for the company for several years before they marry and resign. There are five middle-
aged female high school graduates in Nippon Kaisha headquarters, employees who have stayed on the job for twenty years or
more and who continue to handle clerical work but without managerial rank.

Because the professionals work mostly in the firm's laborato-
ries, there is little personal contact between the two groups.

MERITS AND DEMERITS OF NIPPON KAISHA RECRUITMENT

Because of the tradition of lifetime employment, Nippon
Kaisha workers today are rarely dismissed. The recruitment of
recent school graduates is one of the few means open to the company to adjust for fluctuations in the economy and the labor market. When the economy is in an upward trend, Nippon Kaisha
recruits a large number of recent graduates. When the economy
slows down, the company decreases the number of newcomers
rather than dismissing its employees. The following table shows
the fluctuations in the number of newly recruited workers by
Nippon Kaisha between 1973 and 1985. In this official statistical
report, Nippon Kaisha categorizes formal educational backgrounds of recruits as well as their sexes, thus reflecting their
fundamental philosophy of manpower utilization.

During the late 1960s when the total Japanese economy as well
as most business activities of Nippon Kaisha were rapidly expanding, the company recruited about 150 to 180 recent university graduates annually. After the first energy crisis of 1973 and
the subsequent economic recession, the company decided to
drastically decrease the number of recruits. In 1976 Nippon
Kaisha hired only sixty-two employees, including only nineteen
university graduates. In the early 1980s when the economy was

TABLE 1: NEWLY RECRUITED WORKERS IN NIPPON KAISHA 1973–1985

Year	Total No.	Univ. Grads.		Tech. College		High School	
		M	F	M	F	M	F
1973	154	57	0	3	0	26	68
1974	157	59	0	4	0	26	68
1975	257	50	0	7	0	100	100
1976	62	19	0	0	0	0	43
1977	120	21	0	2	0	33	64
1978	81	11	0	0	0	2	68
1979	183	36	0	0	0	37	110
1980	189	49	0	2	0	43	95
1981	193	63	0	4	0	38	88
1982	173	53	0	9	0	36	75
1983	171	47	4	8	0	14	98
1984	284	53	4	17	0	120	90
1985	251	67	10	22	0	58	94

again in an upward trend, Nippon Kaisha increased the number of new recruits from 200 to 300 annually. Instead of laying off the existing labor force in a recession, Nippon Kaisha prefers to adjust the cost of human labor by changing the inflow of workers as well as the outflow of older workers.

In the past Nippon Kaisha avoided retrenchment or layoffs of employees in an economic recession and preferred to share the cost of labor adjustment by means of managerial pay reduction, decreases in overtime, decreases in new recruits, and encouraging early retirement. Many Japanese companies in addition to Nippon Kaisha pursued this no-retrenchment policy.

At the macro level of the economy, the system helped maintain a higher level of employment and decreased friction associated with structural changes in the economy. It also decreased antagonism between management and labor. At the time of a rapid recovery, the Japanese company could readily utilize the existing labor force to quickly increase production. The morale of employees is maintained through a perception or myth that everybody in the company prospers and suffers together, not just those at the bottom of the hierarchy.

In the 1980s, international competition and industrial restructuring toward a more service and commerce-oriented economy began to change the conventional image of the large corporation as a secure employer. Top students who chose the thriving shipbuilding and aluminum firms of the 1950s and 1960s found themselves stuck in low-prestige, no-growth companies in the 1980s and had to release many employees.

Although not that drastically, many firms transfer excess personnel to subsidiaries. Nippon Kaisha is no exception. The firm has been primarily a chemical products firm, and it is now diversifying into electronics. In the process, a certain amount of rationalization is needed. New employees are aware of the fact that the lifetime employment system is no longer a certainty. Mr. Nakamori, a twenty-four-year-old Waseda university graduate who recently joined Nippon Kaisha, says,

A man who works for the firm for a long time may not get fired, but he may be shipped off to a subsidiary probably with a demotion in terms of status and salary. That is not lifetime employment. We know that lifelong employment is a myth.

Career paths for new recruits are becoming increasingly diversified, and one can no longer generalize that Nippon Kaisha's system is strictly lifetime or seniority-oriented. We will later come back to this important issue of transfer to a subsidiary. At present, let us continue to examine how newly hired employees go though their acculturation process to become Nippon Kaisha men.

SOCIALIZATION OF EMPLOYEES: CORPORATE TRAINING

On the first day of April every year, all newly hired workers of Nippon Kaisha gather together in a big hall of the headquarters of the company to be greeted by President Kubo. Mr. Kubo expresses his heartfelt welcome and describes the long-standing three spirits of Nippon Kaisha: Harmony, Sincerity, and the Pioneer Spirit. The ceremony is a rite of passage as young Japanese move into the "real world," having finished their formal education. Instead of the blue jeans and shirts of college days, they are dressed in new business suits and look up to the platform where the company executives sit while President Kubo stands in front of a microphone. This Nippon Kaisha ritual is very similar to the entrance ceremony of a Japanese educational institution, and as a matter of fact, these young Japanese are going to receive another type of education to become Nippon Kaisha men, this time, both vocational and cultural training. On the surface, the ritualistic arrangements of the ceremony look similar from one year to another. However, a longitudinal study reveals subtle changes in the tone of speeches, suggesting changes in corporate value orientation.

In his presidential speech in 1979, President Kubo used terms of kinship and family and reminded the newcomers of the integrity of the company community. Colleagues, he stressed, were not to be regarded as potential competitors but as friends or pseudo-siblings who would share many years together in the company. Management ideology of industrial familism was clearly reflected in Mr. Kubo's forty-five-minute speech in 1979.

Reflecting changes in the corporate environment in the 1980s, however, President Kubo in 1985 emphasized the pioneer spirit of Nippon Kaisha, where young people were expected to be innovative and professional. Individual creativity was stressed as an important personal quality sought by the company. Mr. Kubo also addressed the globalization of the Japanese economy and Nippon Kaisha's international expansion. He pointed to the competitiveness of the business environment in the future and the need for creative manpower.

Reflecting upon ideology expressed by top management, Mr. Machida, a 40-year-old section chief of Nippon Kaisha's Kamiyama plant, describes the organizational climate of Nippon Kaisha in the 1980s.

> I think that Nippon Kaisha believes in developing 100 percent of individual abilities. We want people who have their own goals, who can think for themselves, and who make their own decisions. We tend to encourage open discussions. You can say whatever you want to say as long as it is based upon good thinking.

In this "open" community, however, status differences based upon formal education become very apparent. We have observed the categorical distinction of school graduates in their official personnel report. This differentiation is practiced in various ways, starting out with training programs.

The very next day after the ceremony, the university graduates and high school graduates are classified in two different groups for their first training programs. The university graduates are sent to the company seminar house for one month in order to obtain practical and theoretical knowledge of the company's operations. During the month of April they are also sent to each factory and work side-by-side with blue-collar workers. They then move to the computer section to learn basic computer operation techniques. In early May they are sent to their respective departments and start working.

High school graduates do not obtain such extensive training. They are sent directly to their own department and are trained by their supervisors on the job. They are, however, asked to write their experiences in diary form for the first month (April). At the end of the month, they stay together in the company's seminar house for a week to discuss their individual experiences with other high school graduates and managers and to attend seminars and lectures provided by senior managers of the company.

Newcomers with university degrees are treated as "trainees" for the first two years by management. They are the potential candidates for managerial positions in the company. Study groups are formed, and some study quality control methods or chemical analysis, while others study production methods, financial analysis, or accounting. Group members voluntarily meet with one another after hours to study and discuss issues.

At the end of the two-year training period, they must present individually the results of their studies at a large meeting attended by senior managers and their own supervisors. This ceremony is crucially important to the trainees because some time after this meeting, some trainees will be moved up to the next grade in terms of salary and position, and others will not. Training programs for a Nippon Kaisha employee continue throughout his life in the company. Nippon Kaisha has its own seminar house in Tokyo, and employees are regularly sent there for training for anywhere from a few days to several weeks. See Table 2.

In addition to the training programs, the personnel department selects promising younger managers to attend seminars outside the organization or in business schools. There are various organizations that provide special business seminars, including the Japan Productivity Center, Sangyō Nōritsu Daigaku, Sophia University, and others. Bōeki Kenshū Center, which is sponsored by the Ministry of International Trade and Industry, provides a one-year course on international business for junior-level managers sent by Japanese companies. The Keio Graduate School of Business Administration also offers a one-year course for junior managers based on the Harvard University case method.

Senior managers of Nippon Kaisha attend training programs provided by Dai-Nippon Inc., while other Nippon Kaisha people are trained at the Nippon Kaisha Seminar House located in Tokyo with modern dormitory facilities and a small Japanese garden.

During a five-day seminar for middle management, which I attended, twenty department heads stayed together in the house. They discussed and studied issues of concern, and listened to the lectures by senior managers and outside speakers. The topics of lectures included a presentation by the personnel director on trends in the Japanese labor market, a presentation by a production manager on quality control, the vice president's assessment of the current situation of the company, a professor of international affairs' analysis of the international market, a discussion of man, life, and philosophy by a Buddhist priest, an evaluation of marketing by the marketing director, an overview of research and

TABLE 2: NIPPON KAISHA TRAINING PROGRAMS

Trainees	Training
Senior Directors	—Japan Fed. of Employers Association Seminars;
	—Management seminars by the Dai-Nippon Group.
Directors	—Management seminars by the Japan Productivity Center.
	—Management seminars by the Dai-Nippon Research Institute of Management Science, Dai-Nippon Inc.
	—Management seminars (6 days)
	—Management seminars of the Dai-Nippon Industrial Group (4 days)
	—Follow-up seminars of the Dai-Nippon Industrial Group (3 days)
	—Basic Management Training Programs (4 days)
	—Management seminars at Nippon Kaisha Seminar House (2 days)
Managers	—Basic Management Seminars at Nippon Kaisha Seminar House (5 days, twice a year)
Assistant Managers	—Basic Management Program (3 days, twice or three times a year), Study groups
	—Seminars on specific topics (law, accounting, statistics, finance, etc.)
	—Management seminars by the Dai-Nippon Research Institute of Management Science (6 days)
	—Assistant manager seminars at Nippon Kaisha Seminar House

White Collar Workers
—White Collar Workers' seminar at Nippon Kaisha Seminar House (3 days)

Foremen
—Sales seminars at the Seminar House (3 days)
—Special seminars on production methods
—New Foremen Training Program
—Study groups
—Quality Control Seminars
—Seminars by the Dai-Nippon Research Institute of Technology (12 days)
—Seminars on labor management (12 days)

Engineers
—Seminars at the Seminar House (12 days)
—Quality Control Seminars
—Seminars by the Dai-Nippon Research Institute of Technology (12 days)
—Seminars on specific topics (production, safety measures, research and development)

Researchers
—Study group
—Saturday seminar on specific topics (voluntary)
—Seminars at Nippon Kaisha Seminar House (4 days)
—Sales seminars at Nippon Kaisha Seminar House (5 days)
—Assistant Manager seminars (4 days)
—Basic Management seminars (3 days)

development by the director of the Dai-Nippon Research Institute of Technology, a presentation on accounting by the finance director, and an assessment of technological innovation by the production director.

The wide range of topics outside the specialized field of a single manager is immediately apparent. A manager from the accounting department must learn about the production process, and a production engineer must learn about the international competitiveness of Nippon Kaisha products.

As part of its management philosophy, Nippon Kaisha clearly believes in the value of combining specialized and general knowledge. Senior managers of Nippon Kaisha emphasize the merit of group seminars among managers of different departments because the managers are encouraged to understand the overall aspects of Nippon Kaisha operations and to develop close working relationships with one another. They believe in the interdisciplinary approach to business problems.

After a day's lectures and discussions, the participants have dinner together at the house, often followed by drinks. At the seminar house, senior managers devote a considerable amount of time to getting to know junior-level people personally; and they associate together rather freely on such informal occasions.

The training of blue-collar workers (who are high school graduates) on the other hand is conducted by foremen and supervisors at each factory. They encourage blue-collar workers to take national qualification examinations in their specialized fields — such as in lathe work, design, quality control, and so on.

Nippon Kaisha conducts intracompany examinations twice a year to help employees improve their individual skills. They reward the winners with prizes and salary increases. The opportunity for promotion by participating in these programs encourages individual competition within production units, contributing to the overall improvement of productivity and efficiency.

REWARDING INDIVIDUALS: THE SALARY SYSTEM

Nippon Kaisha, following standard Japanese practice, pays its workers monthly. The salary is composed of three parts: basic salary, additional salary, and special allowances. The basic salary is decided according to educational background, years of service and age, while additional salary is based on the grade of work and number of work hours. The basic salary and additional salary each comprise roughly 45 percent of the total pay.

The remaining 10 percent of an individual's salary is paid as special allowances, such as for a dependents allowance, overtime and special work. There is no incentive system or commission-based payment even for salesmen or operation center managers.

The basic salary, which is 45 percent of the employee's monthly pay, is calculated on two different bases: (1) salary based on educational background at the time workers entered the company, which automatically increases annually, and (2) salary of the first category multiplied by a particular rate according to the grade of work and number of work hours. Each employee is placed in a particular grade category (such as grade one, planning work for a manager: See Figure 5). The rate has an upper and lower limit. For example, the upper limit for grade one, planning work is 69 percent, and the lower limit is 41 percent. On the other hand, the upper limit for grade 1, factory supervisory work is 76 percent, and the lower limit is 50 percent.

The additional salary is also based on the type of job and the working hours calculated in a different way from the basic salary. The additional salary also has two components: (1) a fixed amount to pay according to the grade of work, which is paid equally to all employees assigned to the same grade of work; and (2) the amount calculated according to the type of job responsibility they hold.

Besides the basic salary and the additional salary, a person gets several allowances for dependency status, overtime, hazardous work, and night work. The biggest allowance for the average worker in the special allowance category is for dependents. Nippon Kaisha has several company housing complexes and dormitory houses for married and unmarried workers. The rent for the company housing is very low compared with the market price.

Figure 5 shows the wage and position grading system for university graduates and high school graduates. The highest position that a high school graduate can assume is deputy section chief in the white-collar section and a supervisory function in the blue-collar section.

FIGURE 5: WAGE AND POSITION SYSTEM OF NIPPON KAISHA

AGE	WAGE RANKING	POSITION	
		(White Collar)	**(Blue Collar)**
64–65	shachō, fuku-shachō	President, Vice President	
60–63	senmu	Head of a Key Division	
60–62	jōmu		
51–61	torishimariyaku	Div. Head in Headquarters	
48–58	riji	Dept. Head, Plant Manager	
47–56	s sanyo	Dept. Head,	Plant Manager kōshi
45–52	h sanji	Dept. Head (buchō)	
42–49	u sanji-ho		
38–42	j fuku-sanji	Section Chief (kachō)	
	i		
35–40	1 Planning 1	Deputy Section Chief	1
31–34	2 2	Deputy Section Chief Supervisory	2
27–30	3		3
24–27	3 Trainee	(university graduates) Supervisory	4
22–23	4 Clerical	Technical	5
	5		6
	6	(high school graduates)	7
	7		

BONUS SYSTEM

A participatory aspect of the Nippon Kaisha culture is manifested in its bonus system. Nippon Kaisha provides a bonus twice a year in addition to the basic salary, supplemental salary, and allowances. The bonus is contingent on the company's economic performance. In boom years, such as in the early 1970s, the company paid bonuses equivalent to several months' salary. In 1985 the company provided a summer bonus equivalent to two months' salary and a winter bonus equivalent to three months' pay. As these bonuses are given to all employees regardless of their performance, it is an important issue in labor negotiations. Every year the amount is decided contingent on economic circumstances and the results of labor-management negotiations.

The bonus system reveals the corporate philosophy of profit sharing among members. Everyone benefits from the company's good performance, and everyone suffers from poor performance.

SALARY SCALE

Evidences of such egalitarian philosophy are also found in the salary scale itself. The salary difference between lower and senior level managers is relatively small: While a 38-year-old junior manager earned $36,500 in 1985, the president's annual income (before tax) was $119,500. It is quite a contrast to the average American firm where the president often earns ten times more than a manager at the lowest level. In United America Inc., for example, the president earned more than half a million with such fringe benefits as stock options and free use of a company jet, while a junior sales manager in the international division earned $43,000 (in 1985). The rate of salary increase of Nippon Kaisha between 1967 and 1985 reflects the general economic trend. See Figure 6.

EVALUATION AND PROMOTION

An employee who entered the company as a university graduate is regularly evaluated through formal channels. Each year in

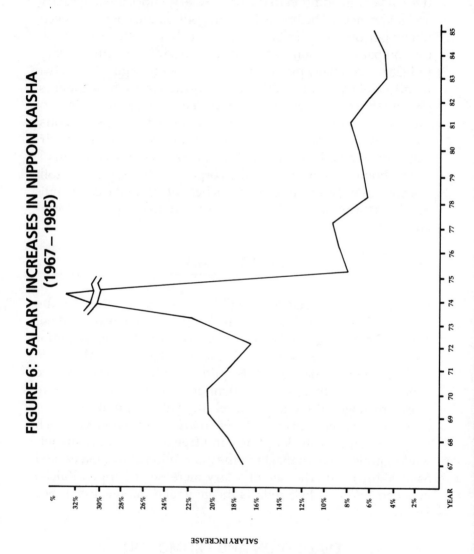

FIGURE 6: SALARY INCREASES IN NIPPON KAISHA (1967–1985)

April, supervisors fill in formal evaluation forms on their subordinates, and report the result to their superiors. Items such as the person's potential, cooperativeness, general job performances, and technical competence are graded as plus or minus from a mean of 100. See Figure 7.

FIGURE 7: EVALUATION FORM

Name: xxxxx
Section and Department: Accounting
Job Grade: 3, planning
Year of Entering the Company: 1976
Major: Economics

(1) Planning Ability
*Does he always plan his job well, and work effectively?
*Does he organize the plan prior to the execution?
*Does he make innovative plans for the achievement of his task?

-20	-10	100	$+10$	$+20$

(2) Accuracy
*Does he act carefully in executing the plan?
*Does he quickly and precisely execute the plan?
*Does he create satisfactory results?

-20	-10	100	$+10$	$+20$

(3) Responsibility
*Does he make enough effort to solve various problems?
*Is he very responsible in performing the task?
*Does he persevere in his effort until the task is accomplished in order
  to fulfill his responsibility?

-20	-10	100	$+10$	$+20$

Within each operation center, managerial discussions are held to balance out the scores of individual employees. Although it is technically possible to score a person as 0 or 1,000, a tacit rule within the company suggests that a person is usually evaluated within the range between 80 (poor) and 120 (excellent).

Employees have access to their own evaluations. When a supervisor rates a subordinate poorly, he usually discusses the reasons for his decision with his subordinate, and he points out possible means of improvement. At the same time, the supervisor must explain the reasons for the poor score of his subordinate to his own supervisor.

The management encourages supervisors to interact frequently with subordinates and give feedback in daily business. A subordinate gains an accurate idea as to how he is being evaluated at the time of formal evaluation.

Unlike some Western companies where the achievement of specific targets is the key for positive evaluation, Nippon Kaisha's evaluation system is more loosely defined and long-ranged. According to Mr. Yamashita, Nippon Kaisha prefers to evaluate a person by observation and interaction at a personal level, keeping in mind the long-range potential of the individual. Mr. Higashi confirms this managerial philosophy. Both personnel directors believe in close communication, both formal and informal, with subordinates, but their styles of personnel management are different.

Mr. Yamashita, who headed the department throughout the 1970s, did his best to make himself available to his subordinates and often invited them out for supper and drinks in order to chat with them informally. Mr. Higashi, who succeeded Mr. Yamashita as personnel director, does not go out with subordinates much because, as he comments, "young people nowadays have their own personal things to do, and I respect that." Nevertheless, Mr. Higashi is also very familiar with each subordinate's personal characteristics, and he sits in the large department room. Mr. Higashi says:

> Individual abilities vary. A person may not be able to perform well because he is in the wrong type of job. In such a case, we try to add or decrease assignments and responsibilities so that his hidden potentiality will be efficiently utilized. While we observe the daily activities of an individual for a long period of time, we can obtain a general idea about the overall quality of the person. Then we try our best to find a suitable position for him.

JOB ROTATION AND PROMOTION

In Nippon Kaisha, like many other Japanese companies, it is not unusual for a university graduate with five years of service in the production department to be assigned to the sales department. The purpose of rotating a potential candidate for managerial position is to give him a wide exposure to various departmental functions and to make him a generalist. A capable younger manager will move up grades of the corporate hierarchy each time he moves from one section to another.

In Nippon Kaisha, there is an unwritten law that a person moving in the circle of production and planning is running upward on an "elite" course. An assignment in the personnel department is also positively regarded because of the emphasis on personnel management by the company and the personnel department's relative power within the corporate hierarchy.

Job rotation can also occur when an employee is judged to be more of a liability than an asset. Although Nippon Kaisha never formally demotes a person, an employee may be moved into a less responsible job while he keeps more or less the same salary as before. Local and overseas branches and affiliates sometimes serve as a place for these people. One person whose performance in an overseas office was judged as unsatisfactory by the top management was brought back to headquarters and then moved into a small office in a developing country in Asia. Mr. Araki, a senior director who told me this story, added that the person was given a second chance to prove his capability in a relatively small business operation. If he proved to be capable, I was assured, he might be brought back to a more responsible job in the future.

Within the corporate headquarters, there are some jobs regarded as a "dead end." It is ironical that corners with a magnificent view, which the Western manager may long for, are usually assigned to excess employees in Japanese offices because they do not need to interact much with other employees in their functions. These people are called *madogiwa-zoku* or windowside executives, i.e., those who have managerial titles but in fact are demoted to auxiliary roles in the organization.

SALARY, POSITION, AND AUTHORITY

The salary scale and positions in the organizational hierarchy do not necessarily correspond at Nippon Kaisha. This is because of the flexibility of job assignments in the organization. The traditional concept of seniority is not completely dead, and salary is generally based on years of service and educational back-ground.[6] In contrast, the idea of meritocracy is often expressed in the scale of positions, which are often assigned based on individ-ual potential and personality. Thus, it is possible for an assistant manager who is ranked grade one, for planning to receive a lower salary than a grade one clerk who happens to be older than the assistant manager.

Today, one can still determine the relationship between salary increase and promotions because of Nippon Kaisha's diehard se-niority rule, especially among younger managers at the lower end of the corporate ladder.

A young college graduate in a clerical job becomes a grade 3 man after completing his initial training. After four to six years, when he is in his early to middle thirties, he generally attains a position of assistant section chief with a salary in the grade one planning category. This is the last nonmanagerial position. Here-after, he will aspire to attain a managerial position of grade three or *sanji* (see Figure 5).

As one goes up higher in the ladder, it becomes more difficult to predict the relationship between age and promotion because of other more influential factors such as meritocracy and political power. At grade one, automatic promotion ends and real com-petition starts with an increasing intensity.

If the man is successful, after twenty-seven to thirty-two years of service, staying within headquarters, he may obtain a position of *sanji*, having worked as an assistant *sanji* and deputy *sanji*. He has now become a departmental head.

The next step is crucial because of the company regulation con-cerning retirement. An ordinary manager should resign from his managerial post at age fifty-six. After resigning, he may move into an advisory position and work there until his official retire-ment at age sixty. When he moves to an advisory post at age fifty-six, his salary decreases to 85 percent of his previous pay.

However, if before the age of fifty-five one attains the *sanyo* po-sition, which is one rank above *sanji*, the retirement from that po-sition automatically moves to age sixty-five. By that time he has a good chance of becoming a board director, heading one of the key divisions.

The board director has no fixed retirement age, which is yet another incentive. The current president of Nippon Kaisha is now sixty-five years old, and it is assumed he will serve several additional years. Fourteen board directors, including four *jōmu* (board directors without executive power) and two *senmu* (senior board directors with executive power) have worked their way up the corporate ladder of Dai-Nippon and Nippon Kaisha for more than thirty-five years.

The youngest board director, someone who does not hold executive power, is fifty-three years old. The average age of the board directors is 63.5 years old, and their average length of service is 38.6 years.

INDIVIDUAL COMPETITION

The overall dynamics of the personnel structure indicate that the real competition among rivals starts at the middle management level. In general, middle management with twelve to twenty years of service who are highly ambitious prefer to stay in corporate headquarters because they consider their chance of promotion is much higher at headquarters than in the field.

The progress of an individual depends very much on what he has accomplished and whether he is judged as a good manager by his seniors. The competition for high positions among middle managers is intense because what is at stake is not only rank and responsibility but their whole livelihood and self-esteem as long as they work for the company. They strive to reach the position of director, board director, and president.

It is at this stage they start to follow certain top-level executives as their mentors, forming factions within the corporate power structure. Factions are usually based on university affiliation, such as *tōdai-batsu* (Tokyo University Clique) or *keio-batsu* (Keio University Clique), or very often because of close personal relationships between a mentor and a follower bound by mutual interests.

It is not uncommon that followers of a particular clique suffer socially and economically if their mentor's rival obtains a high-level position, as the opposing factional leader will certainly attempt to promote his followers.

The hidden fear of losing jobs or of being transferred to advisory functions is particularly strong among middle-aged employees who have been trained to be generalists and have no particular skills to sell outside the company.

A thirty-seven-year-old manager comments on this situation:

> I know that I am a capable and hard-working man in this company, and the company has been treating me fairly decently. I have little complaint about that, but now I am thirty-seven, facing a turning point in my career. I am no longer young, and this may be my last chance to get out of the company. But what can I do if I leave the company? My skill as an engineer has been achieved only by training inside this company. My capability is limited. I can perform well in this company because I know how to manufacture this company's products. But if I am thrown into an open job market, who will pick me up and give me the same salary and position which I am enjoying here?
>
> The competitors of my company will not recruit me because they are big, and they recruit only recent university graduates. I would probably end up working for a small company doing less satisfying work and getting less salary.

So they try their best to stay and to find a good career inside the corporation. Those who are ambitious prefer to stay in the headquarters of the company and do not like to be dispatched or transferred to joint-venture companies or sent to overseas assignments. If the management asks them to do so, they prefer to come back to the headquarters as soon as possible. Being away from headquarters means the possibility of becoming an outsider in the company hierarchy.

Mr. Tsuba, a forty-five-year-old manager who was asked to set up a project of technological transfer involving an American company, had to move out of his position in the production department to become the head of an ad hoc project team. Mr. Tsuba had to spend at least two years working on this project. According to Mr. Tsuba:

> When I moved out of the company to help this project, my former position was filled by a younger manager. I will do my best to make this project successful, but I sometimes fear that I will not be able to go back to the same production department after this.
>
> I am already outside and have lost contact with my former colleagues and bosses in daily business interactions. I am now a little bit off the track of my career advancement. I hope to go back to the right track.
>
> I don't know whether the company can find a suitable position for me after I finish this project. While I will be away for two years, many capable managers will move up the ladder. I will miss a lot by stepping outside the company.

Because higher positions in the company are few in number, the junior management certainly feels competition from other managers to achieve the next position, although they rarely talk about it publicly. A deeper source of frustration is the diminishing chance of becoming a top manager.

An increase in the number of employees with a university degree (currently 1,100 out of 5,100 employees) is causing a problem in the labor management of Nippon Kaisha. If the management tries to maintain its tradition of using the seniority wage and promotion system, they must increase the number of managerial positions to meet the demand, particularly for those who entered the firm a decade ago when the company was hiring fifty or more university graduates annually.

There is already an increase in the number of persons at the top of the nonmanagerial sector, employees who do not hold the title of *fuku-sanji*, which is the lowest managerial title, and who work as deputy section chiefs.

Because of the relative shortage of managerial positions, competition among middle-level managers is intensifying. Losers often have to leave the headquarters as *tenzoku* men — the topic of next section. Because of limited employment opportunities in the Japanese labor market, Nippon Kaisha managers do not have many alternatives in their career planning. Unless one is among those eagerly sought after mid-career specialists, it is a situation in which the individual must find a way to fulfill his self-interests.

TENZOKU AND SHUKKO SYSTEM

There are two systems, *tenzoku* and *shukko*, to move personnel away from Nippon Kaisha to one of its thirty-odd affiliates and subsidiaries. Although many official reasons are given for such a transfer, one significant purpose of the two systems is to trim off redundant personnel at the managerial level. Let us examine this mechanism of manpower rationalization.

Tenzoku

When cherry blossoms have passed their peak and start to fall like snow in mid-spring air, some Nippon Kaisha men receive brown envelopes containing a white rice-paper letter from President Kubo. It indicates the company's wish to appoint him for a new job at its affiliate company.

As explained in chapter four, *tenzoku* or "change of affiliation" is a practice where a person formally resigns from a company to be hired by its child firm, or *ko-gaisha*. Nippon Kaisha, as a *ko-gaisha* of Dai-Nippon, receives *tenzoku* men from its parent company. At the same time Nippon Kaisha has more than thirty *ko-gaisha* of its own to which it dispatches personnel as *tenzoku* men.

Tenzoku men are often managers who are moved to a subsidiary in order to: (1) set up a new operation, (2) strengthen a particular aspect of the company, (3) provide a liaison function between the parent company and the subsidiary, or (4) continue working after retirement from the parent company.

The official retirement age at Nippon Kaisha is age 60, and it is often the case that a retired employee moves to a subsidiary to work for the company for several more years. See Figure 8.

Over the last ten years, the average age of the Nippon Kaisha worker has risen from thirty-three years old to 36.5 years old. The number of employees has also increased from 3,952 to 5,100.

More than any other aspect of Nippon Kaisha's conventional management strategy, the seniority system is now undergoing a drastic change: Nippon Kaisha realizes that the seniority system is too costly and is shifting more and more towards a performance-based salary and promotion policy. Instead of using American type layoffs, however, Nippon Kaisha uses less drastic measures such as *tenzoku*.

So far, Nippon Kaisha subsidiaries willingly accept such transfers of management from Nippon Kaisha, partly because of their wish to strengthen managerial ties with the parent company and partly because of their need for experienced managers; most of Nippon Kaisha's subsidiaries are still relatively young in experience.

The selection of managerial posts in subsidiaries is made through informal communication between the Affiliated Companies Division of Nippon Kaisha and its subsidiaries. For the parent company, it is a means to control the personnel and operations of subsidiaries. For subsidiaries, it is a way to open more communication channels and improve personal relationships with the top management of Nippon Kaisha.

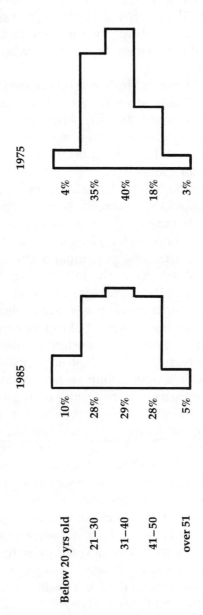

FIGURE 8: AGE COMPOSITION OF NIPPON KAISHA EMPLOYEES (1985, 1975)

Because of the industrial hierarchy, a junior manager who retires from Nippon Kaisha will become a senior manager of a subsidiary. He will work there for several years, usually until age sixty-five (social security payments begin at sixty-five), or he may move to a smaller subsidiary, this time as a senior advisor, an honorary position for a senior executive, who may work there until age seventy.

For example, when Mr. Yamashita retired as personnel director of Nippon Kaisha at age sixty, he moved to a medium size subsidiary as *jōmu* (board director). After several years, he resigned from that company, collected a lump sum retirement allowance, and moved to a still smaller subsidiary of Nippon Kaisha as *sōdan-yaku* (senior counsel).

Nippon Kaisha has an Affiliated Companies Division, which audits the subsidiaries' financial reports. The director of the division regularly meets the top management of the affiliates and subsidiaries to check and advise on financial management, production procedures, and personnal matters. The division produces financial reports on the total Nippon Kaisha Group with the cooperation of the Accounting Division.

The system works not only as a way of eliminating redundant personnel. From the viewpoint of top management, *tenzoku* has a larger and perhaps more important function, which is to consolidate the integrity of the industrial group.

As in the Dai-Nippon group system, *tenzoku* men of the Nippon Kaisha *keiretsu* enhance a sense of in-group feelings among subsidiaries, a key psychological factor for maintaining control and fastening cooperation. On the subsidiary's board, *tenzoku* executives discuss matters with representatives of its major shareholder, Nippon Kaisha. They are ex-colleagues who have shared a number of years experiences in Nippon Kaisha. This interdirectorate network enhances interfirm communication and coordination of business activities. Although *tenzoku* men formally resign from Nippon Kaisha, psychologically they are Nippon Kaisha men; they have devoted more than thirty-five years of service to the parent company. Their pro-Nippon Kaisha mentality becomes obvious if there is a conflict of interest between the parent company and the subsidiary.

Because of such loyalty towards the parent company, none of the member companies would enter on a new venture without the agreement of Nippon Kaisha and its major affiliates.

The advantages of this system are well-recognized by the Nippon Kaisha management, who sent forty-three managers to subsidiaries as *tenzoku* men in 1985 alone.

Tenzoku as a Retirement Program

Personnel Director Higashi considers the practice of *tenzoku* a useful countermeasure against an aging labor force. In the future, the company would like to move older workers into subsidiaries so that they can work until they become eligible for pension payment. This system is particularly attractive for blue-collar workers of Nippon Kaisha, most of whom must retire at age fifty-five although they might still wish to work. With Japan's life expectancy reaching seventy-seven for men and eighty-two for women, many older workers need to work long after the retirement age of fifty-five. Nippon Kaisha founded subsidiaries as a solution to provide financial support for these workers until age sixty-five when Japanese public pension payments begin.

In 1983 Nippon Kaisha established two 100 percent subsidiaries, which are designed exclusively for blue-collar retired employees. One such subsidiary is a packing and delivery company, handling Nippon Kaisha's products. The other is a security and service firm, which provides guards, delivery men, and messengers for Nippon Kaisha and its affiliates. In 1985, Nippon Kaisha added two more firms for retired personnel and plans to establish a few more.

A retired person who moves to a subsidiary of this kind receives a lump sum retirement payment from Nippon Kaisha. He then works for a subsidiary at a lower salary than his previous pay.

The *tenzoku* practice is diversifying as Nippon Kaisha attempts to adapt to changing environmental requirements. The number of *tenzoku* is expected to grow, as Nippon Kaisha searches for ways in the near future to defray the costs of too many older workers and retirees.

Shukko

There is another more temporary method of personnel transfer called *shukko*, which is also widely practiced in Nippon Kaisha. Nippon Kaisha has 970 *shukko* men who are working for affiliates and subsidiaries. *Shukko* is a dispatch of personnel to another firm within the industrial group for a limited period of time.

Unlike *tenzoku* men, *shukko* men may have a chance to come back to Nippon Kaisha, although it is not always the case. Sometimes, a *shukko* man is asked to become a *tenzoku* man due to a change in the policy of Nippon Kaisha management or because of changing economic circumstances.

The official reasons for *shukko* are: (1) to improve the management of a subsidiary (normally one year); (2) to improve sales of Nippon Kaisha products by dispatching salesmen (two years); (3) to improve relationships with other companies or governmental agencies (case by case); or (4) to advise or guide the management by dispatching managers (case by case).

As we have observed, there are multiple meanings of *shukko* and *tenzoku*, both official and personal, in each case of personnel transfer. Nippon Kaisha men often depart with mixed feeling, a sense of sorrow mingled with new hope.

When a man is selected for transfer, his superior notifies him several weeks before the annual official announcement on personnel changes in spring. Nippon Kaisha then issues an official statement written in traditional *sumi* calligraphy with the insignia of the president on special rice paper. According to Mr. Aoki, an engineer who was transferred to Nippon-United, "when you receive it, it is like a *shōshū-rei-jō* (an imperial draft for military service). There is no U-turn."

In "celebrating" such a new assignment, the whole department gives a farewell party. Often the president or vice president attends the party and gives a speech on how great the man's past service to Nippon Kaisha was, how significant his new post is, and how his new assignment will bring benefits to the subsidiary and Nippon Kaisha. The speech ends with good wishes for his *go-kentō* (strenuous efforts to make it successful). His colleagues toast *kanpai!* (bottoms up; Cheers!), lifting beer glasses.

Unlike a typical retirement in this country, Japanese *tenzoku* and *shukko* signify a certain continuity between an employee's past career in Nippon Kaisha and his new task assignment. A *tenzoku* man is no longer officially a Nippon Kaisha man, but he is still a member of the Nippon Kaisha Group no matter how peripheral his new position is.

Conclusion

Upon closer examination of the *tenzoku* and *shukko* systems, one realizes that career development of Japanese *sarari-man* or white-collar workers is not as straightforward as the conventional image of the lifetime employment system suggests. The notion of lifetime employment assumes that workers remain in the same organization until they retire thirty or more years later. In reality, for the great majority of Japanese adults, lifelong job tenure is more a dream than a reasonable expectation.[7] Even for an elite organization man of a large Japanese firm, the probability of remaining within the same firm, and of assuming an executive position in thirty some years, is more like hitting a jackpot.

Japanese managers' career paths are just as treacherous, exciting, and exhausting as those in a large American multinational. It is increasingly difficult to survive and succeed in a large Japanese corporation. Many managers fail and leave the organization. Others take up the challenge of running a new subsidiary operation.

When they leave, however, their relationship with the original firm does not end then, unlike that of American managers who quit a job. Japanese maintain relationships, as they parachute down to smaller less prestigious organizations; these relationships are institutionalized. Accumulated knowledge and historical wisdom possessed by these men are utilized through these institutions for several years to come. From the life-course view, the *tenzoku* men need to modify or perhaps remake occupational goals. They moved before. They moved from one department to another within the original firm. This time the move is from one firm to another in the same *keiretsu*. The man tries to console his soul, justify his past political moves, and rationalize this new outcome.

* * *

We have looked at Nippon Kaisha people from the time of their entry into the firm to the time of their exit. Nippon Kaisha places much emphasis on its personnel management and human resource management, both inside the firm and in its *keiretsu*. The examination of the *shukko* and *tenzoku* system reveals the corporate-level ideology for the cohesion of the group.

My interviews with Nippon Kaisha managers revealed that an overwhelming majority do not regard their jobs simply as a means of earning money or a business contract. Instead, they attach a great deal of meaning to the continuity of relations formed within the corporate framework and derive intrinsic rewards from their work life. They express a relational way of looking at the economic institution.

Nippon Kaisha managers believe that profits, losses, and technology are ultimately dependent on social encounters between individuals and how they perceive such social relationships. In this view, business is confined to neither finance nor technology alone.

A strong centrifugal force operates in this organic entity, spinning off personnel, functions, and divisions from a core of rotation to periphery, while concentrating power, status, and prestige at the center. *Tenzoku* and *shukko* men spread corporate culture and business knowledge from the reservoir at the center to remote corners of *keiretsu*. The concentricity of relations nurture the integrity and communication among *keiretsu* "sibling" firms in a pseudo-Confucian order of vertical relationships.[8]

We conclude that Nippon Kaisha's corporate strategy for personnel is relation-oriented. Despite recent changes, Nippon Kaisha's employment relationship continues to exhibit a system of relational contracting, rather than spot contracting.[9]

What are the economic effects of such relational dynamism? Considering "relational contracting" between *keiretsu* organizations, Dore identifies three effects of such a system[10]: First, the relative security of such relations encourages investment in supplying *ko-gaisha* (child firms). Because their relationships to the parent manufacturing firm is relatively secure, *ko-gaisha*/vendors could afford to take a longer term view on their capital investment or research and development.

Secondly, the relationships of trust and mutual dependency make for a more rapid flow of information. News of impending changes in markets or technological innovation can be passed rapidly through personal grapevines and often widely shared throughout the *keiretsu* system.

Another important byproduct of the system is general emphasis on quality and dependable delivery. What holds the relation together is the sense of mutual obligation. According to the ethic of relational contract, the parent firm expects subcontractors to meet the obligation to provide quality and delivery, while the subcontractors expect the parent to "look after" them.[11] In this long-term relationship, both sides are obliged to do their best.

We have begun to feel the intricately woven texture of the Japanese business world composed of personified corporations. In the next chapter, which is the heart of the present study, one enterprise, "born and raised in America," enters the stage. Our focus will shift from a single-firm study (Nippon Kaisha) in this chapter to a study of intercultural interaction between two firms (United America Inc.-Nippon Kaisha). My methodology will also shift from a conventional Organization Behavior approach to a more process-oriented, interpretive approach.

The joint-venture study, which is the most important part of this book, is an ethnographic case history, chronologically following stages of the joint-venture operation of Nippon United, from the contract negotiation, the establishment of the joint venture, the initial problems, the technical problems, the marketing problems, and the reorganization through the operation of the company up to the year 1985.

The focus of my ethnographic study was on the perception and evaluation of critical past incidents by the Japanese and American managers who had been involved in the decision making and expressed their opinions at the time of research. I recorded their statements regarding the reasons and methods for particular decisions and their modifications in the past, and their retrospective thinking, thus allowing them to "interpret" and create social reality and order that made sense to them.

My research, because of its nature and approach, made them probe their ways of doing business against those of the joint-venture partner. The dialogical process of the joint-venture operation became more salient when the self was identified against the others.

I have stated that in joint-business negotiation, styles and forms of decision making are not that essential. It does not matter much whether the Japanese use consensus-style decision making, while Americans use the majority vote rule, as long as they reach the same decision. The problems of joint-venturing occur when the partners do not agree on the issue of concern. Such business problems, although crucial for the success of the operation, have little to do with the Japanese government's protective policies or tariff barriers. Rather, they have something to do with each manager's values and ideas about how to run his business.

I argued in chapter one that quantitative analyses of decision making or sociological questionnaire surveys, which have been an overwhelmingly favorite approach in past organization studies, cannot fully explain this crucial area of corporate ideology and cultural values. This qualitative, ethnographic study was intended to fill in this area.

CHAPTER FIVE

THE JOINT-VENTURE COMPANY: NIPPON UNITED

INTERCULTURAL MANAGEMENT

Culture consists of symbol-mediated patterns of behavior, attitudes and ideas, which are interrelated, learned, and shared by members of a social group. Our judgment about what is rational or irrational, what is natural or unnatural, and what is good or bad is largely learned through culture. In the previous chapter we observed that Nippon Kaisha's culture emphasizes industrial group solidarity, human resource development, and long-range corporate planning, and that the corporate culture justifies and legitimizes managerial actions. In addition, it is generally consistent with its larger socioeconomic cultural environment.

Managers live in a particular sociocultural environment at a certain historical moment. Born out of the specific cultural milieu of twentieth century Japanese capitalism, Nippon Kaisha's managerial thinking represents one version of possible business "rationality" alternatives. Likewise, United America's managerial thinking, which will be examined in this chapter, is influenced by their American business culture, which tends to emphasize profit optimization and maximum return on investment, and considers human resources as tangible costs.

The underlying theme of this ethnographic case study is that corporate culture is created and developed by organizational members as a subset of larger cultures, and not as an isolated, unique entity. It is a composite process of organizational members' traits, and their perception of environmental factors, of organizational practices, and of macroeconomic characteristics of the historical moment.

When two different corporate cultures meet and interact with each other, the interface of the two cultures reveals not only the differences between the two but also implies differences of larger cultures — namely primary culture and professional culture — where organizational members have been socialized. Primary culture and professional culture serve as background cultures of a corporate culture. Let us examine this relationships between cultures.

Primary culture affects everyone in society and is learned by primary socialization. In this case study, primary cultures are American and Japanese cultures.

Professional cultures, as subsets of the native primary culture, can be found in medicine, law, science, education, etc. The professional culture of business provides the means for business-men to perceive, interpret, plan, and implement particular busi-ness actions. Business culture is constrained by the primary cul-ture in a sense that the codes of business behavior do not usually contradict the codes of behavior in the primary culture, but rather select from the wider culture.

Consequently, a Japanese businessmen's business decisions are partly constrained by their "Japaneseness." Studies show that managers of different cultural backgrounds exhibit different managerial styles and behavioral patterns in multinational cor-porations.[1]

Corporate culture usually stays within the limits of business culture and within the limits of primary culture. It is more spe-cific than professional culture and is directly related to activities of the members of a particular company.

The Nippon Kaisha culture has been created and developed because Nippon Kaisha people perceive, interpret, and interact with their task environments. Individual members bring to-gether their values, attitudes, and norms, acquired through their primary, professional, and corporate socialization processes.

They perceive, interpret, and recreate social and political sanc-tions, rewards and punishments, power relationships, and cor-porate hierarchy that encourage certain behavioral patterns, while discouraging others. The corporate members reflect in action on their jobs and continuously modify, nurture, or change their attitudes, values, and norms on business-related issues. Through symbolic interactions, they share a socially perceived reality beyond individual idiosyncracy.

In this dynamic process, the company as a social group develops a collective history, a common philosophy, and a collective need to process its complexity through symbolic means. Although an organization contains many subcultures, the culture of a dominant group with a learned, shared, compelling set of symbols, often provides an environment for other members to classify, code, and act out social reality and to legitimize certain behavioral patterns.[2]

The relationships between primary culture, professional culture, and corporate culture are not random but of gradual specialization. Diverse professional cultures are subunits of primary culture in the sense that codes of professional cultures agree with those of primary culture, but they are more specific in their application. Unlike general cultural codes set by primary culture, the codes of businessmen usually deal only with business behavior.

Similarly, desirable and nondesirable defined by a corporate culture are more specific compared with those in the wider frame of business culture. The relationship between the three levels of culture is marked by gradual specialization, which is achieved by a step-by-step process of socialization. Persons in any company are therefore socialized first into their primary culture, then into their business culture, and finally into their corporate culture.

By the time Mr. Yamashita of Nippon Kaisha meets Mr. Martin of United America, these two individuals in their triple cycles of socialization exhibit different cultural orientations and act accordingly.

This chapter will show that the organizational culture of Nippon Kaisha clearly differs from that of its American partner because its primary, business, and corporate cultures differ. Organizational cultures of Nippon Kaisha and United America have evolved into the present structures over many years. Both have found legitimacy and effectiveness in their respective environments. When United America attempts to change or modify certain aspects of Nippon Kaisha culture, however, it meets resistance. Two corporate cultures, each consistent with their respective business and primary cultures, meet, collide, and co-operate while trying "officially" to create a hybrid corporate culture in the name of their 50 – 50 joint-venture company. Out of many trials and errors, a new ground of accommodation is slowly formed through acculturation.

This study focuses on an intimate level of intercultural interface to examine not whether culture matters but when and how it matters. It will follow chronologically a case of one corporate culture interacting with another for more than fifteen years. Differences in managerial thinking are highlighted in critical incidents such as the initial joint-venture negotiation, the contract, and technology transfer.

Another important new approach of this joint-venture case study is to reveal the nature of intercultural competition. Insufficient attention has been paid to the competitive aspects of the joint-venture relationship: This study will reveal that international joint ventures are not always cooperative ventures, but rather they exhibit many competitive characteristics. This ethnographic study will show that the two partners very often exhibit discords over managerial control, that they compete for power and control, and that their approaches to managerial control are culturally conditioned: Japanese prefer to exert authority through human resource strategies, while Americans pay greater attention to restructuring organization systems with functional specifications.

It is important to observe when and where cultural factors come to play a role in the joint-venture operation. In general, cultural differences are revealed more saliently when it comes to "software" of the joint-venture operation.[3] For example, differences are observed in goal setting, assessment of personal skills, system of evaluation and promotion, marketing and sales, decision-making time frame and aesthetics.

The American management and the Japanese management of this joint venture can be viewed as two historical layers of cultures that have become opposed as rival models of organization. The emerging culture of Nippon United can be viewed as a historical process where dialogues between two different social groups constantly recreate newer layers of corporate tradition.

Let us look at the ethnographic history of Nippon United Company.

NIPPON KAISHA BEFORE MEETING
UNITED AMERICA INC.

During the 1960s Nippon Kaisha was in the middle of a geographical expansion and diversification of its product lines. The company was looking for foreign technology on various products, which could be introduced to the Japanese market.

Prior to meeting with United America Inc., Nippon Kaisha engaged in a joint-venture project with Hawthorn Inc. of the United States, a multinational conglomerate with seventeen divisions and fifty-seven sales companies located all over the world. Hawthorn Inc. had begun investigating the possibility of entering Japan through its sales agent in Japan. During the 1960s Hawthorn contacted Iroha Kaisha, a smaller Japanese chemical manufacturer established in 1952 by a self-made chemical engineer and entrepreneur. Iroha Kaisha's founder-president had a close business and personal relationship with the top management of Nippon Kaisha. Their relationship went back to the time when a cooperative research and development project on an industrial chemical product was conducted between the two companies. Iroha Kaisha was also a subcontractor of Nippon Kaisha, supplying parts and chemical materials.

Nippon Kaisha management, who were interested in entering a particular chemical field in which Iroha Kaisha was engaged, considered the acquisition of Iroha Kaisha, provided that the quality of the product was to be improved by introducing foreign technology. In 1965 Nippon Kaisha negotiated with the founder and president of Iroha Kaisha, Mr. Horiuchi.

Mr. Horiuchi founded Iroha Kaisha with his wife in a hut with a corrugated tin roof located near the Arakawa River in 1947. From that humble start, Mr. Horiuchi toiled to build the firm. The company grew under his autocratic leadership, the workers of Iroha Kaisha began to unionize, and the union fought for better working conditions and wages. Mr. Horiuchi complained bitterly about the "invasion of the reds" in the late 1950s. By the late 1960s, Mr. Horiuchi was ready to quit. In 1966 he sold the company to Nippon Kaisha with which he had a long-established trade relationship.

Nippon Kaisha tried to fire ten employees while keeping approximately ninety of the previous Iroha Kaisha employees. Although the official reason for dismissal was to eliminate redundant workers, it was clear that Nippon Kaisha wanted to start the firm clean without "ideological" problems. Nippon Kaisha also sent fifteen technical engineers, accountants, and other experts as *shukko* men from the headquarters, together with the four senior *tenzoku* managers. Mr. Horiuchi retired, and one of the four senior managers became the new president.

Negotiations with Hawthorn Inc. started parallel to the acquisition and reorganization of the new subsidiary. In the fall of 1966, Hawthorn Inc. and Nippon Kaisha agreed to form a joint venture using the former facilities of Iroha Kaisha.

The union protested the dismissals of ten Iroha Kaisha employees and sued Nippon Kaisha. It took Nippon Kaisha ten years to settle the problem out of court. During the 1970s a few of the original ten plaintiffs were still fighting the company's decision.

In 1967, Nippon Hawthorn Kaisha, a joint venture between Nippon Kaisha and Hawthorn Inc., was inaugurated. Nippon Kaisha held 50 percent of the capital while Hawthorn Inc. (U.S.A.), and Hawthorn Australia Inc., a 100 percent subsidiary of Hawthorn Inc. (U.S.A.) each held 25 percent.

The management started to straighten out the old labor union problem. A new enterprise labor union was formed, supervised by the Nippon Kaisha union, to rival the old one. In two years, the company union won leadership by election. In 1967 the new joint-venture company built a manufacturing plant to manufacture and sell synthetic resin and polymer products.

COMMUNICATION DIFFICULTIES

In the beginning, the joint venture faced several problems. First, communication difficulties became very acute. On the initial technological transfer, all the documents sent from Hawthorn Inc. had to be translated because Nippon Kaisha's Japanese engineers did not understand technical English. Available interpreters had little specialized knowledge on the chemical formulation procedures. Instructions on technical matters from Hawthorn Inc. were sometimes misinterpreted or ambiguous.

At that time, Nippon Kaisha was mostly domestic-oriented, without an overseas division, and was short of English-speaking employees. They recruited a few bilingual Japanese in mid-career to assist in communication between the two companies. It took them a while to acquire the operational procedures of translation and interpretation. Mr. Holland, an American engineer at Hawthorn who participated in technological transfers said:

> I would explain technical matters to Mr. Kaneko, a man from the Nippon Kaisha overseas division. I knew that Mr. Kaneko had little previous knowledge on the technical matters which I was trying to explain. I would use plain English. Then Mr. Kaneko would talk to Mr. Inoue and other Nippon Kaisha engineers standing besides us. There would be a lot of talk back and forth among themselves in Japanese. They would talk very rapidly, and I could not even catch a single word. They would talk for quite some time. Then Mr. Inoue, through Mr. Kaneko's interpretation, would ask me to explain the matter again. I would get an uneasy feeling and sense of suspicion that Mr. Kaneko did not or could not translate technical English.

SECRETARY'S SALARY

Hawthorn Inc. (U.S.A.) sent an American manager, Mr. Thurow to become vice president of the joint-venture company. Because Mr. Thurow did not speak Japanese, he hired, as his personal secretary, a Japanese female college graduate, Miss Tanaka, who majored in English literature. Miss Tanaka was an attractive young lady with silky long black hair. She spoke fluent English, was very organized, and seemed competent in dictation and typing. Appreciating her intelligence and high level of professional competence, Mr. Thurow decided to pay her rather handsomely.

Mr. Thurow, unfortunately, was not familiar with the Japanese wage and salary system, and he eventually set Miss Tanaka's salary at a level more than three times that of other Nippon Kaisha female clerks and secretaries. Because the accounting of the joint-venture company was handled by Nippon Kaisha's Accounting Division, stories about Miss Tanaka's extraordinary salary level soon spread among Nippon Kaisha's female employees. Much social pressure, informal but persistent, was put on Miss Tanaka, finally forcing her to resign from the company.

CUSTOMER CLAIMS

Nippon Hawthorn started to sell synthetic resin and polymer products in the Japanese market using Nippon Kaisha's distribution network. Japanese customers started to complain about the slight odor of the product, which was not related to the product performance. Hawthorn Inc. (U.S.A.), which had never encountered such a problem in the American market or in many other foreign markets, ignored the complaints, arguing that the removal of the odor should not be the main concern of the chemical engineers of the joint-venture company.

The American side, to whom the product market in Japan was still very small, did not wish to invest time and money in removing the odor. Nippon Hawthorn had several competitors who were engaged in price competition, and the sales margin was small for the joint-venture company. The Japanese side, however, argued that the company should provide what the Japanese customer wanted because the sales of the product depended heavily upon the customer's taste. Because Americans did not extend technical assistance for this problem, Nippon Hawthorn's Japanese engineers, with the help of Nippon Kaisha's research and development scientists, spent much effort to remove the odor by themselves. Hawthorn management complained that they were making unnecessary modifications in the product, which had nothing to do with its excellent functional quality.

VOLUME OF ORDER

The differences in the market size posed another serious problem. Hawthorn Inc. in the United States was used to a huge volume business with large clients. They considered it less important to measure precisely the content of an individual package. When Nippon Hawthorn ordered a certain number of packages, they found that some packages contained more of the material, and others less, although the total volume was the same as the volume ordered. The Japanese, who had to produce more finely measured products because of the smaller volume of individual orders, had to adjust the volume of material themselves.

In the United States, large users with direct access to the consumer make annual plans based on projected demands, and order the products accordingly. On the other hand, many Japanese clients/users of Nippon Hawthorn products are actually middlemen in the long chain of distribution. They tend to adjust orders to market demands in a shorter time.

In the initial phase of the operation when Nippon Hawthorn was still importing some products and materials from the United States, this difference became a problem. While Hawthorn preferred to send a large volume to Japan, due to transportation and cost problems and expected an annual order system from the joint-venture company, Nippon Hawthorn Kaisha needed a more finely tuned adjustment to supply the products when users asked for them, or "just in time."[4] When a Japanese user asked for immediate delivery of products, Nippon Hawthorn Kaisha could not get them from America and had to give up the business. Such failure in delivery damaged the credibility of the new joint-venture company in the eye of its customers.

GOVERNMENT INDUSTRIAL QUALITY STANDARD

The Japanese governmental standards on chemical products were more strict, and in order to receive the Japanese Industrial Standard (JIS) mark for guaranteeing the quality of the product, Nippon Hawthorn had to raise quality standards above those required in the United States market. The American parent company believed that the product could sell even without governmental guarantee because the standard of quality was adequate. The Japanese side, on the other hand, insisted that obtaining a guarantee label from recognized authority, or *o-sumi-tsuki*, was essential. Without much support from the American side, the Japanese engineers again spent a considerable amount of effort in order to receive the guarantee.

Having overcome such initial problems, Nippon Hawthorn is now operating successfully in Japan. The product, without odor, is of an excellent quality, better than that of comparable United States manufacturers, and is now being sold overseas.

Because of the critical past incidents described above, Nippon Kaisha managers had formed certain presuppositions about difficulties involved in a cross-cultural joint venture before they met United America. The preceding incidents and their outcomes had been registered in Nippon Kaisha's management mentality as accumulated historical knowledge, and they influenced the managers' subsequent dealings with United America.

A corporate culture and its value orientation are created, developed, and modified through a continuous process of learning. When managers in action try to interpret, analyze, and solve a particular issue, they are already conditioned and programmed to think in a certain way because of their past learning experiences. They do not approach a problem fresh every time. Instead they consciously or unconsciously reflect and rely upon their repertoire of past collective memories, examples, legends, myths, and experiences. Although a joint venture with United America is different from that with Hawthorn, it is understandable that Nippon Kaisha management used their only previous experience with an American firm as an important reference point.

Likewise, United America's management carried its own cultural baggage when they crossed the Pacific Ocean to meet Nippon Kaisha. Let us briefly look at United America Inc., with its own reservoir of accumulated information ready for future application.

UNITED AMERICA INC. BEFORE MEETING NIPPON KAISHA

United America Inc. is a multinational corporation with 40,000 employees, 100 profit centers, more than 300 manufacturing plants, 600 business locations, and more than 7,500 products. The company is listed among the top fifty United States manufacturing companies on the Fortune list with worldwide sales of over $4 billion.

In the late nineteenth century, the company started as a family-owned consumer products business. At the beginning of the twentieth century, United America Inc. expanded geographically within the United States. Diversification of product lines started in the late 1920s, and the company entered the chemical field. In the 1930s, the stock of United America Inc. was listed on the New York Stock Exchange.

Following a study of opportunities abroad, United America Inc. started in the 1950s to establish overseas operations, first in Canada and Mexico, then in Denmark, Holland, and other European countries. The company then entered into South American countries, including Peru, Brazil, Argentina, Venezuela, Colombia, and Puerto Rico. In the late 1950s, they established the first Asian base in the Philippines, and then in other South Asian countries as well as in Australia. Most of their foreign operations were in the form of 100 percent subsidiaries or sales offices. In the 1960s, United America formed a 50–50 joint venture with a family firm run by a strong-willed entrepreneur in Spain. Besides this successful venture, United America did not have previous experience in running an international joint-venture operation.

United America's history of expansion fits the common pattern for America firms to move into the European market after investment in Canada and Mexico. Like many American multinationals, United America preferred 100 percent subsidiaries to joint ventures in their direct overseas investment.

Together with direct investment, exports from United America grew. By the mid-1960s, the business of the company's foreign operations had grown to about 15 percent of total sales.

Since the beginning, United America Inc. had been regarded by the employees and the general public as a steady and conservative company. The image of the company had been associated with several major consumer products, which were commonly found household brands.

The year 1967, however, saw a significant change at United America. Mr. Lang who had ascended the corporate ladder through its chemical division became president. Mr. Lang wanted to change United America's domestic orientation. The new management under Mr. Lang's leadership, set in motion a long-range program designed to change the corporate image: to transform the firm from a fiarly successful, regional company with a few identifiable major product lines, to a dynamic, well-diversified international corporation. Mr. Lang wanted to put the company on a world map and to position United America Inc. in the public mind as a manufacturer and distributor of a broad range of consumer and industrial products of high quality.

Looking at United America in retrospect, it was also the time when the concepts of business administration, strategic management, profit centers, and management by objective began to infiltrate its corporate board rooms. In a wider environment of United America, business schools began to thrive, with Harvard Business School at the pinnacle. MBAs, equipped with "sophisticated" management techniques and financial know-how, were hired to plan strategy. United America was no exception.

For the first time in the history of United America Inc., the office of the president was established and moved into a new building with a newly created presidential staff of MBAs. Their job was to develop, through corporate policy, a new image for United America Inc., to provide close control of the decentralized management of the company's increasingly diversified activities, and to broaden the executive role in short- and long-range corporate planning and in the appraisal of operating performance.

The name of the street where the corporate office was located became a generic term for the power center among United America managers.

Mr. Lang, through energetic and inspiring speeches, publications, and corporate announcements, guided United America's takeoff for greater diversification and globalization. He also started buying many smaller firms to serve as new divisions on United America's growing lists of internal organizations. This was a move totally opposite to Dai-Nippon's spinning off its divisions to create *keiretsu*, while keeping the parent firm thin and trim, during the same time. In United America Inc. the Chemical Division was expanded both by the acquisition of other firms and the establishment of new business.

Another important decision by the office of Mr. Lang was to create a United America Inc., International. The newly created division took full responsibility for foreign affiliates and subsidiaries and for exports. The International Division was put under the direction of Mr. Murray, corporate vice president, and was organized according to product groupings. Mr. Murray was in his early sixties, and because of his age, people gossiped about possible successors after Mr. Murray's retirement in the near future. (In contrast, Nippon Kaisha managers start their race for upper management positions at Mr. Murray's age.)

With the new International Division, the other divisions also went through a restructuring: The division's product lines were organized into profit centers and grouped according to the sector of the industry each served. Each profit center was assigned re-

sponsibility for the production, marketing, and profit performance of its products. The profit centers were provided by the division with centralized staff services such as engineering, quality
assurance, accounting, legal services, and research and development.

In 1969 the Board of Directors in United America, Inc. was reduced from fifteen to thirteen members. (In 1985 they had eleven
board directors, including seven outside directors and one advisor to the board: In contrast, Nippon Kaisha has no outside
director).

In 1971, Mr. Murray was moved up to the corporate office to
become vice chairman, while keeping the position of International Division president. He was to keep the position for a few
more years before retirement. Because of this move, United
America Inc.'s International Division was again restructured,
this time along geographic lines, in order to more fully develop
overseas market opportunities without distinction as to products. The division was divided into three geographical areas,
each under the direction of an area president: United Europe,
United Latin America, and United Asia. The Canadian operation
was transferred from product divisions to the International Division as another subdivision. Under Mr. Murray's supervision,
major operations included the European operation headed by
Mr. O'Leary, the Latin American operation, headed by Mr. Lo-
pez, and the Asia operation, led by Mr. Franklin.

Mr. Franklin, a slim, tall, intelligent man in his late forties,
came from a United America family—his father had worked for
United America and had retired as a vice president. After graduating from a prestigious East Coast university, Mr. Franklin
started out as an assistant sales manager at United America and
moved quickly into exports and international operations. He
lived both in Europe and Asia and was one of a few truly international men in United America. Mr. Franklin had a graceful
gentlemanly mannerism and was known for his analytical ability
and meticulous attention to details. He was a classy individual,
ambitious, and aspiring to become president of United America
someday. The office rumor said that Mr. Franklin and Mr.
O'Leary were in a deadlock rivalry as each man headed United
Europe and United Asia respectively. Mr. O'Leary had been involved in the chemical field for more that ten years. The reader

may recall my encounter with Mr. O'Leary at Hotel Ōkura in Japan. As head of Europe this Irish American gentleman aspired for the presidency of the International Division as his next promotion.

The headquarters of the International Division (United America Inc., International) is located in New York with approximately 150 members. More than 12,000 employees reside outside the United States. The International Division is responsible for the operation of 130 plants in 32 countries and exports to more than 130 countries. The division's profits account for roughly 25 percent of the whole company; its sales represent 20 percent of the total. United America was ready to go global, and Asia was one area where opportunities seemed to be enormous.

With the enthusiastic support of President Lang, the International Division expanded geographically in the late 1960s. United America's previous experiences in international operations, however, were mostly in Latin America and Europe. In Asia, the Philippines was the only country where United America established a chemical manufacturing operation. Mr. Lang handpicked Mr. Franklin to head the Asia Division. Mr. Franklin knew that his rise or fall in the corporation depended upon the Asia operation. Japan was virgin territory for him.

UNITED AMERICA INC. MEETS NIPPON KAISHA: INITIAL CONTACT

United America Inc. had been exporting various products to Japan, using Japanese *sogo-shosha* or trading companies as their sales agents.[5]

Mr. Martin, who later became the second president of the Japan operation, was working for the Machinery Division of United America at that time. Through his export efforts of United America machinery to Latin American countries, Mr. Martin began to know many Japanese trading company men who were forerunners of Japan's globalization. When the International Division started looking for someone to expand their business in Japan, Mr. Martin recommended one of his Japanese acquaintances, Mr. Ōbayashi, a San Francisco branch manager of Kakubeni, a large *sōgō-shōsha*.

It took several weeks for Mr. Ōbayashi to accept the job offer from United America. Acceptance meant leaving the security of lifelong employment of his company, but Mr. Ōbayashi considered the financial rewards and managerial challenges offered by United America hard to refuse. In 1969 he resigned from Kakubeni and became United America's sales representative in Japan. Mr. Ōbayashi also suggested that a more significant presence of the company than a sales agent would be necessary for further penetration of the Japanese market.

It was the time when President Lang told Mr. Franklin about the decision of the top management of United America Inc. for an eventual capital entry into the Japanese market: The capital liberalization movement was underway in Japan—up to 50 percent of ownership was permitted in an increasing number of industries; United America Inc. had joint-venture companies in other countries; and a 50–50 joint venture in Japan would be a good start, the management thought.

Three years after Mr. Ōbayashi's appointment, the International Division decided to establish its Asia headquarters in Tokyo. Mr. Franklin did not want to move out of the power house of New York. He instead appointed Mr. Hart as the first Asia vice president and sent him to Japan as United Japan representative president.

THE HART FAMILY'S INITIAL DIFFICULTIES

Although Mr. Hart had been in the international field of consumer division of the firm for more than ten years and had traveled extensively, this was his first foreign assignment. He knew very little about Japanese society and its people, and he did not speak a word of Japanese. When Mr. Franklin called him to discuss this new and challenging assignment, he did not have any past experience as a yardstick for assessing the enormity of his new task. The company did not give Mr. Hart or his family any preparatory training before sending them to Tokyo.

Every cultural community maintains an "unspoken understanding of the way the world is"—a frame of reference from which behavioral rules can be understood, anticipated, and predicted. Upon arrival in a host country, expatriates like Mr. Hart find themselves confronted on a daily basis by behavioral signals they have no means of interpreting.

The lack of formal training programs for international managers was/is a common phenomenon in American multinationals. This is in spite of the fact that the American expatriate would represent the company in the eyes of the local people, and that his task was to establish initial contacts and to start an operation considered of crucial importance for the company. Many American firms assume English to be the universal language of business, and therefore expect the American business culture to be the universal culture of business. Others profess the belief that the culture of the corporation is distinct from and more significant than that of the host community.

The maintenance of such misconceptions is detrimental to the success of multinational corporations both in terms of finance and public relations. The estimated cost of relocating an unsuccessful expatriate alone falls within the range of $100,000 to $200,000. The significance of this figure is not fully appreciated until one considers that an estimated 30–40 percent of all overseas assignments result in early returns due to the failure of the expatriates to cope in the foreign business environment.[6] Even within a culture perceived to be as similar as that of England, the early return rate stands at a notable 18 percent.[7]

United America was typical of many multinationals, which annually uproot managers from American soil, fly them across the Ocean, drop them in an alien environment, and hope they will do their best. United America gave Mr. Hart three weeks to move from his residence in California to Tokyo, Japan. Mr. Hart did not have enough time to sell his house in California, and his wife stayed behind for an additional month to organize their move.

When his family (a wife and two school children) arrived in Tokyo, Mr. Hart had already rented a condominium in a central district of the metropolitan area. Back in California, Mr. Hart had a four-bedroom house, but a house that size could not be obtained in Tokyo. At that time there were few Westernized apartments in Tokyo, and those available were very expensive, ranging between $3,000 and $6,000 a month for a two-bedroom apartment. Mrs. Hart, who like her husband did not speak the Japanese language, had to organize family-related matters alone without the assistance of an interpreter. Her husband was already involved in many new business projects and was striving to initiate the operation in Japan. Consequently, he was often absent in the evenings and on weekends.

Because of a more distinct sexual divison of labor in Japan, the worlds of Japanese husband and wife are often separate and independent of each other. Although it is changing, particularly among young couples, Japanese couples do not share or entertain their friends together. American expatriate managers are often entertained by Japanese men alone without wives. It is therefore difficult for American executives' wives to meet Japanese businessmen's wives. In addition, Japanese do not entertain guests at home, unless they are intimate friends. Japanese men generally go to bars and clubs with hostesses. In such hostess bars, it is difficult for women to join men. Very often Mrs. Hart found that she was the only woman at company-related receptions and parties.

The Tokyo American Club and parties among American nationals often become places for American wives to complain about their isolation from the rest of the community, their frustration when their husbands alone are invited and entertained by Japanese hosts in Geisha parties and hostess clubs, and their loneliness while their husbands are on business trips.

In spite of a waiting list, Mrs. Hart managed to put her children into English-speaking Nishi-mach Elementary School in downtown Tokyo. Because of the language barrier, it is rare for American children to attend a local public school, which is free. American schools and other missionary schools, which educate English-speaking children, are private schools without Japanese governmental subsidies. The tuition is expensive, ranging for elementary school from $5,000 to $8,000 annually per child.

While Mrs. Hart settled herself and her family in Tokyo, Mr. Hart started immediately to learn about the Japanese ways of doing business. With the consent of the Domestic Division, Mr. Hart moved Mr. Ōbayashi to his office in Tokyo and appointed him as vice president of the Japanese operation.

Mr. Ōbayashi started assisting Mr. Hart in investigating the Japanese market and searching for potential partners for joint venture. United America Inc. had been testing the Japanese market by exporting a number of products allowed entry through Japanese government import regulations.

INITIAL SEARCH

Mr. Ōbayashi used his personal connections in the Japanese trading industry and school/university cliques in his search of joint-venture partners. Because Mr. Hart had no command of the Japanese language, it was the task of Mr. Ōbayashi to make an initial contact with Japanese companies. In addition, he often served as an interpreter in delicate negotiations and important meetings with Japanese firms. He also gave advice on the market and potential partners.

Mr. Martin who succeeded Mr. Hart later and who participated in some of the negotiations recalled:

> We gave Mr. Ōbayashi a considerable amount of responsibility to become a bridge between the Japanese companies and us. He was not, however, a professional interpreter. He not only interpreted for us, but also expressed his opinions on the issue at meetings. We did not know how much was the opinion of the Japanese company and how much was Mr. Ōbayashi's opinion.

During 1969, United America Inc.'s Japanese office negotiated with a number of Japanese companies on the possibility of technological licensing and joint-venture agreement. Three joint-venture negotiations together with that of Nippon Kaisha were under way simultaneously.

The product in which Nippon Kaisha was interested was a wrapping material made of synthetic resin. The material was first introduced to Japan in the early 1960s when other Japanese companies started importing the product from large foreign manufacturers. Nippon Kaisha, in the late 1960s, also started importing the product from a few American manufacturers as a sample to test the market. The product of United America Inc. was one of them.

During that period, another Japanese company, which belongs to a powerful and competing *keiretsu* group, started local production. While there was less competition, the company quickly gained 30 percent of the market, which was expanding rapidly. Several Japanese manufacturers, some with technical agreements with foreign corporations, followed the successful one in local production. Two Japanese companies formed joint ventures with foreign firms for local production.

The market was getting hot, expanding at a tremendous speed in the last stage of the Japanese chemical industry's boom before the energy crisis.

Nippon Kaisha, observing the growth potential of the market and seeing other companies going into local production and making handsome profits, felt anxious and started its search for foreign technology.

The general corporate policy of Nippon Kaisha in the late 1960s was to diversify its product lines and to enter into new fields. The joint-venture agreement with Hawthorn Inc. of America was signed at that time. It was also before the energy crisis: The Japanese economy was booming with a two-digit growth rate, far exceeding that of other industrialized nations.

Mr. Ōbayashi's ex-employer, Kakubeni, is a trading company within the Dai-Nippon Industrial Group. When Nippon Kaisha started importing sample products, Mr. Ōbayashi introduced the United America product to Nippon Kaisha through his ex-colleagues at the trading company. Mr. Ōbayashi knew that Nippon Kaisha would be interested in the production technology of wrapping materials possessed by United America Inc.

The management of United America Inc., however, did not want to simply sell the technology; they wanted to enter the Japanese market through a joint-venture agreement.

When United America Inc. expressed its wish, Nippon Kaisha was rather reluctant. Nippon Kaisha did not wish to join in a joint venture. Mr. Shimada, who was a director of Nippon Kaisha at that time, said:

> We knew that joint-venturing would cause problems. We wanted only technological licensing. It is very difficult to have two decision-makers who have equal power, even in the same cultural environment. Because of the differences in thinking between the Americans and the Japanese, there would be many conflicts of opinions, as we had seen in our Nippon Hawthorn operations.

Mr. Franklin, President of United Asia, stated:

> The top management of United America Inc. was eager to enter Japan in a major way. We realized that selling technology without managerial participation would be a disadvantage to us. We wanted a significant managerial participation, and therefore would not accept minority ownership. Since the Japanese government restricted foreign ownership in Japan, 50 – 50 joint-venturing was the only solution.

Managers of both companies held several formal meetings to discuss the possibility of a tie-up. The American corporation, from the beginning, asked for a joint venture.

Mr. Shimada continued:

We needed the technology held by United America Inc. in order to diversify our product lines. Our competitors were already engaged in local production and were achieving success. The demand was growing. Our need for technology overrode our concerns with the problem of joint-venturing.

Mr. Martin added:

We were optimistic about the potentiality of the market, and were confident about the capability of Nippon Kaisha backed up by Dai-Nippon. We found that Dai-Nippon Kaisha, the parent company of Nippon Kaisha, was a well-established company and were impressed by its management and performance.

Concerning the logistics, we thought it advantageous to utilize the distribution network of Dai Nippon-Nippon Kaisha Group.

After almost a year of negotiation, Nippon Kaisha agreed to a joint venture because of the strong wish of United America Inc. for a joint venture and because of Nippon Kaisha's need for United America's technology.

FEASIBILITY STUDY

The International Division of United America conducted an economic feasibility study on a possible joint venture involving Nippon Kaisha and United America. Basic economics analyzed by the financial expert of United America Inc. did not seem optimistic: Nippon United Company would be a latecomer in the market where strong competition was projected.

Serious questions about quality arose when United America Inc. exported its product to Japan through Nippon Kaisha on a trial basis. Because the product was shipped from the northern part of America through the Panama Canal to Japan, the tremendous changes in temperature caused deterioration of the product by the time it reached Japan. These two major factors clouded the Nippon Kaisha-United America joint-venture project.

From the viewpoint of Nippon Kaisha, the quality problem was not only the deterioration caused during shipment, but also uniformity and the aesthetic appearance of the product, which Japanese clients would consider important. The wrapping material was delivered in rolls. The product was, however, not rolled up in a uniform manner; the rolled edges were not neatly cut, and trapped air bubbles created a wobbly appearance, which was aesthetically not acceptable to the Japanese.

Mr. Higashi, who was working for Kamiyama Lab at that time, recalled that Nippon Kaisha's engineers and chemists were, however, confident of their ability to improve the quality because "the company had been producing chemical products for more than fifty years."

They were also confident about the strength of their distribution network and sales organization. "Once the quality of the product proves to be good, we can sell it to the users" was the opinion of the Nippon Kaisha management.

MR. HART'S TROUBLES

While the negotiations were still under way, a personnel change in United America Inc. took place: United America, Inc. had already established one joint-venture company and a few technical agreements with other Japanese companies. This particular joint-venture company founded in the late 1960s was called Yamato United. Yamato-United was struggling with a poor market performance and a large loss in profits. Inside the Japanese parent company of the joint venture, an internal power struggle for leadership was raging among top management. A substantial deficit caused by Yamato-United adversely affected the overall balance sheet of United America's Japanese operation. United America's other Asian operations in the Philippines were reporting poor financial results. Mr. Hart was held responsible for these poor performances. Pressures were put upon Mr. Hart to improve the overall performance of the Asia Division.

In 1972, Mr. Hart was suddenly recalled to the United States. In two months, Mr. Hart resigned from United America Inc. (Mr. Hart had been in Japan for only two and a half years).

APPOINTMENT OF MR. MARTIN

President Lang, still anxious to make Japan operations a success story, wanted a major overhaul of the Japan operation to cut the losses and to speed up the company's further penetration into the Japanese market. Mr. Franklin of United Asia was put under severe pressure from the top management. Mr. Franklin still did not want to move out of New York himself to head the Asia operation in Tokyo. He could not afford to leave the power center when Mr. Murray, president of International Division, was just about to retire, and the company was expected to nominate his successor. At the same time, Mr. Franklin needed desperately to improve the performance of the Asia Division. He needed a trustworthy trouble-shooter with solid international background. He selected Mr. Martin, a veteran international sales manager of the Machinery Division of United America Inc., who had originally suggested to the International Division hiring Mr. Ōbayashi.

Mr. Martin had been selling United America's machinery all over the world. He possessed a financial background but also had worked in the fields of marketing and sales and had headed a few regional operations in the United States. Because of the international sales transactions of machinery, he had visited Japan several times, and had been involved in a joint-venture negotiation with another Japanese company, which was related to his machinery field.

Mr. Franklin told Mr. Martin to bring a solution to the mess of Yamato-United as soon as possible. Mr. Martin moved from the Machinery Division to the International Division. In the summer of 1972, the new American representative landed in Tokyo. Like his predecessor in Japan, he did not speak the Japanese language and possessed only a limited knowledge of Japanese society, culture, and people. Like his predecessor, neither Mr. Martin nor his family received any training before arriving in Japan. For him, it was a "learn how to swim quickly, or drown yourself" situation. Before his hasty departure, Mr. Martin had read about twenty books on Japan, but his real learning about Japan had just begun.

By the time Mr. Martin landed at the crowded Haneda airport, Mr. Hart had already left Japan. Consequently, Mr. Martin did not receive any briefing on the operation from Mr. Hart personally. He had to find his way by himself with the assistance of Mr. Ōbayashi.

This practice of United America Inc. to put a new man in the operation without a briefing session contrasts sharply to the general Japanese practice. When a manager of an important field operation is replaced by another, the Japanese company customarily gives several months' notice before its annual announcement of personnel change. The company appoints a successor several weeks before the departure of the manager who has headed the operation. The new man is given detailed information about the operation, is introduced to major clients, banks, and business associates with the personal introduction of the predecessor, and is assisted in planning the future operation.

If the personnel change involves top-level management of the operation, the ritual-conscious Japanese hold an elaborate farewell party in a banquet hall of a major hotel, inviting clients and trade associates to witness the formal shift of authority and power into the hands of the new man. At the same time, again in a formalized manner, they express their continuous commitment and effort in the business, and assure the continuous corporate policy regarding the operation. They assure their customers that the organization and their long-range relationship with clients will continue regardless of personnel changes.

In contrast, Mr. Martin, the new American representative of United America Inc., arrived in Tokyo without a ceremony, just as his predecessor quickly and quietly flew out of the country.

END OF YAMATO UNITED

Since his first day on Japan's soil, the new vice president of Asia had to work hard to grasp the peculiarities of this alien business environment. His immediate task was to put the Tokyo operation into manageable shape, to deal with existing joint-venture companies, and to begin the United-Nippon joint-venture project.

Mr. Martin, who had an accountant background among other things, started out with some drastic cost-cutting in the United Japan office operation: He dismissed translators and receptionist/tea girls, sold the company's limousines, and drastically reduced expense accounts. Mr. Ōbayashi was not particularly pleased with these new measures. He believed that a high corporate image should be maintained through smooth customer relationships. After all, the Japanese expense/entertainment account as a total is larger than the national defense budget which is about 1 percent of Gross National Product (GNP). Expense accounts were necessary parts of operation in Japan, Mr. Ōbayashi argued. Differences in opinion started to grow between the two immediately.

As for the crippled Yamato-United, Mr. Martin negotiated with Yamato for some time but finally decided to sell the United's half to Yamato. The first Japanese joint venture of United America had a short, troubled life and a sudden death, at a total loss of several million dollars.

PRESIDENT'S VISIT

United America's President Lang was eager to look at the Japan and Asia market himself. In the fall of 1972, three months after Mr. Martin arrived in Japan, United America's chief executive officer-president visited Japan. He flew into Japan on a corporate jet plane together with the head of the International Division and the Asia president, attended business meetings and receptions, made speeches concerning the importance of the Japanese market to United America Inc., and emphasized his commitment to doing business in Asia. (I was his interpreter.) During his whirlwind one-week stay in Japan, the president decided to sign the agreement with Nippon Kaisha, despite the previously mentioned difficulties in the feasibility study.

Following the visit of President Lang, United America Inc. sent two experts — a chemical engineer and a financial analyst — to update the 1970 study. The net effect of their visit was a reappraisal of the investment proposal, which tended to substantiate that the economics of this project were good. The American chemical engineer, who was sent from the Chemical Division upon the request of the International Division, felt rather strongly that the quality problems involving the deterioration of the product shipped from the United States to Japan should not be a problem for local manufacturers. He tended to agree with the optimism of the Nippon Kaisha management that there would be no major technical problems in the local manufacture of the product for the Japanese market. Then both companies went ahead in deciding the details of the operation.

PREPARATION OF THE CONTRACT

The new company, which I call Nippon-United Kaisha, was to be established with the capital of 100 million yen or $400,000 provided equally by United America Inc. and Nippon Kaisha. Together with the joint-venture basic agreement, they were to sign a license agreement.

In Nippon Kaisha, the *bunsho-ka* or documents section of the General Affairs Division prepared the basic outline in the Japanese language. Staff members in this section were not professional lawyers, although most of them held B.A. degrees in law. Their knowledge of commercial and corporation law had been acquired while working for the company.

In Japan there are approximately 11,000 attorneys available to serve a population of over 117 million, or about one attorney per 10,250 people. By contrast, there is one lawyer for every 630 citizens in the United States. The scarcity of lawyers in Japan is partly due to the extremely high standard set to pass the National Legal Examination. Less than 2 percent of the applicants pass the annual examination. Although the number per capita of Japanese taking the judicial examination is slightly higher than that of Americans taking bar examinations, the difference is that more than two-thirds of American applicants pass the bar exam.

Partly due to the institutionally created shortage of lawyers, and partly because of cultural and historical factors that have led the Japanese to prefer extrajudicial, informal means of dispute settlement, the Japanese use litigation markedly less than most Westerners. Since the Second World War, the annual rate of litigation has remained stable at between 140 and 180 formal trials per 100,000 persons.

To Americans, who use lawyers in almost every contractual transaction, it may be revealing to know that an ordinary Japanese would probably never see a lawyer in his lifetime; the Japanese rarely use lawyers in divorces, seldom draw up a will, virtually never consult a lawyer to purchase land or a house, or to get a bank loan.

During the 1970s, there existed a few — no more than twenty — foreign lawyers formally practicing in Japan, who could handle legal matters concerning American direct investment in Japan. Until 1955, Japanese language competence was not a requirement for foreign lawyers to be admitted to the bar. But in the 1970s, the chance for a foreigner to pass the bar was almost nil, considering the enormous difficulty in fulfilling the language and other requirements for the bar, unless he was born and raised in Japan as is the case of several Korean lawyers in Japan.

Quite a number of Westerners were, however, practicing informally in Japan even before the change in law in the 1980s, which finally permit American lawyers' practices in Japan. Many international law firms had established offices in Tokyo in the 1970s and employed both Japanese and foreign lawyers, the latter sometimes under the guise of law clerks.

In contrast to American reliance on professional lawyers, most large Japanese companies have their own legal staff members, who are law faculty graduates but have not passed the National Legal Examination. They work as staff of the *bunsho-ka* or documents section and do much of the work handled by corporate legal counsel in the United States. Although clearly they do not possess the professionalism or cross-industrial expertise of members of the bar, their technical knowledge of corporate law is often greater that of many Japanese lawyers.

While preparing the draft, the *bunsho-ka* staff of Nippon Kaisha had constant contact with the senior managing director, who was the head of the Chemical Division and was to be the president of the new company, the director and managers of the International Division, and the other directors of the Executive Committee.

In United America Inc., on the other hand, the responsibility for writing the draft fell to the general manager of the Japan office, the area president, and a lawyer of the legal department of the International Division. They also hired a Japanese lawyer in Japan to check on their decisions. The general manager of the Japan office, with help from Mr. Ōbayashi, studied the regulations imposed by the Japanese government.

The regulations were more strict during the early 1970s before the 100 percent capital liberalization in principle was announced by the government. The application had to go through a case-by-case screening by the Foreign Investment Deliberation Council. The decision to select a Japanese as president of the new company was made due to such considerations. They also followed Federal Trade Commission (FTC) regulations in the United States and the Antimonopoly Act Guidelines for International Licensing Agreements (May 24, 1968). The terms and amounts of royalty payments and restrictions or obligations on using the technology were also settled.

JOINT-VENTURE AGREEMENT

It is common to have separate joint-venture agreements and technical licensing agreements. The joint-venture agreement is generally regarded as permanent or long-term, while the technical licensing agreement may need to be changed as technological innovations take place. Usually, joint-venture agreements are signed by the parent companies that invest in the new company; technical agreements are signed by the company and the foreign investor that provides the technology.

Under Japanese law, inspection by the court is conducted only when there are articles regarding the benefits for the promoters, such as dividends, priority rights to subscribe to newly issued shares of the company in the future, fees for promotion, etc. In order to avoid the intervention of the third party, i.e., the inspector from the court, some companies include such a clause as:

New Company shall be established by an association of seven promoters designated by Japanese Company. Subscribers of the promoters shall be limited to one share each, and their shares shall be transferred to Japanese Company immediately after the incorporation of New Company.

During the time there were several areas where the Japanese legal system differed from the American.

(1) While the payment of dividends on the capital share can be authorized by the board of directors in the United States, the decision-making authority on the payment of dividends lies in the hands of the shareholders and is decided by a majority vote at the

shareholders' meeting in Japan. The upper limit of the dividend payments is also regulated by the Commercial Law (Article 290). This means the American shareholder (United America) has to be present at an annual shareholders' meeting in Japan for items that could be decided at a regular board meeting under United States Law.

(2) The Japanese Commercial Law does not recognize the validity of voting by proxy or letter for decisions at a board of directors' meeting (Article 260–(2)). The requirement of attendance in person poses a problem for a foreign firm whose headquarters are usually located outside of Japan. Some joint-venture agreements state that the decision-making procedure can include proxy voting, but it is, in fact, a violation of Commercial Law.

(3) The Japanese Tax Law favors dividend payment over retention of the income, but the tax rate on dividends, not to mention the tax on profits, is much higher than in the United States. In 1978 the overall tax when a part of the profit was paid as dividends rated 55 percent in Japan. The United States Tax Law does not make such sharp differences as the Japanese; if the profit was paid as dividends, the rate was 46 percent, and if not, 48 percent in the United States in 1978.

These legal differences looked innocent at a first glance, but each had important implications for joint-venture operations. For example, the requirement of the personal presence of directors at every board meeting in fact meant that very busy American executives had to find time to fly to Japan to vote or that important decisions were postponed until such a meeting could take place.

The high tax for dividend payments meant that the flow of profit back to the United States was discouraged, and reduction of dividends or reinvestment of corporate profits back to the joint venture was encouraged.

LEGAL DOCUMENT

Following the above legal regulations, the contract was signed in the early 1970s. The United America-Nippon Kaisha joint-venture basic agreement has sections on definitions, general, organization of the new company, capital, transfer or sale of shares, directors and management, management of the new company, production and sales, technical assistance (for which they signed a separate technical licensing agreement), notices (addresses), effect of invalidity, government approval, integration (the authority of the contract), arbitration, and interpretation.

In retrospect, the joint-venture basic agreement did seem to lack precision in some clauses; for example,

Section: Management of New Company   Article XX

New Company shall use its utmost effort to maintain good financial condition and achieve, as promptly as practical, independent management.

Because of the lack of an independent distribution network for the company, the Sales Division and the Marketing Division of Nippon Kaisha were to provide services to the new joint-venture company in terms of the delivery of the product, the sales, and distribution. The American side, nevertheless, insisted on the future independence of the joint-venture company from the Japanese parent corporation and asked to include this clause of the contract. What the term "as promptly as practicable" meant, however, was that the Japanese side could maintain its control over the new joint venture as long as it was "practicable," according to Mr. Martin. He says,

Because of the vagueness of the terms of the contract, we could not act to pursue the perceived best interest of the joint-venture company which may have been in conflict with Nippon-Kaisha's objectives.

According to the United America management, there are other clauses that could have been more precise, if they had known the actions likely to be taken later by the Japanese.

Section: General   Article XXXX

Both United America and Nippon Kaisha shall give reasonable assistance to New Company in connection with management, administration, personnel affairs, services, and other.

The "reasonable" assistance can be judged subjectively. In some cases "reasonable" actions by Nippon Kaisha were interpreted by United America Inc. as intervention in the managerial power of the new joint venture.

Mr. Franklin agrees with Mr. Martin, saying:

Because of the lack of a time limit, we could not start or stop the actions taken by the Japanese. Although we have 50 percent ownership, the Japanese side seems to have more control over the new company.

Mr. Shimada, who later became United-Nippon President, justifies Nippon Kaisha's action:

The new company is organized and exists under the laws of Japan, having its office in Japan. Although it is jointly owned by both companies, we believe that the new company should be administered mainly by Nippon Kaisha because we have more experience in operating a Japanese company. It was difficult to persuade United America's management on this issue. They insisted on 50–50 managerial participation.

Regarding personnel management, United America gave the authority to assign employees for the new company to Nippon Kaisha. Because there was no time limit in the contract regarding the term of this responsibility, United America was often frustrated by getting seemingly unqualified personnel. The contract continues:

Nippon Kaisha shall provide such possible assistance and guidance as from time to time may be necessary. Until independent management is achieved, Nippon Kaisha shall assign employees to perform the day-to-day management functions in accordance with the directives and resolutions of the board of directors on New Company.

This clause gave Nippon Kaisha the authority to appoint operators and employees. United America could not assign employees until "independent management is achieved." United America Inc. had to rely on hard bargaining and negotiating when the personnel appointed by Nippon Kaisha are not acceptable.

ORGANIZATION OF THE JOINT-VENTURE COMPANY

As the Japanese government insisted that the position of the president should be held by a Japanese, Nippon Kaisha suggested that Mr. Shimada, a senior director with a mechanical engineering background should be appointed as president. Although the contract stated, "The representative director, who in performing his function as such, shall have *primary* responsibility to New Company," (underlined by the author) Mr. Shimada was to continue his work as a senior manager of Nippon Kaisha as well as fulfilling the new position at Nippon United. The managers of United America nevertheless approved his nomination.

The vice president of the new company was named by United America Inc., and Mr. Martin, the American representative of the Japan Office, held the position. Four Americans and four Japanese sat as board directors of the new company. The American side was composed of Mr. Murray (the president of the International Division), Mr. Franklin (the area president), Mr. Nickolson (the general manager of the Domestic Chemical Division in Hammond), and Mr. Martin (the general manager of the Japan Office of United America Inc.).

On the Japanese side, Mr. Shimada (a senior managing director), Mr. Hosono (the director of the Chemical Division), Mr. Yamagi (the director of the Sales Division of Nippon Kaisha), and Mr. Kihara (the plant manager of Nippon United's Kamiyama Plant) were appointed as board directors. Three out of four American board directors lived in the United States, and the operation of the new company was generally handled by Mr. Franklin and Mr. Martin (the American side) and the Japanese managers.

Mr. Kihara who was the plant manager of the new company had a mechanical engineering background. In order to assist Mr. Kihara in the chemistry area, the researchers of Nippon Kaisha's Chemical Laboratory became closely involved in the project. Mr. Higashi, who later succeeded Mr. Yamashita as personnel director of Nippon Kaisha, was a section chief of general affairs of the Kamiyama plant at that time. He remembered the enthusiasm of the Kamiyama lab staff members, who talked about the launch of the new product, which they would develop to suit the local market.

The new company's products were sold through Nippon Kaisha because of the lack of a distribution network of the infant company. It was, however, stated in the contract (without time limit) that the new company would eventually have its own sales division.

Nippon Kaisha appointed Mr. Kawamura, thirty-two, as sales manager for handling the Nippon United product, but Mr. Kawamura was located inside the Nippon Kaisha Sales Division with an additional post of sales manager within Nippon Kaisha. The real control over the sales of the product was, therefore, in the hands of Nippon Kaisha, not Nippon United. Accountants and production engineers as well as quality control staff also came from Nippon Kaisha as *tenzoku* men.

PRESIDENT AND VICE PRESIDENT: A BIG DIFFERENCE

Concerning the board of directors, the contract reads:

New Company shall have the representative director nominated by Nippon Kaisha, who shall be the president. One of the directors nominated by United America shall be the vice president of New Company.

United America underestimated the power of the Japanese president, partly because they were preconditioned by their knowledge of the power of American board directors, shareholders, and other stakeholders over and beside the president, and partly because they were ignorant about the actual workings of Japanese corporate decision making and could not interpret "what it meant to be a Japanese president" correctly.

Contrary to the stereotype image of Japanese group decision making, Mr. Martin and other United America managers soon learned that Nippon United president had almost an unlimited authority as the representative executive officer of the company. Likewise, President Kubo of Nippon Kaisha and their top management seemed to exercise tremendous power over the entire corporate community without many checks and balances. First of all, Mr. Martin learned that the representative officer, such as President Kubo of Nippon Kaisha, was almost free of pressures from stockholders.

Under Japanese law, shareholders have a right to a small dividend, but beyond this they have few rights. In the case of Nippon Kaisha, the percentage of dividend to net profit is 14 percent (in contrast to usually about 50 percent earnings in United States companies), and profits available for reinvestment is 86 percent. Because Nippon Kaisha management was/ is committed to the long-term growth of the company, the cash left after dividend payment was/is mostly reinvested in the company. Abegglen and Stalk believe that this difference contributes greatly to the competitive advantages of Japanese *kaisha* over American firms (1985). Their thesis is as follows: The American shareholders receive a significant share of profits in the form of dividend payments, which are taken to be a sign of successful operations and competent management. Share price is strongly influenced by the rate and level of dividends paid.

In United States companies, the board of directors was created, at least theoretically, to represent the interests of the shareholder-owners, where directors are named to the board from outside the company in the majority of cases. At the same time, in order to link the interests of management with that of the shareholders, profit-related bonus plans, stock options, and similar plans to reward management for imported earnings and increased share price have become widespread in this country. Because of this, American management has a strong incentive to maintain steady improvement in earnings, even on a quarterly basis. In the process, the company becomes a vehicle for profit optimization or for profit maximization. Implicit is the view that the success of the company depends upon executives who should be appropriately and handsomely rewarded. Corporations become a financial property—a vehicle for personal gain.

LONG-TERM GROWTH COMMITMENT

In contrast, it is important to understand the mechanism of the Japanese shareholder and the board of directors. The common stock shareholder of the Japanese company is legally entitled to dividends in Japan. The first major difference is, however, that dividends are paid not as a percent of earning, but as a percent of the par value of shares in the company. Usually dividend yields as a percent of market value of Japanese shares are low, about one or two percent. But dividends are paid to ensure the company's ability to raise equity funds in the future.

The second important difference is that the board of directors of the Japanese company consists almost entirely of inside board members, that is, of the senior management who have moved up in the executive ranks as career employees. These senior executives represent the will of their constituency — not the shareholder but the employee community.

With no specific shareholder representation on the board, a highly profitable Japanese company can meet its dividend requirement with only a small percent of its total earnings. Most of its earnings will be available for reinvestment for the company. With the shareholder in the position of investor rather than controller, and with dividends not critical to share price, Japanese management are "free from the tyranny of accountants, and from the terrible pressures throughout the U.S. organizations for steady improvement in earnings per share."[8]

In addition to freedom from shareholders, financially successful Japanese companies are also free of bankers' interference. Nippon Kaisha is one of these successful ones with improving finance, whose debt-equity ratio was 0.7:1 in 1985. Nippon Kaisha President Kubo sat at the corporate pinnacle. Basically, Mr. Kubo's major constituency was his own group of career employees, who were his subordinates in the firm. He would try to allocate resources to ensure the best possible path for corporate growth and prosperity. Not pressed for immediate return on investment, Mr. Kubo and his management could afford to look beyond quarterly or yearly profit figures. Another influential partner of Mr. Kubo, Dai-Nippon Inc. also shares this view for long-range prosperity of Nippon Kaisha-Dai Nippon group. They are not interested in short-term return on the shareholder's equity.

KEIRETSU FOR GROWTH

Dai-Nippon management had spun off their divisions into new *ko-gaisha* subsidiaries, which included Nippon Kaisha. Nippon Kaisha in its turn spun off its divisions into new *ko-gaisha*, attracting new capital for further growth. One of the reasons for past spinoffs of divisions was to solve the problem of limits on capital because of massive and wide-ranging growth opportunities in its corporate environment in the 1960s and early 1970s.

When there are massive and wide-ranging growth opportunities in the environment and the yet the firm is limited in capital, one solution is to set up subsidiaries only partially owned by the parent company and ask these subsidiaries to seek their own capital sources for further expansion. The management philosophy behind it is that the greatest leverage for increased total return to the company and eventually to shareholders lies with growth rather than with dividends or reported profits.

President Kubo of Nippon Kaisha and his internally selected corporate board basically shared this view for *keiretsu* growth. When they saw an opportunity to move into plastic wrapping film business, there were many other promising areas of expansions competing with this project. A logical move for Nippon Kaisha was to tie up with another company, in this case, United America.

In the joint-venture *ko-gaisha* corporate board of Nippon United, the same pattern for growth was repeated. *Tenzoku* and *shukko* men from Nippon Kaisha eventually formed the core management of the new joint-venture company, working for the growth of the overall *keiretsu* group.

The American vice president, Mr. Martin, who might not share the same view, did not have the power to represent the company under this contract (power was in the hands of Japanese president). Mr. Martin's and United America's control over the new company was limited from the beginning, partly because Mr. Martin was the only expatriate manager physically present in Japan who could represent United America's view in daily contacts with the Japanese.

Mr. Martin's "profit now" philosophy hit a stone wall of Japanese executives who preached for a long-term perspective for growth in unison.

VOTING POWER

The new company was to have six directors at the time of its incorporation, although a later amendment increased the number to eight. The voting power was equally distributed between the two parties. When there were six directors (three from Nippon Kaisha and three from United America), each resolution or action presented for approval to the board of directors had to be adopted only upon the affirmative vote of at least four directors, including at least two directors each nominated by Nippon Kaisha and United America. The concept of majority voting did not change in essence after they increased the number of directors (four from Nippon Kaisha and four from United America).

Mr. Franklin recalled:

One of the problems was that we did not limit the power of the board of directors against the shareholders. Since we could not use proxy voting at a board of directors' meeting, and we could at a shareholders' meeting under the Japanese law, we could have made major decisions at a shareholders' meeting without bringing in all the American directors. Another problem in this contract was that we did not state clearly which issues had to be discussed either at a board of directors' meeting or at a shareholders' meeting. Since the Japanese directors were also the operating managers of the new company, it was implied that many decisions were day-to-day operational decisions without requirement of a board of directors' meeting.

Both Japanese and American managers stated that the contract lacked a method of settling disputes between the parties. It stated that disputes should be settled by arbitration pursuant to the Japan-U.S. Trade Arbitration Agreement of September 16, 1952, by which each party is bound. If one followed the Arbitration Agreement, an outside "public" arbitrator had to be brought in to solve disputes between the parties, which certainly creates an additional problem concerning the leakage of confidential information to outsiders. Besides the problem of confidentiality, bad publicity on the dispute would certainly affect the company's reputation.

The two parties had to find a meeting point in a board of directors' meeting, without making the problem publicly known. However, the split in voting power between board members did not help much to reach solution. Because the allocation of final authority in each field, such as marketing, production, and finance, was not clear, both parties had to spend considerable energy and time in trying to persuade the other to their way of thinking.

UNITED AMERICA REALIZED THE MEANING OF TENZOKU

It was soon after the contract was signed that Nippon Kaisha's *tenzoku* men started to operate the new joint venture. United America managers presumed that a man who quits one job and starts another would psychologically turn a new leaf in life and begin a brand new career, just like many do in the United States.

They quickly learned that in Japan *tenzoku* do not act like that. Mr. Martin recalled:

> We signed the contract which gave Nippon Kaisha the authority to appoint middle management and lower ranking employees. We were unfamiliar with the Japanese labor market, and it seemed best that Nippon Kaisha handle the personnel issue. In order to start the operation, we immediately needed professionals and engineers. Nippon Kaisha's *shukko* and *tenzoku* systems appeared to serve our interest.
>
> We did not realize, at that time, that the employees of Nippon Kaisha in which United America has fifty percent ownership would be so loyal to Nippon Kaisha in their parent-child relationship. They tend to follow the directions of Nippon Kaisha, which may not be in the best interests of Nippon United Kaisha.
>
> We also found out later that it was almost impossible to dismiss an employee, even when the employee is incompetent. It seems that there are a lot of political bargaining and negotiations within Nippon Kaisha to select a man to be transferred to an affiliate company. Since we are isolated from the personnel management, we have no idea what is going on politically within Nippon Kaisha. The only thing we could do was to meet the man appointed by Nippon Kaisha and to evaluate the man as we saw him. We have no veto power, although Nippon Kaisha would reconsider the choice if we object strongly.

Mr. Yamagi, superior of Mr. Kawamura in the Sales Division of Nippon Kaisha, said:

> Nippon Kaisha and United America Inc. management agreed in the beginning that the everyday operations and personnel issues would be handled by the Japanese side. Since we are operating in Japan, it was natural to employ the Japanese style of personnel management. We consider the new company as Japanese, although 50 percent of capital came from the U.S.

Mr. Yamashita backed his statement by saying:

> Nippon United became a part of the Nippon Kaisha Group. Many of its members came from Nippon Kaisha with a strong sense of attachment to the parent company. We were ready to work together to make the company successful in Japan.

Mr. Franklin later commented on this issue of corporate groupism:

> We did not know what mutual obligations among the members of *keiretsu* really meant. We vaguely understood that the organization of an industrial

group is comparable to that of the profit center system. A profit center in our company has sufficient autonomy in decision making. We, therefore, considered that Nippon United could make decisions independently since it was a separate company.

We later found out that management of an affiliate company always takes the group's interests into consideration and tries to follow the intent of the Japanese parent company. The Japanese employees consider themselves as part of the Nippon Kaisha-Dai Nippon Group, and they openly express their pride as a part of the group.

They faithfully follow the regulations and codes of behavior set by the group, which is tacitly understood among the members. In order to justify their actions, they often state that it is the way that the group operates. Their conviction to follow the group's rules is so firm even when it seems more rational to take an alternative action.

PERSONNEL POLICIES

Regarding the selection of managers, both parent companies' management showed differences in opinion. Nippon Kaisha, as part of a corporate culture emphasizing group solidarity, takes the selection of senior managers as an issue of paramount importance. Mr. Shimada, who negotiated with the Americans on personnel matters, mentioned:

For managerial positions, we still consider that age and years of service are important. In the U.S. a young, aggressive manager may be able to fulfill the leadership role because of the close relationship between the position and the job. In Japan, where a title or position does not signify leadership, a manager must gain the respect and support from his subordinates. A young, inexperienced manager may find it difficult to gain such support, since the subordinates are accustomed to senior-aged managers.

Without support from subordinates, it is impossible for him to work efficiently because the job requires teamwork and cooperation in the Japanese organization.

We also take into consideration that friction may occur in the organization if we pick up a junior manager, passing over those senior to him. Because of such restrictions, the number of candidates for managerial positions is limited.

Mr. Franklin recalled:

Since the contract gives the authority to appoint middle managers to Nippon Kaisha until the new company becomes independent, we have no means to take action on our side in order to select the right man. We have to wait for Nippon Kaisha's selection and comment on it. It is frustrating.

There was already an obvious difference in opinion between the partners as to what constituted capable leadership, and we observe the seed of conflict being sown at this time. The American side wanted a dynamic, aggressive leadership to initiate this challenging operation. They wanted someone who could push the firm towards high profitability. The Japanese side on the other hand wanted a mature leadership, very knowledgeable individuals, who could gain respect from clients, workers, and industrial associates. United America was not familiar with the Japanese situation; therefore, they more or less went along with Nippon Kaisha's recommendations at this stage. We will observe some serious problems concerning personnel later, but the initial operation of personal management progressed without much conflict.

COMPLETING THE STAFFING

After the appointment of the management of the new company, Nippon United recruited the clerical staff from Nippon Kaisha. As for the factory work, they hired thirty male workers and seven female part-timers from the Kamiyama area where the new company plant was to be located. They also hired two young girls as assistants and secretary-receptionists. The recruitment of the workers was done mainly by Mr. Kihara, the newly appointed plant manager.

Mr. Higashi, as personnel man of Kamiyama, assisted the recruitment of local workers. Mr. Yoshida, plant manager of the Chemical Division in Kamiyama, became involved in the general administrative work of the new company because of the geographical closeness and the similarity in the field of operation.

The Chemical Research Laboratory of Nippon Kaisha was also located within the chemical plant, under the supervision of the Kamiyama plant manager. United Nippon, from the beginning, had a close association with Kamiyama plant and lab people.

ORGANIZATION OF THE JOINT VENTURE

With regard to the organizational structure of the new company, various people were involved in decision making. The close relationship between the new company and Nippon Kaisha was quite obvious as Nippon United received services and guidance from Sales, Accounting, Affiliated Companies, Personnel, and Chemical divisions of Nippon Kaisha.

All the services provided by United America Inc. came through the Japan Office of its International Division. Its Chemical Division located at Hammond acted upon the request from the International Division. Although Mr. Nickolson, the president of the Chemical Division, sat as a board director of the new company, the major decision-making power lied in the International Division. See Figure 9.

PLANT LOCATION IN KAMIYAMA

Nippon Kaisha owned several plants in the vicinity of Tokyo. One of the plants, the Kamiyama Factory of the Chemical Division, was in an industrial complex in Kamiyama, about two hours and fifteen minutes by train from Tokyo.

Kamiyama City was developed as one of the postwar bedroom towns of the metropolis. When you get off the train from Tokyo, you see a modern department store and retail outlets facing a plaza in front of the railway station where local buses stop to let passengers get off at the terminal. Seven or eight taxies stand near a sunny pedestrian sidewalk, where numerous bicycles are parked in neat lines, leaving little room for pedestrians. At one end of the plaza starts the main street of the Kamiyama Ginza. Nearby is a small police booth. Many people come daily to the station, riding bicycles, or using one of the suburban bus lines.

A five-minute drive from Kamiyama railway station brings you to a two-way country road, as a car passes by colorful faces of pachinko parlors (Japanese pinball game centers), drive-in restaurants, blue-tiled roof houses, and small rice paddy fields. Soon you can see an industrial park with various size factories and office buildings.

In the early 1960s, Nippon Kaisha acquired a vacant lot in this industrial park, within twenty minutes from the railway station and fifteen minutes from the Kamiyama Factory. Nippon Kaisha considered this investment prudent, predicting the future expansion of the Chemical Division and the increasing price of land in

FIGURE 9: NIPPON UNITED KAISHA'S ORGANIZATION
MAJOR PARTICIPANTS IN DECISION MAKING

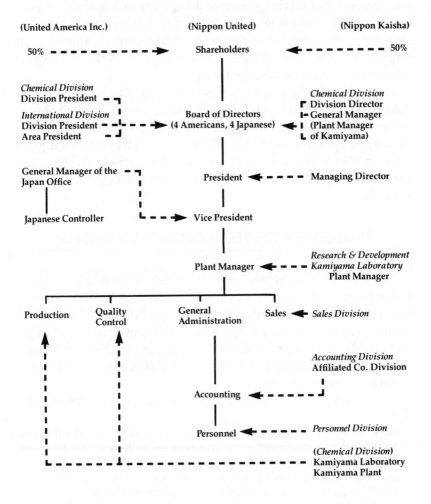

the area. During the economic boom of the 1960s, many Japanese companies purchased land, sometimes without concrete plans for construction, due to skyrocketing land prices and unbounded optimism about continued growth of the company.

As of 1972 the land was still vacant, and Nippon Kaisha offered to lease it to the new company for its plant. The decision on leasing this particular land in Kamiyama was due to: (1) its geographical advantage in transporting materials and goods; (2) its closeness to Nippon Kaisha's Kamiyama Chemical Factory and Laboratory; and (3) the economic advantage of leasing over purchasing land for the new company with small capital. The American side, knowing the high cost of land in Japan, agreed with Nippon Kaisha. Nippon Kaisha as a landowner was to receive an annual rent from the new company.

As you recall, the headquarters of Nippon Kaisha is located in Tokyo, and so is the Japan Office of United America Inc. Sales of the products manufactured by the new company were to be handled by Nippon Kaisha's Sales Division, which is also headquartered in Tokyo. Two-hour train trips to Kamiyama from Tokyo became a routine for Japanese and American managers of Nippon United.

PROBLEMS WITH TECHNOLOGICAL TRANSFER

In the fall of 1972 the new plant manager, Mr. Kihara, was sent to the headquarters of the Chemical Division of United America Inc. in Hammond in order to receive technical and chemical training for several weeks. Mr. Kihara had never been out of Japan and did not speak English. Mr. Imai from the Nippon Kaisha Overseas Department and its New York Office accompanied Mr. Kihara as an interpreter.

Mr. Weaver at Hammond, who trained Mr. Kihara, recalled:

We were told by our International Division to provide technical training to Mr. Kihara. It was difficult for us to communicate with each other even with interpreters because discussions were highly technical. I could see Mr. Kihara becoming exhausted trying to understand what we were telling him about our patented formula in English through interpretation.

Mr. Kihara was a mechanical engineer, and we do not know why Nippon Kaisha did not send chemical experts to learn the formulation side of the operation. But he was the only one we got. We taught Mr. Kihara all the chemical formulations of our products.

Mr. Nicholson, Director of Chemical Division, continued:

As we believed that Nippon Kaisha people wanted to produce the same product as we manufactured in the U.S., our training concentrated on concrete know-how and actual operational techniques. We did not teach him much of the basic chemical theories or the historical process of our operation, i.e., the past trials and errors in order to reach the current stage. If we knew the intention of Nippon Kaisha for adjusting the formula and operational process, we could have taught him more about the chemical principles. Nippon people could have avoided reinventing the wheel a lot by learning from our past errors. Communication barriers seemed to be largely responsible for this problem.

Mr. Yoshida of Kamiyama stated:

We have a chemical laboratory and plants which are producing other chemical products. We were confident of our capability to adjust the United America product to the needs of the Japanese Market. We believed that sending Mr. Kihara to receive the original chemical formula of the product would be enough. We were prepared to do the rest of the work.

After the return of Mr. Kihara from the United States, Kamiyama people immediately started testing the American formula and adjusting it to serve their purpose. The reasons why they tried to modify the formula instead of adopting the American original are important. Let us examine this issue.

DIFFERING GOALS ON PRODUCT QUALITY

Nippon Kaisha people were interested in modifying the product for local requirements rather than following the American specifications. The Chemical Research Laboratory in Kamiyama knew about the need for adjusting the formula to produce a suitable product for the Japanese market. The adjustment was necessary, according to Nippon Kaisha, in the area of heat resistance, uniformity, aesthetic appearance, and softness of the film.

At that time the plastic film wrap business was dominated by major *keiretsu* giants, and in addition, there were about ten other competitors. Because of the growth of large Japanese retailers, supermarket, take-out food shops, and fast-food restaurants, the market for plastic wrapping was expanding rapidly. Nippon Kaisha's competitors, compelled by their overall profit pictures, were competing in the film segment of the market by maintaining heavy price pressure on all others so that smaller ones would be squeezed out of the market.

Nippon Kaisha wanted to jump into this fiercely competitive

but growing market in a major way to seize a large portion of the pie from its competitors. Comparing United America's product with those of its competitors, however, Nippon Kaisha people concluded that their first problem was the appearance of the film.

According to Nippon Kaisha, the product must appear clean, transparent, shiny, and tightly rolled with clean edges. To the Japanese customers, the appearance of the film was crucial, they concluded. In comparison to other products in the market, United America's roll looked wobbly and silvery, with a few air bubbles trapped between the sheets, and it had messy edges, according to the Japanese. Their suspicion about the product's aesthetic problem was confirmed when the imported products from the United States were troubled in the market before domestic production commenced. Obviously such an aesthetic problem did not exist in the United States.

Managers rarely judge events independently, but often rely upon their past experiences as reference points. The reader will recall Nippon Kaisha's past experiences with Hawthorn Company, where technical problems involving odor were eventually solved by Nippon Kaisha's engineers without help from Hawthorn. Partly because of this experience, the engineers in Nippon Kaisha's Kamiyama plant were ready to solve technical problems by themselves. They were very proud of their skills and technical expertise, confirmed by the fact that they previously had solved the odor problem.

In the Hawthorn case, they felt that much time had been wasted asking the Americans to solve the odor problem. This time they believed that all they needed was the original chemical formula from United America and that the rest could and should be handled by the Japanese.

Mr. Yoshida of Kamiyama Factory and even Mr. Hosono, director of the Chemical Division of Nippon Kaisha, were involved in the formulation side of the project. They worked until early hours to test and retest modified formulations. Their intention was to make a perfect product to be introduced to an already highly competitive market. Quality was their key word.

During Mr. Kihara's visit to Hammond, the United America Chemical Division, not knowing Nippon Kaisha's intention to "fool around with the formula," gave Mr. Kihara the formulation of the product, their recommended flow diagrams of the plant, and other specifications.

From the viewpoint of members of the Hammond group such as Mr. Nickolson and Mr. Weaver, Nippon people were to study them and to sent their plans back to them for approval. They were willing to teach them exactly how to make this product successfully. All the Japanese had to do was to follow their instructions faithfully. Hammond people were proud of the fact that United America's plastic wrap was selling very well, commanding a major share of the domestic market. The American customers were satisfied with the product.

Nippon Kaisha back in Japan, however, started modifying the product with their own methods, which they had acquired in the production of other chemical products. Because they had chemical facilities and a laboratory in Kamiyama, the research work was conducted under their supervision.

PROBLEM OF PRODUCTION FLOW DIAGRAM

Nippon Kaisha had affiliated *keiretsu* companies in the construction field. They decided that the new plant construction in Kamiyama would be handled by them because they had experience in constructing other plants for Nippon Kaisha.

Mr. Martin commented:

> These construction people, however, did not realize the specific plant requirements for producing our products. We later found out, for example, that the air ventilation system was inadequately installed, which created contamination problems. On producing the film, we needed an extremely clean environment. Even a tiny bit of dust could be stuck onto the film which would ruin the product.
>
> Unlike American plants, however, the Japanese emphasis was on how to minimize the floor space because of Japan's high land cost. For instance, the use of forklifts for transporting materials and goods within the company, which seemed so natural to Americans, was rejected by the Japanese due to the space problem.

Nippon Kaisha changed the production flow diagram, based on their experiences in the Kamiyama plant. They decided to use a layout with closely lined up machinery to save space on the floor, against the recommended floor plan, which specifically requested the straight lining up of major machines with ample space in between.

In the Japanese production system, where one worker attends several machines on a rotating base, the shorter the distance between machines, the more efficiently the worker can move from one machine to another. The Kamiyama plant people mistakenly thought that the machines in the Hammond plant were lined up because of a one man-one machine principle, "imposed by trade union specialization." The truth was that the straight line of machines could save much time for smoother flow of the operation. The straight line with much space around would also make maintenance and checking of products much easier in case something went wrong in the production.

The Hammond technicians did not explain every logical detail behind the diagram to Mr. Kihara because they were unaware of Nippon Kaisha's intention to change the floor diagram so drastically.

Mr. Weaver and other experts of the United America Chemical Division in Hammond recommended a two-line operation at the initial stage of production based on the fact that "our normal plan would call for putting in two lines and starting up on the first line. The second line serves as a source of spare parts. It is extremely useful during periods when significant changes need be made to the first line."

Nippon Kaisha, considering the fact that the initial stage of operation should be on a trial basis and would require possible adjustments on formulation and production procedure, did not wish to invest in a second line and insisted on installing only one line.

When the drawings of the operation were sent from Nippon Kaisha to the United America Chemical Division, Mr. Nicholson, Mr. Weaver, and technical experts of the division could not believe it. Mr. Nicholson sent a curt letter through the International Division saying:

> We could not approve the flow diagrams presented by Nippon Kaisha since we had no experience in manufacturing the product by this method, and this was the first knowledge we had that substantial changes were being made. As professionals who are proud of the successful operations of United America's products in the U.S., we could not accept the plan.

The layout is confining and inflexible with respect to operations, expansion, and the manufacture of a new product. While we cannot say their methods of production flow will not work, it is a major departure from the recommendations, and no provision has been made in the layout for alternative handling methods if their system should fail.

Mr. Martin said:

Our people in Hammond believed that Nippon Kaisha engineers had tried to take their knowledge of other chemical products and apply this know-how to this product in process layout and equipment selection.

United America considered this technological transfer as a normal one, in which they gave instructions for material tests, formulations, operations, etc. in practical terms. All the know-how was exactly what they were doing in the United States. They refrained from going into fields in which they had no experience.

United America had been selling the product all over the world without difficulty, and they had a large share of the market in the U.S.

The Chemical Division experts of United America rejected the flow diagrams presented by Nippon Kaisha, which deviated greatly from their recommendation. They also considered that the two-line operation was an absolute necessity for the beginning of operations in Japan.

Mr. Shimada, in reply to the opposition from Mr. Nicholson of United America, stated:

Our plan was made based on our careful study and long experience in similar fields. We are confident, and we would like to proceed with Nippon Kaisha's own plan.

Now Mr. Nicholson and chemical people were very upset. They could not understand why the Japanese would not follow their advice. After all it was United America's technology, wasn't it?

As the Chemical Division of United America and Nippon Kaisha could not agree on the flow design and the number of production lines, the start of the operation was delayed. Both insisted that they were correct. Finally, Mr. Franklin and Mr. Martin could wait no longer. The International Division people decided to go ahead with the Nippon Kaisha plan, accepting their Japanese colleagues' full confidence in the success of the plan.

Having heard their decision, Mr. Nicholson sent a letter to Mr. Franklin saying:

> We accept these drawings with reservations only because Nippon Kaisha will be responsible for making the plant operate as predicted.

DISCUSSION OF CHEMICAL FORMULA

In 1974 the Chemical Division of United America sent Mr. Weaver and another technical expert to help start up the plant. Much equipment had been imported from the United States through the United America Chemical Division, and the two experts were to help the Japanese assemble the equipment and start the operation.

Mr. Kihara (Nippon United plant manager), Mr. Konishi (production section chief of the new company), Mr. Yoshida of Kamiyama plant, and senior researchers of Kamiyama held discussions with the two Americans. Much time was spent discussing Nippon Kaisha's product requirements. The Japanese chief lab researcher of Kamiyama mentioned that the Japanese customers wanted a specific type of product different from the previously imported ones. He explained in detail the aesthetic preference of the customer. The American side argued that it had nothing to do with the function of the film.

Mr. Kihara was concerned with the deterioration of the product due to temperature changes. The formulae of the American and Japanese were compared and examined. Using the Japanese formula, the product would meet the aesthetic requirements imposed by the Japanese customer but would create other technical problems. The American original formula was very sensitive to temperature and humidity, which had to be taken into consideration for the operation in Japan. This led to many hours of meetings.

They eventually decided to modify the Japanese formulation, and several chemical compositions were tried in the Kamiyama Laboratory with advice from the American chemist.

START-UP OF THE OPERATION

Nippon Kaisha decided to use their own layout in the operation, which was different from the American system. Necessary corrections relating to the system were recommended by the American experts so that such a layout could be utilized.

The engineers and workers stayed in the factory from early morning to evening to learn the operation techniques taught them by the Americans. Several adjustments were made prior to the initial run. The Americans demonstrated the operation techniques, explaining the methods one by one to the eagerly listening Japanese. Mr. Imai of the Overseas Division of Nippon Kaisha provided interpretation.

Mr. Weaver later made a technical report for the International Division in which he recalled these days in Japan:

> We felt that the management people of the new company were capable of handling each phase of the operation precisely. We appreciated their hard work and long hours spent learning the necessary technology. We were impressed by the hard work and intelligence of the Japanese managers with whom we spent hours discussing issues.
>
> The employees of the new company seemed to have a a strong sense of dedication to the project. We stayed in the plant until nine or ten o'clock at night teaching them how to run the machines. Everyone was so serious and eager to learn.

After experimental runs, everyone was intently looking at the transparent sheet coming out of the machine. It looked even, smoother, and beautiful! The machine continued running for four more hours before the experts declared the success of the operation. *"Banzai, banzai!"* (Hurrah, hurrah!) Everyone was smiling.

The American engineers stayed in Kamiyama for ten more days until they were confident that they had taught essential handling techniques necessary to manufacture the product efficiently.

In the report, Mr. Weaver also wrote:

> We must conclude that with the technical confidence demonstrated by our partners at Nippon Kaisha, that the Nippon-United Chemical Plant will prove to be an excellent addition to our markets in the Far East.

Nippon United was to increase the production capacity to several lines in the future. The layout of the plant was such as to provide space for future expansion, and a vacant lot attached to the plant was to be used for further expansion in the future.

PERSONNEL SHUFFLE AT UNITED JAPAN OFFICE

In mid-1972, Mr. Ōbayashi of United America Japan Office left the company. With Mr. Martin's tightening of the budget of the Japan office, Mr. Ōbayashi increasingly felt uncomfortable. Mr. Martin did not seem to allow Mr. Ōbayashi much elbow room. Mr. Ōbayashi felt that he had given Mr. Martin much knowledge about the Japanese market and ways to do business in the Orient, but that he now saw little chance of promotion in the company with Mr. Martin directly above him.

Mr. Ōbayashi's experience in the international field was a well sought after commodity. Once he made his intention known in the circle, he was immediately recruited by another American company, which had started several joint ventures in Japan. Mr. Ōbayashi was offered a job of president of its Japan operation with a 50 percent salary raise.

After the departure of Mr. Ōbayashi, Mr. Martin, who had been in Japan for a total of one year, decided not to hire a new Japanese vice president. He felt that it was time for him to deal directly with Japanese clients and partners without an intermediary. He would handle Nippon United himself.

FINANCIAL REPORTS

The first problem between Mr. Martin and the new joint venture was in the area of financial reporting. Mr. Kihara, plant manager of the new company, recalled:

> We were used to giving oral reports to Nippon Kaisha management regarding day-to-day operations. We were surprised and sometimes even annoyed by the frequent requests for reporting from Mr. Martin regarding figures, tables, and charts. He also wanted to use the straight line depreciation rate. We had to explain that the Dai-Nippon Group was using the accelerated depreciation rate, and we alone could not change the method.

Mr. Martin commented on this issue:

> It was so difficult to communicate with the Japanese people in Kamiyama. They would ask us to send information on technical or other matters from the U.S., and we promptly answered them either by telex or letters. When we needed some information from them, however, it took them weeks to reply. Sometimes they did not reply at all, and we had to visit, call, or write to them again.
>
> For example, to get simple financial data for our quarterly profit and loss statement, we had to get in touch with the Sales Division, the Marketing Division, the Accounting Division of Nippon Kaisha plus Nippon-United Kaisha. They seemed to lack a formal financial reporting system regarding day-to-day operations.
>
> We asked the Nippon Kaisha management again and again to change the method of calculating the depreciation rate, but their answer was always the same: all Nippon Kaisha affiliates and subsidiaries follow the accelerated depreciation rate, and they could not make one affiliate change the method.

FINANCIAL REPORTS: DIFFERING OPINIONS

Regarding the financial reports, the contract of the joint venture reads as follows:

> New Company shall keep all books of accounts and make all financial reports in accordance with the standards prescribed by Japanese laws and regulations and generally accepted accounting principles in Japan.
>
> New Company shall prepare and forward to United America and Nippon Kaisha a balance sheet and profit and loss statements made pursuant to books of account so kept as provided in the above section.

The new company naturally followed the practices of Nippon Kaisha and its *keiretsu* group to maintain a uniform financial system among them. For example, the new company followed the accelerated depreciation rate, which had been used by the Japanese parent company. The accelerated depreciation rate system makes the initial depreciation of equipment and facilities much larger than that in later periods.

The accelerated depreciation rate had been used uniformly among Dai-Nippon Group members that had a tremendously rapid technological advancement and frequent change of equipment and facilities. Quick write-offs of facilities was the norm.

United America had quite a different approach to this issue. At the initial stage of the joint-venture operation when they had losses rather than profits, it seemed reasonable (according to the American side) to use the straight-line depreciation rate. Using the straight-line system, you depreciate the same amount every year. Both the straight depreciation rate and the accelerated depreciation rate are accepted accounting principles in Japan.

Mr. Martin argued that the accelerated depreciation rate would enlarge the amount of the firm's initial expenses too much, ending up with little or no profit in the first few years. To Mr. Martin (and Mr. Franklin in this matter), whose career depended upon the profit performance of the Japan operation, it was very important that this joint-venture would turn out to be profitable, as soon as possible.

The Japanese management disagreed. They argued that this new company, Nippon United, was going to be a part of Dai-Nippon/Nippon-Kaisha *keiretsu*. Uniformity with the Nippon Kaisha-Dai Nippon industrial group in accounting procedures was very important. The Japanese management also argued that they expected losses for the new company for the first few years anyway, and that they were not very much concerned about the initial loss, because they took a much longer term view of this operation.

PROFIT MAKING: OPPOSING VIEWS

These two opposing views can not be fully appreciated unless we look at the past experiences and perceptions of the two management cultures regarding profit making. As far as the American side was concerned, profit was vital for maintaining the operation and for advancing the careers of managers in charge. Mr. Franklin was facing a very important career turning point because of the anticipated retirement of Mr. Murray, International Division president. Mr. Franklin had observed numerous occasions when the company had dismissed incompetent managers who were not producing profits. Recently, Mr. Franklin himself had dismissed Mr. Hart for this very reason. Likewise, Mr. Martin was keenly aware of the significance of profit making. If Mr. Martin did not produce profits in Japan very quickly, his head would be the next one to roll.

On the other hand, no managers in Nippon Kaisha were

threatened personally with dismissal due to a low profit of the joint venture. They might be moved to different subsidiaries or affiliates as *tenzoku* men, but they would still be Nippon-Kaisha *keiretsu* men. As we have observed in the previous chapter, their corporate culture was based upon the solidarity of the industrial group. This gave them a different perspective upon running the joint-venture company.

To the Japanese management, one of the most important initial tasks of this newly created subsidiary was to develop good relationships with the parent firm and member firms. The uniformity with the *keiretsu* in its accounting procedure was regarded as vital by the Japanese managers.

Concerning profit, Nippon Kaisha's corporate strategies was long term and centered on cultivating human relationships. Nippon Kaisha was eager to move into the new market of plastic wrap, and they were ready and willing to sacrifice a few years of profits for the sake of market expansion. Their approach to the depreciation issue reflected this line of thinking in sharp contrast to that of United America representatives.

Mr. Franklin and Mr. Martin, after several weeks of negotiations, finally gave up on the idea of the straight-line depreciation system. Nippon Kaisha management just would not do it. The Americans at that moment judged that cooperative relationships with Nippon Kaisha management would be more important at this stage of the game and went along with the Japanese.

FINANCIAL REPORTS: A SECOND AND RELATED PROBLEM

The second area concerning difficulties in financial reporting of the new company is that only the balance sheet and profit and loss statements were specifically requested in the contract. United America management were used to weekly reports, monthly budgets, and quarterly forecasts, all in written forms, and they automatically assumed that the Japanese did the same thing. They did not. Nippon Kaisha relied far less on written reports for short-term operational data, partly because Nippon Kaisha employees share information verbally through intense personal contacts among themselves and partly because they were more long-term-oriented as discussed above. They were annoyed that they had to make special formal reports to United America management almost every week. Preparation of written reports in English also took time, adding to their aversion to number crunching.

Finance-oriented Mr. Martin, following the American headquarter's custom on the other hand, wanted to receive exact operating data on the new company in order to measure strategies or assess progress or efficiency. He also wanted written reports and confirmation for his own file, just in case.

Mr. Martin learned that it was next to impossible to get necessary operating data on short notice from the new company, the Nippon Kaisha Sales Division, the Marketing Division, or other relevant departments of the Japanese parent company. He had to establish a new financial reporting system with divisions concerned. Because many were located within Nippon Kaisha, and not in Nippon United, Mr. Martin had to count upon the good will of Nippon Kaisha personnel for timely reporting. Mr. Martin himself was obliged to report on the United America Asia Division performance to New York; he spent many frustrating days in collecting necessary data from Nippon Kaisha personnel and compiled the final report for the American headquarters.

In order to help solve this problem of financial reporting, Mr. Martin hired a Japanese controller, Mr. Ōta, who had been working for another joint-venture company as an accountant. Mr. Ōta's task was to receive financial reports from the Japanese side and to "translate" them into English, following the methods used by United America. Japan was the only country where the financial reports of the operation had to go through the local office to the headquarters, rather than being sent directly from a subsidiary to United America in the United States.

Mr. Ōta explained:

I became, in many ways, the cushion between the Japanese and American sides. Because of the differences in financial systems, I decided to get only basic data from Nippon United and to make financial reports myself for the American company.

Nippon United makes reports basically for Nippon Kaisha, not for United America. I am the one who restructures the reports, calculating translation gains or losses, and adding royalty payments, etc.

In the Dai-Nippon Group, a member company has to follow the group's rules, and acts within the framework set by the group. They are very proud of being a member of the group.

On the other hand, United America is a multinational, and they are also proud people. It is hard to have two proud people with different opinions agree on an issue.

The only thing that saves us is that the two companies at least try to understand each other without getting too excited about smaller problems.

Mr. Ōta was a devoted Christian in his mid-forties. After graduating from Aoyama University in Tokyo, he worked for Japanese aluminum manufacturer. When he became a section chief, he decided to move out to a foreign affiliate because, he said, "I needed more freedom and challenges." Mr. Ōta had worked for two other foreign affiliates before he landed in the present position. He became directly involved in the financial side of the joint venture.

About the time when Mr. Ōta was ready to take up his new position in the United Japan's office, the Organization of Petroleum Exporting Countries (OPEC) oil embargo shook the whole world as a devastating energy crisis. The "oil shock" caught Japan, which was 99 percent dependent on imported oil by surprise. Panic-stricken housewives grabbed foodstuffs from store shelves and stockpiled them in cupboards. Toilet paper disappeared from stores overnight. Neon signs of nightly Tokyo districts were turned off. Long lines of automobiles were formed for gas. A science fiction novel called *The Submergence of the Japanese Archipelago,* by Sakyō Kobayashi, became a bestseller.

These were particularly difficult years for chemical companies. In spite of the reduced profit of the parent company, the second line of production was put on stream in the Nippon United plant as planned. The plant geared up for full capacity operation at this unpropitious time. During the following months, sales did not improve much because of the general economic depression. What was worse, the product proved to be poor in quality, and the rate of rejects from users increased.

HIGH REJECT RATE

Mr. Martin faced one of the most difficult problems since the start of the operation — rejection of the product by the Japanese customer. He said:

We had expected a loss in profits for the first year of operation. During the first several months, I visited Kamiyama regularly and noticed that the rate of rejects from users was high. But I was optimistic about the capability of the Nippon United people and thought the quality of the product would improve after the initial stage was passed.

There were several problems influencing the product quality: Lack of uniformity, uneven thickness of the film, the existence of air bubbles, and generally poor appearance. One cause for poor appearance was contamination. Because of the way the plant building was originally constructed by a *keiretsu* member firm, the building was not completely airtight. Consequently, there were occasions when small pieces of dust got trapped in the film compound. The building had to be completely resealed at considerable additional expense. Special insect screens and orange lights to ward off tiny bugs from neighboring rice paddy fields also had to be installed.

There had also been a major misunderstanding concerning the method of cleaning extruders for maintaining uniform pressure. While Mr. Kihara was in United America's Chemical Division, he thought that the American group did not stop the machine for several months. In reality, the Americans checked and cleaned the machines whenever contamination occurred. Nippon United engineers, while complaining about poor quality, did not frequently stop the machines for such checkups. Instead, they tried to modify the chemical formulas and other production processes.

FIRST CASUALTY: SOLVING THE PROBLEM OF QUALITY

Mr. Shimada, president of United Nippon, and other top Japanese directors were, nevertheless patient with the new company. Mr. Shimada publicly said to the plant people in one of his speeches that their first task was to improve the quality of the product and that they expected no profit until the quality problem was solved. The American side was not that patient. Mr. Franklin urged Mr. Martin to take some concrete action in order to remedy the situation. According to Mr. Franklin, he had waited long enough to conclude that Japanese engineers could not solve the problem themselves.

Mr. Martin reported to Mr. Franklin that the company needed

a major improvement in production and technology, as well as in management. Based mostly upon his experiences in United America, Mr. Martin concluded that the issue was not only that of poor production techniques but that of poor management. He therefore suggested a change in key personnel. Mr. Franklin agreed with Mr. Martin. The American side wanted to hold someone responsible, because, in their view, the management of the new company was in charge of quality issues and they should take full responsibility for the quality problem.

Neither Mr. Martin nor Mr. Franklin was impressed by the performance of Mr. Kihara, the plant manager. They concluded that Mr. Kihara should be replaced by a more dynamic and competent "chemical engineer."

Nippon Kaisha management was shocked to hear the suggestion that Mr. Kihara be dismissed. They opposed the "hasty removal of the top personnel" proposed by United America after such a short period of time. Mr. Shimada and other Japanese directors argued that Mr. Kihara was a good team leader, and that it was not his personal incompetence that caused the poor sales result and the high rejection rate. Mr. Franklin and other American directors were not persuaded, however. They insisted that the company needed to bring in profits rather quickly and that it needed a competent, dynamic leader to surmount these obstacles. The argument continued. It took three months for Nippon Kaisha to accept the proposal by United America.

Mr. Shimada recalled that the American side was very determined on this issue, and that Nippon Kaisha had no alternative if they wanted to continue the good relationship with United America, and they did.

Mr. Shimada said:

> We were reluctant to change the personnel of the new company after only a year and a half in operation. But United America Inc. pressed us very hard, showing their discontent with the poor sales result of the new company. They believed that the present Nippon United management was not capable of handling the problem which was mainly in production areas. We had a lot of discussions within the company (Nippon Kaisha), but our top management finally decided to replace the plant manager.

In early 1976, both sides agreed that Mr. Kihara should be

called back to Nippon Kaisha. Mr. Kihara was later dispatched as a *tenzoku* man to another smaller affiliate company of Nippon Kaisha.

SELECTING A NEW PLANT MANAGER

Mr. Franklin and Mr. Martin strongly felt that this time they should carefully monitor the selection process. They informally negotiated with Mr. Shimada in a Japanese tea house and in a hotel restaurant to make sure that Mr. Shimada understood the type of manager that would be acceptable to United America.

Mr. Franklin said:

> We told the Nippon Kaisha management that we needed a young, aggressive, and intelligent manager who had enough experience in running a chemical plant. Nippon Kaisha people explained about different Japanese management policies on personnel issues, but we pressed them hard.
>
> We told them that we could not continue having poor sales results and that we needed a major improvement in the new company management. It was the first major crisis in our joint-venture operation.

Mr. Shimada finally came up with a candidate: a 42-year-old mechanical engineer, Mr. Mochida. Mr. Mochida had worked for Nippon Kaisha since its establishment. He first entered Dai-Nippon's Chemical Division in 1955 and was put in charge of machinery used in that division. When Nippon Kaisha spun off from Dai-Nippon Inc., he was also transferred to Nippon Kaisha as a *tenzoku* man.

During the late 1960s he worked as production section chief of the Chemical Division of Nippon Kaisha in Kamiyama. In 1973 he was again moved to an affiliated chemical company, which was spun off from the Nippon Kaisha Chemical Division. During the early 1970s he worked as production manager of the affiliate located on the Japan Sea Coast. Mr. Mochida recalled:

> One day I had a visit from Mr. Hosono, director of Nippon Kaisha headquarters. He told me that Nippon United was having some troubles, and asked me if I could help them by becoming the plant manager of the company. It came to me out of the blue. I had no choice but to say 'yes.' I had been working in the chemical field all my life, although my educational background is in mechanical engineering. I know enough of machinery used for

chemical operations. I had worked for the Nippon Kaisha plant in Kamiyama and knew many engineers and researchers there.

It was like going back to my old territory. Besides, it was a great promotion for me. I would be the youngest plant manager among all the affiliates of Nippon United. I was immediately transferred to Kamiyama.

TECHNICAL HELP FROM HAMMOND

Mr. Martin felt that unless some immediate action was taken, the new company would become a disaster. Consequently, he requested through Mr. Franklin that technical assistance be obtained from the Chemical Division of United America.

Mr. Weaver and a machinery expert of the United America Chemical Division were selected by Mr. Nicholson of the Chemical Division to be sent to the new company's plant in Kamiyama. Their assignment was to analyze the operation, to determine the underlying causes for the plant's inefficiencies, and to make recommendations for improvement. Based on this information, Mr. Martin would discuss the production, sales, and marketing of the new company with Nippon Kaisha people. They would modify their methods of operation to insure a profitable joint-venture operation.

Mr. Weaver mentioned:

We were sent to Japan for trouble-shooting for ten days. It was not a particularly pleasant return for me. It was cold and windy in Kamiyama. When we arrived at the factory, Nippon United people treated us coldly as if they wanted to blame our technology for producing poor quality products. I thought I would be pushed to the wall there.

I immediately started working. I stopped the operation and started cleaning up the machines. Nippon United people looked surprised. They started taking notes and asking millions of questions of me.

I have been in this business long enough. I knew what was wrong and what should be done. Once they realized that it was worthwhile listening to me, their attitude changed completely.

Mr. Aono, an engineer at Kamiyama at that time, recalled:

Before the American engineers came, Nippon Kaisha's and Nippon United engineers had tried everything to solve the contamination problem. But because of the initial misunderstanding, we did not clean up the machine. We thought it was not necessary, and believed that the machines should be checked only once every several months. We were shocked when Mr. Weaver stopped the whole operation and started cleaning up the machines. We then realized that it was an important cause for the contamination problem.

According to the American experts, one of the problems was that the engineers of the Nippon United operation lacked understanding of the chemical formulations, raw materials, and basic principles involved in the production of the particular chemical product, which was different from Nippon Kaisha's other chemical products. Numerous meetings were held at Kamiyama with Nippon Kaisha personnel and Nippon United quality control and production personnel to discuss issues relating to raw materials, formulations, testing, finished product quality, equipment, and processing. A prepared list of at least seventy questions, written in Japanese and translated for the Americans, were fully discussed. In accordance with the organizational structure of the United Kaisha plant in Kamiyama, many people were involved in this technological problem. See figure 10 *Participants in Decision Making*.

In addition, Mr. Weaver gave a talk on formulations and raw materials while the American mechanical engineer gave a course to production personnel on the methods of trouble-shooting, minimizing and controlling defects, as well as a means of determining operation problems. A trouble-shooting guide for specific problems prepared at the American Chemical Division was presented to the Nippon United operation staff.

The American experts found the operating staff at Nippon United very hardworking people "who always seem to keep themselves busy on the job. The supervisory and management personnel were working 98 hours — seven days a week — in the plant."

In the course of discussions, they began to realize that several problems had caused the inefficiency.

CAUSES FOR INEFFICIENCY

Nippon United had departed from the original recommendations made by the United America Chemical Division so far as plant layout and material was concerned. Nippon United had in-

FIGURE 10: PARTICIPANTS IN DECISION MAKING

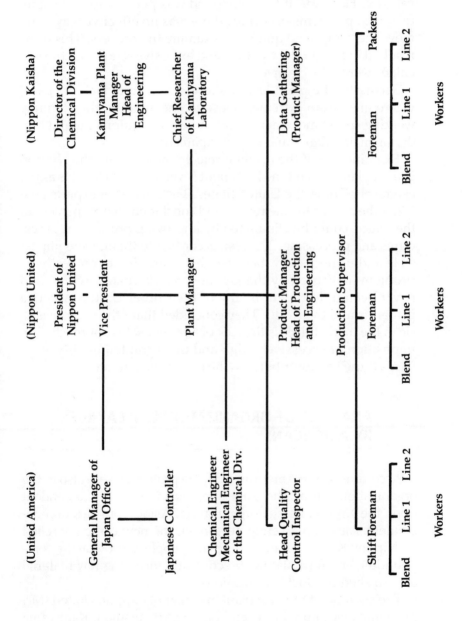

sisted upon their own layout. The American experts had reluctantly agreed that Nippon Kaisha's system might be worthwhile when the operation was running smoothly and no problem developed. However, if the compound was poorly mixed or other technical problems occurred, there was no effective way to remove the compound quickly to examine the process. This delay resulted in nonproductive time and excessive scrap until the machines were fully cleaned.

Secondly, the plant layout showed a general lack of space, where lines were extremely close to one another, thus limiting working space, movement of machinery or equipment, and hindering maintenance and future expansion.

Examination of the in-plant rejects showed that the Nippon United plant at that time had about seven times the rejects as the chemical plant in the United States. The American experts analyzed the causes for the rejects and concluded that 80 percent of the rejects could be eliminated by improving production procedures and processing. The rest, according to them, were impossible and unnecessary, because they were due to an aesthetic problem instituted by the Japanese marketplace, which had never been a detriment in any of their other United America plants around the world. They concluded that "the major obstacle in the marketplace is the lack of a proper sales approach. The imposition of excessively high and unwarranted quality standards is the key contributor to the high rejection rate."

ANALYSES OF ORGANIZATIONAL WEAKNESS BY AMERICANS

According to the American side, the problems were also in the organization setup. The plant operation was highly dependent upon the Nippon Kaisha organization. Aside from lack of independent sales or marketing personnel, the new company relied on Nippon Kaisha's Kamiyama plant people to provide the compounding and formulating direction and incoming raw material and finished product specifications.

The position of the new plant manager of Nippon United (Mr. Mochida) placed under the authority of Mr. Yoshida, Kamiyama plant manager of Nippon United, did not permit Mr. Mochida to exert full control over the Nippon United operation. Judging from this organizational setup, the American side concluded that Mr. Mochida was highly dependent upon the Nippon Kaisha organization for services. Because of this dependence, the Nippon United operation was regulated by a number of people, without any "one man in charge."

In late March, Mr. Weaver, Mr. Martin, Mr. Ōta (controller of the Japan Office), Mr. Mochida (plant manager of Nippon United), Mr. Yoshida (plant manager of Nippon Kaisha Kamiyama), Mr. Yamagi (Nippon Kaisha's sales director) and Nippon United sales and marketing people met in the Nippon Kaisha headquarters in Tokyo. Mr. Imai (section chief of the Overseas Department) and his assistant also attended the meeting.

According to the American side, it was apparent that the difficulties in Nippon United Japan could be divided into two separate areas. The first area was technical difficulties related to formulation and process. The second set of difficulties were related to sales and marketing.

Mr. Martin stated during the meeting:

> A number of our technical problems can be traced back to Nippon Kaisha's failure to follow more precisely the engineering recommendations made by United America at the time of plant construction and the installation of the equipment. Nippon Kaisha does have considerable know-how in other chemical products and perhaps felt that this knowledge could easily be translated into our particular product field without difficulty.
>
> Time has proved that this is not so, and some of our difficulties can be traced back to this mistake. While Nippon Kaisha men were trained at our Chemical Division in the preinstallation stage, and we believe that we had adequately explained the chemical and engineering principles governing our know-how, considerable gaps in understanding existed, due again to the language and communication problem and partially to the wide cultural differences in both organization and structure.
>
> These problems can never be totally resolved and will always impact our work in Japan to some extent.

After this opening remarks, the two American engineers explained the causes of the technical problems and recommendations for improvement on about ten major items in the operation. They agreed to send a more complete technical analysis of these difficulties as soon as they went back to the United States. The Japanese agreed to follow this technical advice in the future. The problem of aesthetic appearance, however, remained unsolved.

MARKETING AND SALES

As the discussion moved to the problem of the high rejection rate, Mr. Franklin stated:

> For some reason users have equated the appearance of the product with quality. Apparently Nippon Kaisha has not tried to reeducate the market and convince them that it has nothing whatever to do with the quality of the product.
>
> Rather than taking this more difficult approach saleswise, they have instead placed an unreasonable burden on the production facility to produce products which suit the user's taste.
>
> This has resulted in many production problems, rejects, storage difficulties, inventory problems, not to mention the vast amount of time and effort spent trying to manufacture such a product.

Mr. Martin recalled the meeting:

> I pointed out to the managers of the Sales and Marketing Divisions of Nippon Kaisha in particular that United America could not and would not accept a situation where our profit results were deteriorating due to the failure of our partner to properly organize and manage their sales and marketing efforts.
>
> I implied that, if this situation did not rapidly improve, I would unquestionably meet the President of Nippon Kaisha and convey to him United America's total dissatisfaction with the cooperation in the sales and marketing areas from Nippon Kaisha.

Although Mr. Kawamura and Mr. Yamagi of the Sales and Marketing Divisions of Nippon Kaisha promised that they would put their utmost effort to expand their sales and improve the profit, they knew the difficulties involving the "reeducation" of the users. Mr. Kawamura said privately:

> Our distribution network is very complex, and it is the task of salesmen to develop a close relationship with large wholesalers in order to sell the product. The Japanese business is still very much dependent on the human relationship. Because of the hard competition, including a price war, salesmen have to give even seemingly unnecessary services to large users. For us the user is the king. Reeducating them sounds unrealistic to us.

Mr. Yamagi added:

> The reason why many Japanese products become highly competitive in the international market is partly due to the severe demands on the quality of the

products in the Japanese market. We have to strive for high quality, even higher than anywhere else in the world. The Americans still think that their product would sell well in Japan because it is selling well in the U.S. But the taste of the market is different here. It is our task to meet the requirement of the market, rather than forcing the market to change its taste.

Mr. Kawamura, section chief of Sales in Nippon Kaisha, had a direct responsibility for the sales of the product manufactured by Nippon United, but he had an additional position as sales manager of Nippon Kaisha and could not fully occupy himself on the sales strategy of Nippon United.

Mr. Martin complained that the Nippon Kaisha Sales Division people were interested in the overall sales of Nippon Kaisha products, not specifically the products of Nippon United. Salesmen in local Nippon Kaisha sales offices handled various products and worked for overall sales results.

Mr. Kawamura said:

The Americans should realize the fact that they could not sell the product without using the Nippon Kaisha distribution network. We were the ones who had been trying to sell the product. They should listen to us.

They should have understood the fact that it was the user who said the product had an aesthetic problem. This was the reason for the poor sales results. But the Americans could not solve the aesthetic problem, although they were the ones who were supposed to provide the technology.

GENERAL MANAGER OF NIPPON UNITED

According to Mr. Martin, on the other hand, the unsatisfactory result of the new company was mainly due to the lack of individual responsibility and accountability. Mr. Martin started to press Nippon Kaisha to appoint a full-time general manager and marketing manager for Nippon United, so that they would be totally responsible for the profits and sales of the Nippon United product. He wrote to the top management of Nippon Kaisha:

With respect to the General Manager's job, I would particularly like to point out that the General Manager is responsible not only for the development of both short and long-range objectives, but the preparation of the total annual budgets and has the full responsibility of carrying out the budget in fact.

It has occurred to me that the pinpointing of responsibility with respect to individual managers is an aspect of American management thinking. I am aware that, in Japan, group decision making, consensus opinion forming and diffused responsibility are the norms.

In the case of a new company fighting to establish a viable market position, it is my belief that a strong, determined, and fully responsible leadership is a mandatory requirement for success.

As I have stated to various Nippon Kaisha executives on several occasions, I believe that Nippon United is sorely in need of a General Manager and a Marketing Manager who will pull together into a concerted program the various functional aspects of our business which will result in a well coordinated plan for growth and profit achievement.

Nippon Kaisha was rather reluctant to appoint a general manager. They said that this would involve a major organizational change in the relationship between Nippon Kaisha and Nippon United. Mr. Martin, with the backing of Mr. Franklin, was very insistent on this issue. After several months of negotiations, Nippon Kaisha finally agreed to look for a competent marketing manager, not a general manager, within the company.

SENDING JOB DESCRIPTION OF MARKETING MANAGER

Knowing that no job description for a marketing manager existed at Nippon Kaisha, Mr. Martin sent a job description prior to the appointment of a marketing manager. See Figure 11.

DISTRIBUTION NETWORK

Mr. Martin believed that one of the basic problems was the lack of marketing knowledge in Nippon Kaisha sales and marketing people. He said:

In America, we are selling service as well as a product. Our marketing people try to develop close relationships with the end-user, and analyze the needs of the market. In Japan the distribution network is very complex so that Nippon Kaisha cannot and does not have direct contacts with the end-user. They are selling the product to the large wholesaler or the trading company which again sells it to the secondary wholesaler. The communication chain is too long for the manufacturer to get an accurate grip on the needs of the end-user. When I discussed this problem with Nippon Kaisha people, I stressed the need for direct relationships with end-users.

FIGURE 11: JOB DESCRIPTION OF MARKETING MANAGER

Basic Function:

Develops policies, procedures, and programs for the marketing of the product. Plans and directs the efforts of marketing personnel toward obtaining profit center objectives. Counsels profit center and divisional management in the field of marketing activities.

Organizational Relationships:

Reports to: General Manager or President

Directly Supervises: Marketing Analysis, Field Service Engineer, Marketing Staff

Scope of Responsibility: Directly responsible for all marketing of the product in Japan

His Specific Responsibilities:

(a) Sales:
1. Assists in formulation of policies and procedures to insure sales force has proper tools to accomplish our sales objectives.
2. Appraises sales programs against planned objectives and recommends corrective action where necessary.
3. Develops forecasts with General Sales Manager.

(b) Pricing:
1. Recommends product pricing.
2. Counsels in individual pricing questions which may have policy implications.
3. Keeps abreast of competitive pricing actions and their impact on Nippon United price policy.

(c) Advertising:
1. Directs advertising and sales promotion activities.
2. Approves copy for conformance to company policy.

(d) 1. Directs market research activity to identify and evaluate market potential.
2. Analyzes sales records for trends.

(e) New Products Development
1. Develops recommendations for new products and product modifications.
2. Reviews plans for new product introduction and makes recommendations.

(f) Packaging
1. Cooperates with Distribution Dept. in developing packaging for the product.

Mr. Shimada, president of Nippon United, explained:

> Of course it is important to know the needs of the end-user. But it is also true that the success of our business depends on the decisions of the large wholesaler to buy or not to buy our products. We are now trying hard to develop the chain of wholesalers who will have exclusive dealings with Nippon Kaisha Sales Division.
>
> Our business is now 50 percent dependent on a large trading company, and we are trying to decrease our dependence on them while increasing the number of exclusive wholesalers. The number of large retailers in Japan is still small. Our business, therefore, must depend on the wholesalers who have numerous retailers under them.

The distribution network of the Nippon United product can be categorically divided into two. One is through large trading companies, and the other is through exclusive wholesalers. See Figure 12. Upon the request of United America, Nippon Kaisha is trying to establish direct channels with large retailers, but their number is still small.

The large and exclusive wholesalers handle not only the Nippon United product but also related products and machines, which are bought by large retail stores. They own their own storage houses and have exclusive contracts with large retail stores to provide various goods to them. Making a direct and exclusive sales agreement with such large wholesalers will give a large volume of business to Nippon United.

In the first distribution network, each middleman takes a few percentages of sales commission, and therefore the end price becomes higher. However, it covers a large number of smaller retail stores all over Japan. Nippon Kaisha sales people consider that keeping the first distribution chain is also important in the present situation in order to keep in contact with the smaller retail stores scattered all over the country. The number of small retail stores selling and using the Nippon United product exceeds 8,000 shops.

Mr. Kawamura said:

> If large retail stores continue to grow in Japan, and direct contracts with them become possible, we will certainly change our present strategy. We realize the need for direct public relationship with the end-user is growing.

FIGURE 12: DISTRIBUTION NETWORK

(1) Distribution Network: Type 1

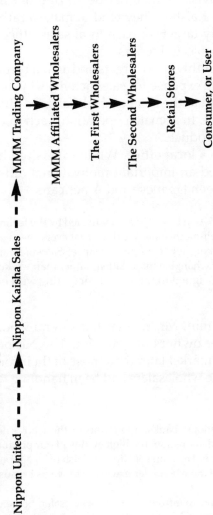

(2) Distribution Network: Type 2

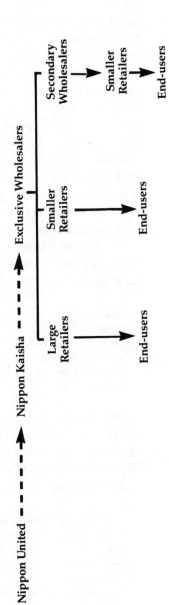

Nippon Kaisha's sales operations are as follows. Nippon Kaisha has twelve sales offices all over Japan, and the sales headquarters is located in Tokyo. The president of Nippon United, the plant manager, and the production manager meet once every month with the Nippon Kaisha Chemical Division to discuss the montly budget. The Industrial Chemical Division together with the Sales and Marketing Divisions then decide an overall sales and profit target of Nippon Kaisha. They tend to make a rather optimistic target. A monthly target for each local sales office is given based on the overall projected orders.

In each local office the monthly sales targets and actual results are indicated in a graph. The expense for sales activities by individual salesmen are reported to the chief of the local sales office and then to the headquarters. In a smaller operation, each salesman handles three or four products.

Mr. Kaji is a salesman in a local office. While we visited his clients together, he indicated an important motivational difference for salesmanship between Japanese and Americans:

> We are not working on a commission base. We are motivated by the feelings of comradeship and need for self-motivation. We think that everyone in our office is cooperating and working for team performance. Salesmen are, therefore, helping each other, exchanging information, rather than working separately on the products assigned to them, and competing with one another.

On a day I accompanied him, Mr. Kaji visited several wholesalers and chatted with the owners or manager. The Nippon United product came to the market later than those of their competitor's products, which the wholesalers had been handling. Mr. Kaji said:

> We investigate business associations, banks, and clients of the wholesaler who has been using them, and demonstrate the high quality of our product vis-a-vis those of the competitor's. The name of Nippon Kaisha-Dai Nippon Group is of great value, because the wholesaler may want to see us because of the renowned name.
>
> Sometimes we ask bank people to introduce us to a wholesaler. Some of our affiliate companies may have business with them. If we hear any complaints on the competitor's products, we feel it gives us a good chance to demonstrate the superior quality of our product. We may call the plant people to demonstrate the use of the product to the wholesaler.

We have to gain their confidence. Sometimes it takes a few years to get a trial order from a wholesaler. We have to develop human relationships and trust from them.

Mr. Kaji visited a wholesaler and sat in his office over a cup of tea, chatting on seemingly unrelated topics with the clerks and managers. He then went to a storage house behind the office and helped them in their inventory checkup. He knew a great deal about the family backgrounds of the clerks and workers and talked casually with them.

APPOINTMENT OF A NEW MARKETING MANAGER

In early 1978, Mr. Kawamura, sales manager of Nippon United, was given the new title of marketing manager. Although United America had wanted to have him independent of Nippon Kaisha, he continued to hold an additional section chief position in the sales department of Nippon Kaisha. According to Mr. Yamagi (head of the Sales Division of Nippon Kaisha), Mr. Kawamura was a very competent manager. Mr. Yamagi believed that it was a good decision to keep him in Nippon Kaisha.

Mr. Yamagi explained:

Since Mr. Kawamura would be closely coordinating with our sales people, we thought it would be better to have him as a Nippon Kaisha man. His task was, however, to concentrate primarily on the Nippon United product.

He had been a competent sales manager in our domestic division and knows the local salesmen and the market very well. We gave him the new title of marketing manager because that was a strong wish of United America.

Mr. Martin accepted Mr. Kawamura's new assignment and stressed the company's need for direct relationships with end-users: The new marketing manager should be out in the field with local salesmen most of the time to develop close and direct relationships with wholesalers and large retailers as well as to learn the market situation. Unlike Nippon Kaisha salesmen who have to worry about other products they are handling, the marketing manager of Nippon United can concentrate on one major item. The combined efforts of the marketing manager and the

Nippon Kaisha sales office force should contribute to the overall sales of the United Nippon products.

Mr. Martin recalled:

> The real task of the marketing manager is to build up overall marketing strategies for the company. Right now Mr. Kawamura is fulfilling a sales function, not that of marketing. He is busy visiting end-users, trying to establish direct contacts with them. But in my opinion, this should be the task of Nippon Kaisha sales people. In the future we would like him to concentrate more on marketing strategies and long-range marketing plans.

PERSONNEL CHANGES IN UNITED AMERICA

In the New York corporate headquarters of United America International, Mr. Murray was concerned about the company after his imminent retirement. He had actually stayed longer than he had planned as president of International and as corporate vice president. He wanted to prepare the organization for a new era without himself at the helm.

Following United America President Lang's advice, Mr. Murray decided to move Mr. Franklin to Europe and to give Asia to Mr. O'Leary, who had been heading the Europe Division. This rather unusual exchange of major area positions in the division, once announced, stirred up an unusual amount of office rumors. Several versions of the meaning of this exchange were circulated among them. It was an old story that Mr. Franklin and Mr. O'Leary had been rivals throughout their career advancement. They represented different styles of management and different styles of life in this matter. Everyone joined in predicting which one of the two, Mr. Franklin or Mr. O'Leary, would be the next division president.

It was no doubt that the top management wanted Mr. Murray's successor to have both European and Asian experiences and that this move was their way of preparing the man as next International Division president.

Mr. Martin received the news back in Tokyo, through international calls from various "friends" in New York. Mr. Franklin called Mr. Martin from New York in person to break the news, which Mr. Martin already knew. A few days later, Mr. Martin received another international call, this time from Mr. O'Leary. Mr.

O'Leary wanted a complete briefing on the Japan operation immediately. The next day Mr. Martin flew to New York.

THE QUALITY PROBLEM FINALLY RESOLVED

Meanwhile in the Nippon United plant, Mr. Mochida and Mr. Aono, who had been transferred from Nippon Kaisha as a new production section chief, had been working hard in order to solve the aesthetic problem.

Mr. Aono had both chemical and mechanical engineering backgrounds, and Nippon Kaisha management felt that he could help Mr. Mochida solve this important quality problem. Since Mr. Aono's transfer, both men had conducted numerous experiments in the plant and the Kamiyama Laboratory with the help of Kamiyama technical experts. Very often the two men stayed overnight in the factory.

Their combined efforts finally brought some solution to the problem. It was the combination of modifying the chemical formulation, changing the pressure, and the temperature. They innovated some changes in machines provided by United America and came up with a system of adjusting temperatures with a much finer tuning. With this new method, they finally succeeded in producing transparent, clean, clear film without air bubbles. It had uniform texture and thickness. In other words, it finally represented the product that the Japanese client wanted.

Mr. Aono said:

All the work for improving appearance was done solely by the Japanese, since United America could not teach us how to solve this particular problem. We sometimes felt that buying the technology alone would have been much better than joint venturing, because we had to improve the technology by ourselves anyway, and we would not have had foreign participation in our management.

Some of us wondered why we had to pay royalties when the foreigner could not help us solve such technological problems. Technological problems are to be solved, and we solved this particular one all by ourselves.

Mr. Mochida recalled:

Once the quality of the product was improved, it was easier to sell it to the user. The Nippon Kaisha-Dai-Nippon Group has a tremendous organization and prestige in Japan. We are very much united for the success of the total group.

The original confusion was due to the inexperience and shallow knowledge of running a joint venture. Within three or four years of the joint-venture company history, our sales started to jump up. It proved that the product finally met the demands of the market, and that it had nothing to do with our organization. Our organization had been working smoothly.

Mr. Shimada, president of Nippon United however, pointed out many benefits of having United America as a partner in the joint venture:

The American side was always eager to improve every month's sales. At board of directors' meetings, American executives stressed the need to increase the market share up to 30 percent, and they were always pressing us for it.

As far as Nippon Kaisha was concerned, the business of this joint-venture company was still small. But the constant urge from United America, as a result, helped us exert greater efforts to improve. The Americans had a realistic calculation of goal attainment, and pressed us to achieve our goals as much as possible.

NEW GENERAL MANAGER

Mr. O'Leary after an intensive briefing by Mr. Martin on Nippon United, decided that the company needed a general manager. With the appointment of Mr. Kawamura as the marketing manager, it was time for United America management to bring up the issue of the general manager again.

Mr. O'Leary believed that the independence of the new company could be achieved by having a full-time general manager who was also the president of the joint-venture company. The current president, Mr. Shimada had an additional post of senior director in Nippon Kaisha, and his function as the president was often limited in day-to-day operations.

Mr. Martin was also keenly aware of the fact that his position as vice president did not have representative power. He had many other responsibilities besides Nippon United. United America ran a few more joint ventures besides Nippon United in Japan, and there were other Asian operations to look after. It was not practical to make Mr. Martin president of the company.

United America nevertheless considered that at least a full-time Japanese president could take the overall control of the company's policies in production, marketing, sales, and finance.

They had been rather impressed by the ability of Mr. Mochida, the young Japanese plant manager who had solved many technical problems particularly that of aesthetic appearance at the plant. United America suggested to Nippon Kaisha that they appoint him president of Nippon United rather than having Mr. Shimada as the part-time president.

Mr. O'Leary recalls:

> We thought Mr. Mochida was a very competent production man and that he was capable of developing his ability in all fields of running the company, which included finance, marketing, and sales.
>
> One of the problems of our structure was the segmentation of responsibility. Nippon United was dependent on the Nippon Kaisha sales people for sales, on the Kamiyama plant for technical advice, and the Nippon Kaisha Accounting Division for financial advice. We thought that it would be better to have a one-man decision maker above all these functions so that the company would be guided by an overall plan created by one man.

The top management of Nippon Kaisha, opposed the plan, however. Mr. Mochida, no matter how capable, was still relatively junior in their hierarchy, and giving him such a significant responsibility would not work out. Mr. Shimada, president of Nippon United, was senior and well-respected. The joint-venture company was doing well. They should leave things as they were, Nippon Kaisha people said.

Mr. O'Leary and Mr. Martin insisted on appointing Mr. Mochida as president and general manager because they needed a strong, competent person to take full charge of the company operation. Mr. Shimada was very nice, but he was at best a part-timer. The company needed an innovative leader.

After much dispute, Nippon Kaisha finally agreed to appoint Mr. Mochida as the new president (the first full-time president).

MR. MOCHIDA'S TROUBLE

It turned out, however, the warning of Nippon Kaisha was accurate. Mr. Mochida, in spite of his capabilities, could not fulfill his responsibilities, partly due to the fixed organizational hierarchy. Mr. Mochida had to deal with directors of Nippon Kaisha Division who were by far his superior. His title of president of the joint-venture company did not carry much weight in the Japanese organization, and he could not get an equal position with the directors of Nippon Kaisha.

Mr. Mochida tried to be aggressive against such odds, which did not work well with Nippon Kaisha people, whose service and cooperation Mr. Mochida needed. Resentment against Mr. Mochida grew among Nippon Kaisha people who were in sales, accounting, administration, and technical labs.

Mr. Martin recalled:

> We learned from this bitter experience that we have to appoint a relatively senior man for a top managerial job. A young manager, no matter how capable, cannot get other managers to work for him because he is not regarded as equal or superior to them.
>
> We faced a dilemma of having a senior and less imaginative manager who can work more smoothly with others, or having an aggressive and capable one who has a hard time being accepted by others.

Mr. Hosono commented on this issue of mature leadership:

> In Japan the company is operated by the cooperative work of its members, not by the chain of command. The manager, therefore, must earn support from subordinates and colleagues in order to fulfill the function. The title of the job alone cannot give him authority.
>
> Nippon Kaisha was not trying to control the joint-venture company. We give them advice, since the everyday operations of Nippon United was very much dependent on the services provided by Nippon Kaisha.
>
> The plant manager (Mr. Mochida) was very competent in the production field, but he still needed assistance in finance, sales, and marketing. It would take time. In the long run Mr. Mochida could be able to function more fully as general manager. We should take a long-range perspective on personnel management. The Americans are too impatient.

Since 1974, international petroleum prices had been increasing rapidly. In 1979 the Japanese petroleum and petrochemical industries experienced the so-called second energy crisis. That year Japan reported a trade deficit of $18 billion mainly because the cost of imported oil had doubled.

Nippon United had been forced to enter a severe price-cutting war with competitors for the sales of products in spite of an increase in production cost. Nippon United product gained about

10 percent market share by that year. However, the company did not have a strong enough market position to influence the price structure and was therefore compelled to compete pricewise while still attempting to enlarge its market share and remain profitable. One dominant competitor, backed up by a different but powerful *keiretsu* group, had continued its high-volume, low-cost, low-price strategy to squeeze out less powerful ones, and the market was becoming increasingly oligopolistic, 60 percent of which was dominated by a few major firms.

The sales of Nippon United in the industrial sector were adversely affected because of the gloomy state of the chemical industry at large and the market itself, which had come to a stop. The company's profits started to decline.

PERSONNEL CHANGES AT UNITED AMERICA

At the United America Inc. headquarters in the United States, Mr. Lang decided to pass the corporate reign to his successor and to step down. Mr. Lang retired at the age of sixty-five, and so did Mr. Murray of the International Division.

Mr. Herb, a corporate vice president and the next man in the line, became president and chief executive officer. He was fifty-nine years old and held an M.B.A. He had been a corporate vice president for seven years, always in the shadow of President Lang.

A subsequent reorganization of the company structure led Mr. Franklin to become president of United International, much to the shock and grave disappointment of Mr. O'Leary.

The changes in United America's top management trickled down to the local level. In 1980 the general manager of the United America Japan Office, Mr. Martin, after nine years of stay in Japan left the country to head another United America foreign operation. Mr. Martin was replaced by a thirty-seven-year-old man from the United America Philippine operation, Mr. Gilbert.

While these personnel changes were still under way in the American company, Mr. Ōta, the Japanese controller of United America Japan, was approached by another foreign firm, which offered him a position as general manager of its Japanese operation. Mr. Ōta had worked for United America Japan for several years. He had hoped that he might head United America Japan someday. The decision by United America's top management to assign another American to its Japan office was a shock to him, especially because Mr. Gilbert was more than ten years junior to him with no business experience in Japan. Within a few months after Mr. Martin's departure from Japan, Mr. Ōta resigned from the company. Two top men left the office of United Japan, leaving only clerical staff to help Mr. Gilbert.

Mr. Ōta's case is not atypical of those who work for American affiliates in Japan. Those who have made a conscious decision to work for foreign firms may have a different value orientation, perhaps more individualistic than the rest of the Japanese, and as a strong demand for such personnel exists in the labor market, they would not hesitate to change firms for their personal benefit.

The change in personnel also brought in quite a different management perspective on the future of United America. Mr. Herb, the chief executive officer of United America, set a primary goal of his corporate policies to be the improvement of the firm's return on investment. More than ever, profitability became an important word for judging United America's many operations.

The change was felt throughout the corporation. Instead of continuing an international expansion, Mr. Herb's policy was to consolidate the company's efforts into profit-making ventures, sell unprofitable operations, and change acquisition policies.

Believing in a strategic management philosophy, he stressed the development of a strong balance sheet, low-cost production, and modified acquisition policies. The corporate office produced a list of pullers and draggers; Pullers were the operations producing profits, draggers were the losers. Symbolically, each operation head who made the puller's list received from the corporate office a navy blue necktie with a hand-embroidered red rose at the bottom: The president congratulated them for having achieved a great Return on Stockholder's Equity (ROSE).

Mr. Herb was not happy with the performance of Nippon United, which showed two consecutive years of poor performance. His dissatisfaction was communicated to Mr. Gilbert who now represented United America in Japan. Mr. Gilbert turned to the Japanese management and expressed United America's concern over the joint venture's poor performance. He did just as his predecessor had done: He pointed his finger at an individual responsible for the poor performance. Mr. Gilbert meant Mr. Mochida, general manager of the company, whose appointment had been at United America's insistence, only a few years earlier.

Mr. Gilbert stated that Nippon United needed a better leader to get out of the slump it was in. The Americans' corporate goals of pursuing short-term profits and their practice of seeking individual responsibility and accountability were evident in his argument. Mr. Gilbert proceeded to discuss the possibility of changing the head of the company with Nippon Kaisha management.

Nippon Kaisha management reminded Mr. Gilbert that it was United America's insistence that made Mr. Mochida president in the first place. Nevertheless, they agreed to replace Mr. Mochida, partly because Mr. Mochida had become rather unpopular among Nippon Kaisha people because of his continuous aggressive ways of handling matters. They suggested to Mr. Gilbert that an older and more senior executive of Nippon Kaisha should become the new president of Nippon United. In 1980 Mr. Mochida was replaced by an ex-board member of Nippon Kaisha, Mr. Kitazawa, who was in his early sixties. Mr. Mochida, bitterly disappointed, moved to another subsidiary on the Japan Sea side as a *tenzoku* plant manager.

The management of Nippon Kaisha at that time informally hinted that they were willing to buy shares of the joint-venture company from United America so that Nippon Kaisha would become the majority owner of the joint venture. Mr. Shimada said:

> We were concerned about such abrupt changes in United America's organization, and started worrying about their long-term commitment. Nippon Kaisha had improved the production technology and the product quality of Nippon United. We could say that the product quality was superior to its American counterpart in terms of uniformity, softness, and neat appearance.
>
> In addition, Nippon Kaisha had been providing sales, accounting, and other services to the joint-venture company. As the company was operating in Japan, we felt it advantageous for both Nippon Kaisha and United America that we should become a majority owner. Under a majority ownership, we could bring in much needed stability in personnel and other management issues.

United America Inc., on the other hand, was still adjusting to the many organizational changes made by the new top management. Mr. Herb, who was against expansionism, nevertheless believed in continued managerial participation in its Japanese ventures. Mr. Franklin, the new president of the International Division, also opposed the withdrawal. Mr. O'Leary informed Mr. Shimada that United America had no intention of becoming a minority owner. Instead, Mr. O'Leary restated United America's wish for the unification of the sales and production forces of Nippon United, thus assuring a continued/greater independence of the joint-venture company from the Japanese parent.

Having learned this idea through informal channels, Nippon Kaisha management felt that the timing for the Nippon Kaisha majority ownership might not be ripe, and instead decided to go along with United America's proposal. Nippon Kaisha had a history of spinning off units to form subsidiaries. The management considered that Nippon United could follow the course of other subsidiaries of Nippon Kaisha: A subsidiary is originally formed around certain production technology or products with a backup service from Nippon Kaisha. As the subsidiary continues to grow, the service functions provided by the parent company are transferred to the subsidiary, eventually making it an independent firm equipped with sales, marketing, administration, research and technology, and production units.

In 1981, the negotiation on the transfer of supporting functions was finalized: The sales, accounting, and personnel functions were moved from Nippon Kaisha to the joint venture. All the personnel previously involved in the joint venture within Nippon Kaisha were also moved as *tenzoku* men. The joint-venture company, however, continued to receive assistance from Nippon Kaisha in the field of production technology, research, and the procurement of raw materials.

NIPPON UNITED AFTER THE REORGANIZATION

The new president of Nippon United, Mr. Kitazawa, had a wider range of experience, not only in production, but also in sales and marketing. He had been a senior member of Nippon Kaisha and was well-respected by others. This would be the last part of his career with the Dai-Nippon Group. Mr. Kitazawa would give his best for ensuring the success of the firm. Nippon United needed a new type of leadership with administrative skills and general knowledge of the new organizational structure, with its own sales and marketing people as well as administrative staff. See Figure 13.

The new president, Kitazawa, who realized Nippon United's difficulties in further penetrating the industrial sector of the market, started to shift the company's sales efforts into the large retail industries and consumer market. Mr. Kitazawa could utilize long personal connections to promote this idea. He personally negotiated with many Dai-Nippon Group members, and Nippon United started to sell wrapping material to customers of member companies of the industrial group.

The company's major business operations were geographically concentrated in the Tokyo metropolitan area. The Tokyo Sales Office was divided into four subdivisions: industrial, large retail, consumer, and special sales via member companies. This change was to concentrate each subdivisions' efforts in a particular market segment and thereby improve the overall sales figure. Although industrial sales continued to be a major source of income, other new sectors started to grow, enlarging their shares in the total sales. In 1985, the industrial sector contributed 70 percent of the total product sales, while the other 30 percent was more or less equally divided among the other three sectors.

The management of Nippon United considered diversification of its product line as they saw the market for wrapping material reaching maturity.

United America Inc., having agreed on this point, suggested that Nippon United should become their sales agent for an automobile-related chemical product manufactured by United America. In 1985, the two sides began discussing the details of the agreement. This signified the beginning of the firm's diversification of product lines.

Following Nippon Kaisha's move into electronics, Nippon United also considered a possible entry into the electronics material field. Several members of the Dai-Nippon industrial group also had electronics divisions. The top management of Nippon United in 1985 began studying the possibility of subcontracting with these firms. Mr. Kawamura, marketing manager of Nippon United, said:

FIGURE 13: NIPPON UNITED KAISHA ORGANIZATIONAL CHART

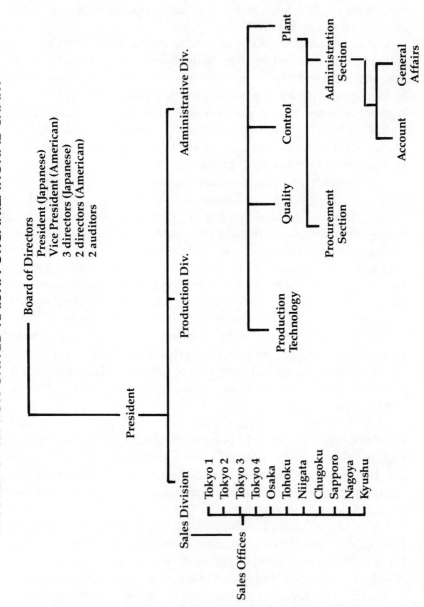

Becoming independent of Nippon Kaisha had both positive and negative effects. The positive side was that we could take initiative for our operation. Nippon United is still young and small, but there is potential for growth.

The negative side was that we moved out from under the protective umbrella of Nippon Kaisha. We can no longer fully rely on the prestige and credibility of Nippon Kaisha: No more *oyakata-hino-maru* (following the rising sun). For our business, using the name of Nippon Kaisha-Dai Nippon is important. We still use the company logo and name when we deal with important clients.

In the early 1980s, Nippon United annually hired several university graduates who formed a bottom layer of managerial candidates below the existing *tenzoku* men. After the "independence" in 1986, the company recruited forty college graduates, in an effort to get ready for more business in new areas. Understanding the importance of human resource development, they also established formal training courses for newly recruited university graduates with help from the parent company: They participated in Nippon Kaisha's orientation seminars and Kamiyama Factory's training courses. The new recruits were also trained by Nippon United management. At the same time, since 1984, the company annually sent a few young employees as technical trainees to a large subsidiary of Dai-Nippon, which manufactures electronic components.

The top management of Nippon United set the company's future course in such a way that "Nippon United will become an independent member of the Dai-Nippon Group, not just a subsidiary of Nippon Kaisha."

ANOTHER PERSONNEL CHANGE IN UNITED AMERICA

In 1984, Mr. Gilbert was recruited by another foreign company in Japan and suddenly resigned. Mr. O'Leary did not replace him and kept only a small liaison office in Tokyo. Mr. O'Leary decided to handle Nippon United himself as he continued to visit Japan regularly and frequently (at least once a month) from New York to discuss matters with the Japanese side. Nippon Kaisha welcomed this move as a show of United America's confidence in the Japanese management. As a matter of fact, there was not much for the American side to do concerning the day-to-day operation because the Japanese side had mastered the technology and they handled routine operations. The company was making profits. In 1987 Nippon United had a capital of 250 million yen ($2 million) with annual sales of about 350 million yen ($2.9 million). As the company expanded into different market sectors and diversifying its product lines, Nippon United was optimistic about its future prospects.

According to the Japanese side, the success of the joint-venture company was due to the high quality of the product and the strength of the Nippon Kaisha sales and marketing force. Mr. Kawamura of Nippon United said:

> Many joint ventures fail when the foreign side becomes too much a meddler. Fortunately, United America shares a long-term view with Nippon Kaisha in terms of future production and marketing strategies.
>
> The American side is happy as long as we are making profits because they tend to judge the company by the figures rather than its qualitative aspects which are difficult to quantify.
>
> Over many years of our association with United America, we are happy to say that we have finally come to understand each other pretty well. United America lets the Japanese side handle most of the day-to-day operations, and they are more appreciative about our wyas of doing business. A cooperative spirit is the key to a successful joint-venture operation.

Mr. O'Leary said:

> We believe the success of the joint-venture company has been due to an extremely high quality of the product, the strong distribution and sales network due to the company's affiliation with the Dai-Nippon Group, various support from the parent companies to the joint-venture company, and the improvement and changes in the management of the company.
>
> We will attempt to diversify the product lines of the joint-venture company, and we project a good future for Nippon United.

In order to achieve its corporate objectives, the American side considered such organizational tactics as: (1) Shortening the distribution chain by concentrating more on the development of the chains through exclusive wholesalers and direct sales to large retailers; (2) Developing several product lines and continuously introducing new products to the market; and (3) Establishing their own research and development lab in the future.

Nippon Kaisha managers still privately expressed their wish to obtain a majority ownership (51 percent at least) of the joint-venture company. So far, however, they had not brought it up at formal meetings.

CHAPTER SIX

ORGANIZATIONAL CULTURE

BINARY OPPOSITION

The preceding chapter illustrated the historical process of the joint-venture operation. The Americans and the Japanese of Nippon United could be viewed as two historical layers of cultural tradition that often became opposed as competing models of management. In this chapter we will first discuss the notion of opposition. We will then examine the fundamental premise for different viewpoints stated by the two groups, and summarize the problems of this particular joint-venture operation.

Strictly speaking, there is no logical means of determining which, if any, of the different social systems can claim to be the ultimate type of opposition (Needham 1987). In many cases it is logically imprecise to assert that a particular social phenomenon is opposite of another social phenomenon — for example, Japanese groupism versus American individualism; or Japanese consensus-oriented decision making versus American majority voting rule — when these phenomena are each made up of diverse components, internal counterpoints, and variations.

In most cases, each term to define a social phenomenon makes a multiple conceptual class, rather than containing an intrinsic and distinct meaning. Words that contain general ideas are each like a little chaos filled with "linguistic contention and contradiction" (Swedenborg 1955).

Of course, not all statements involve opposition, and not all terms are regarded as possessing opposites. Often the contrast-

ing terms turn out to be not of absolute opposition but of variation within a spectrum of possibilities.

The science of comparativism has uncovered an array of conceptual hazards. It has proven that social analyses carried out in
terms of opposition are often not reliable, and that the concept of
opposition itself is "intrinsically disputable" (Needham
1983:112).

Social scientists who compared Japanese and American firms
have revealed both differences and similarities between the two
systems. For example, the employment practices of Nippon
Kaisha are not opposite of the employment practices of United
America. Upon examining the systems in detail, one finds many
"functional equivalents" (Cole 1971:12). The long years of service
and internal promotion are not unique features of Nippon
Kaisha, but are common among the core employees of United
America.

Koike (1981 and 1988) ascertained that the employment pattern
of Japanese blue-collar workers is similar to those of white-collar
workers in Western Europe and the United States. The Japanese
age-wage profiles for male blue-collar workers in large companies
resemble in shape the Western European age-wage profiles for
white-collar males. Koike explained the labor patterns from the
way in which skills are formed in large Japanese firms. He proved
that the differences between the American and Japanese employment systems are at best tendencies, not opposites. He rejected
the hypothesis that so-called seniority wages are a unique feature
of the Japanese wage system.

As for the historical development of Japanese labor practices,
the systems of lifelong employment, seniority, and internal promotion were relatively new innovations, based upon the shortage of skilled workers (Taira 1970). These systems are applied
only to a minority of the total work force in Japan, excluding
those working for smaller firms, female workers and temporary
workers.

Concerning corporate strategies for profit making and growth,
distinction between the short- and long-term goal orientations is
a matter of gradation. There are also differing tendencies in corporate strategy, technology, and organizational structure between Japanese and American firms. According to a survey of 518
large Japanese and American firms, the structure and process of

Japanese firms tend more to be organic in nature, while those of American firms tend to be mechanistic (Kagano et al. 1984). At the same time Kagano et al. noted that these differences also consistently correlate with differences in corporate strategy, technology, and environment of the respective firms within each society.

In spite of the fact that differences between social systems are not of an absolute nature, there seems to be an almost ideological need for human groups to categorize many dyadic group relationships as metaphorically opposing, perhaps because the human mind seems to prefer simplicity, and binary opposition appears to be a simple concept. Opposition is a convenient and consequential idea for categorizing a pair of reality, only it is far from being incisive and trustworthy. Culture is not science, and people are not always rational.

A simple but consequential fact for knowledge is that it takes at least two somethings to create a difference. Bateson writes:

> To produce news of difference, i.e. *information*, there must be two entities (real or imagined) such that the difference between them can be immanent in their mutual relationship. . . . There is a profound and unanswerable question about the nature of those "at least two" things that between them generate the difference which becomes information by making a difference. Clearly each alone is — for the mind and perception — a non-entity, a non-being. (Bateson 1979:72)

In this joint-venture study, a story about a past critical event given by one group is always contended by the other's narrative as if they were engaged in an argumentative dialogue: The two talk alternatively, describing events and expressing ideas, while sharing the same temporal and spatial locality. Each presents an alternative and distinctive way of running a business operation.

In terms of goals, profit making, product quality, firm-to-firm relationships, human resource utilization, managerial accountability, and other significant operational issues, United America and Nippon Kaisha claimed that they had different corporate ideologies. They contrasted each other as antithetical, and their self-identity was formed against the perceived opposition.

By polarizing the world into the two, and by searching for a symbolic victory over the other, the contending narratives of American and Japanese managers weave memories of past critical events into their present: Recollections of the past are given newer connotations, in the light of the present situation, and in competition with alternative interpretations presented by the other party. Thus organization culture can be seen as a historical process where debates between opposing social groups are constantly recreating newer layers of cultural tradition.

Their debates over critical pieces of memories in this joint venture covered many topics: the formula modification; the plant layout; the system of financial reporting; the terms of profit making; the selections and/or dismissals of key personnel such as Mr. Kihara (their first plant manager), Mr. Mochida (the second plant manager, and later the president), and Mr. Kitazawa (the new president); and the definition of the product quality.

One could trace the formation of two battling doctrines — the "American" way and the "Japanese" way in this joint venture. Each side in its quest for sanction resurrected the imaginary "ancient wholeness" of the American or Japanese corporate traditions, ignoring variations and contention within each tradition. The managers blended their almost mythological images of the cultural unity into their storytelling.

The signification of past events serve two objectives: The newly interpreted selective memory either makes the current account more persuasive or may help define subsequent events, particularly in an organizational crisis.

For example, a major crisis took place when the rejection rate of the product became too high. The reader would recall that Nippon Kaisha managers told past events concerning an odor problem at Nippon Hawthorn, their joint venture with Hawthorn Inc. of the U.S.A.

This story about the quality issue served as an allegory for Nippon Kaisha managers who wished to justify their ideology for Japanese technological supremacy. Nippon Kaisha's organizational legend about the "odor" problem of Nippon Hawthorn made the subsequent story about the "aesthetics" problem of Nippon United internally more persuasive. In their mind, the two sporadic quality-related incidents at two separate joint ventures became a set aggregated by their serial resemblances, partly because the human mind comprehends events by means of association.

When the product rejection rate became very high, both sides seized on this crisis and presented their versions of the solution to the problem. They both hoped to persuade the other into their ways of thinking. In their dialogues, which resembled ideological warfare, each side drew an imaginary boundary that extricated it from the other. Each placed the other at the opposite end of an axiom.

The Japanese side considered the improvement of the product aesthetics should be the major means to overcome this crisis, while the American side proposed the establishment of a centralized managerial structure to be the remedy.

In their chronicles, they decorated the event with meanings, while revealing the "ineptitude" of the other. The Japanese reasoned that the rejection was due to the failure of United America's technology to elucidate the aesthetic issue. The Japanese proceeded to emphasize their arduous and original research, which eventually led to a solution.

In contrast, the Americans referred to the past "foolish" modification of the chemical formula by the Japanese and recounted the "competent" technical assistance provided by the Hammond experts, which ultimately rescued the business.

At the time of a crisis when the very existence of the organization is threatened, a possibility of "hell" with its implied retribution surfaces to the group's consciousness. Figuratively speaking, this is the time when organizational senior members need to diagnose an organizational illness and to give a correct remedy. Some may suggest a surgical operation in order to revitalize the organization.

Each tale of an organizational crisis by the American and Japanese managers follows a plot as to: how their wise men prescribed a cure; how they claimed their supremacy over the other's "pagan" method; how they transmuted the other into their ways of thinking; and how they finally saved the soul of the organization.

As a means to legitimize their prescription, sometimes a new text (a sacred document) was written and presented to the other party. For example, Mr. Martin, who was convinced that Nippon United needed a strong centralized marketing policy, wrote a detailed job description in order to appoint a marketing manager. With this document at hand, United America pressured Nippon Kaisha to select a full-time marketing manager.

United American managers attempted to "reform" Nippon United with this newly created job description document. This job description metaphorically served as a scripture or a text of authenticity to implement a belief system. The document sanctified managerial performance against objective goals, clear functional division, and individual responsibility. These were part of the corporate canon of United America perceived by Mr. Martin. The verbs frequently utilized in this text to define the role of a marketing manager were "direct," "develop," "counsel," and "accomplish."

However, the American canon was always challenged by an alternative presented by the Japanese, who questioned the authenticity of the Americans' view and argued back. Neither side could completely dominate the process between these rival traditions.

Let us look at these separately enacted traditions, "ours versus theirs," that served as group ideologies. The following American versus Japanese ways simulate ritual texts because they are defined monologically as the only reliable truth. They are by nature dogmatic and sermonizing.

THE AMERICAN BUSINESSMAN'S IDEOLOGY

We at United America Inc. considered the growth and maximization of profit as the most important consideration: Profits must be made so that the company can provide a solid return on investment and internally generate the funds with which it can operate and grow.

Growth may be reflected in many ways, in sales, market share, and product extensions. United America expected to see progress in all areas.

From the beginning, we attached considerable importance to the joint venture as a vehicle for further expansion and growth in Asia. We were anxious to establish a base of operations in the rapidly growing Asian market.

Active and direct managerial participation was emphasized from the beginning. At the initial stage, we were very ambitious to develop its operational base in Asia.

We formed a joint venture with Nippon Kaisha to obtain access to the Japanese market. In our mind, trade-offs between our technology and market access made sense.

Another important aspect of our philosophy concerns operational management: We expect operations that we own, or in which we have an equity, to be properly managed in all areas. We expect that people appointed to positions responsible for these functions will be professionally competent. If such personnel do not, in our opinion, perform satisfactorily, we will replace them promptly with competent people.

Our organizational strategies were explicit. We gave primary focus on coordination of each functional unit (production, sales, marketing, etc.) and tackled problems in each unit one after another. We viewed the organization as a system composed of formal units placed in lateral and vertical relationships of functions. Each unit should effectively pursue its functional specialization for achieving an overall corporate goal. United America management utilized financial analyses based upon quantitative data to make each unit responsible for its outcome and to contribute to the overall economic output.

We reserved and exercised the right to monitor, control, direct, and modify any policy decisions made by the management of an operating division, including a joint-venture company if necessary. When the joint venture did not operate satisfactorily, the management of United America took decisive steps swiftly to remove "incompetent" people, to reorganize the structure, and to streamline the operation.

When problems occurred in an operation, we expected solutions and options to be provided by the managers of the operation. We considered this problem-solving function to be one of the prime responsibilities of the manager. We expected the manager to be decisive, to have the ability to reach a decision among alternative courses of action rapidly, to be achievement-oriented, pragmatic, and professional.

United America's top management in New York expected local American managers to produce profits, no matter how difficult and different the Japanese situation was, because we considered that it was the primary job responsibility of our field managers.

Managers can be dismissed if the "bottom line" numbers are poor. United America managers all had target figures assigned each year and worked toward that goal. For example, Mr. Franklin, Mr. O'Leary, and Mr. Martin were evaluated according to their performance vis-a-vis specific goals. We responded to the corporate norms of individual accountability, monetary and other rewards on high performance, and negative sanctions on poor performance.

Mr. Hart was called home because of the poor profit result of the Asia Division after his short stay in Japan. When Nippon United did not perform well, Mr. Martin had to bring forth some solutions, which often meant key personnel changes among his subordinates.

When product rejections from customers were high, we considered that Mr. Kihara should take responsibility because he was the first plant manager of the new company. Mr. Kihara was replaced by Mr. Mochida. When the operation did not improve, Mr. Mochida was also dismissed.

United America recognizes its social and other responsibility as a company, but social responsibility should be defined primarily in economic terms. For us the company is the place to work and to produce results. We as United America managers feel a great sense of accomplishment when we meet our targets, but on the other hand we face consequences if we do not meet the targets. The rules of the game are very clear. United America does not like excessive outside intervention, nor does it favor taking an overly paternalistic approach toward its employees.

※　※　※

The preceding account summarizes the general thinking of the United America managers. They believed that United America's corporate culture was developed through its dynamic interaction with American business culture within its primary (basic) American culture. Their presumed home environment, against that of the Japanese, was a unified one.

The American managers could recall a number of past instances when the previously mentioned assumptions had been effectively applied to real issues and problems. Through many years of symbolic interactions within the firm, Mr. Franklin, Mr. Martin, Mr. O'Leary, and other American managers had come to share values of a powerful and dominant subgroup (i.e. management) of United America. In their mind, the previously mentioned assumptions and corporate ideologies had become United America's ways of doing business, in contrast to those of Nippon Kaisha.

When they started the joint venture in Japan, the individual managers of United America started to clarify these cultural assumptions, which, they believed, were correct and rational. Let us now take the same issues and describe the Japanese businessman's outlook regarding the joint venture.

Nippon Kaisha's cultural ideology in comparison with that of United America can be characterized by their pro-market share mentality and emphasis on quality and human resource management. In the following section, the personal pronoun "we" (rather than "they") will be used to enhance the reader's awareness of binary opposition.

THE JAPANESE BUSINESSMAN'S IDEOLOGY

We at Nippon Kaisha would certainly like to make profit for the joint-venture company, but the management had to take a long-range perspective for the company in our attempt to increase our market share step by step. We were willing to sacrifice our short-term profits for this goal of market share expansion.

In order to compete successfully in the market in the long run, the quality of the product must be excellent. Consequently, our initial efforts were concentrated on upgrading of the product, which included the improvement of product appearance to suit the taste of Japanese consumers.

Like many other Japanese companies, Nippon Kaisha took an original foreign technology and attempted to "improve" it. We did not hesitate to spend time and money in innovating and upgrading production technology, increasing overall production costs, over United America's protests.

Our strong interest in the product's appearance was not a unique phenomenon among Japanese manufacturers, who often pay considerable attention to aesthetics (including packaging) of the product.

With respect to product extensions and new products, we would like to introduce as many new products as possible. This was the main reason why we wanted to introduce foreign technology and production methods in the first place.

While United America's motive for joint-venturing was to gain access to the Japanese market, our main motive was to gain access to the technology developed by the American company. Actually, we preferred licensing because it seemed to be the most flexible and least expensive way to gain our objective.

Throughout the history of the joint venture, we preferred that the foreign investor keep a low profile. We would have appreciated it if the Americans had given us total control over the joint-venture company and participated as little as possible, especially in personnel management.

We wanted to and did supply all the management and other personnel for the new company. However, the selection of management personnel was limited because we practiced a system of promotion by seniority of service, and most of our directors were over fifty years of age, with a lifelong commitment to the company.

We did not develop specialists: our managers were college graduates whose specialized experience was confined to the training they had been given in the company. It was difficult to recruit professionals in the free market because labor mobility was low and good prospects were already committed to other Japanese companies. When it came to personnel changes, firing employees or dismissing them was very difficult regardless of the circumstances.

Our top management recognized that the joint-venture company was a separate entity with its own management. Our concept of authority was different from that of their American partners. We considered it inappropriate to interfere directly in its operation or in the decisions of its appointed management. We preferred indirect assistance and personal advice. We believed that we had to develop formal and informal communication channels with the joint-venture management first.

We believed in the long-range development of human resources and in the extensive use of personal communication.

We put great importance on good will and cooperation among those involved in the operation. We believed that a smooth interpersonal relationship and the sharing of information were the key factors for a successful project. Because of this belief, we asked our managers to create an environment conducive to teamwork. United America's way of hiring and firing key personnel was disturbing to our management.

We believed that our managers should be equipped with the leadership ability to guide their teams. They should be intelligent, hard working, and loyal to the company. We did not accept aggressive individualism, which might have been considered as a positive characteristic by United America.

Our management did not see the organization as a system of analyzable components. Rather, we saw it as a community of individuals who are related to one another in continuously changing relationships of human obligation, affection, loyalty, trust, duties, and friendship. We did not view our corporate structure as a rationally constructed entity in abstract terms. We did not put individuals and human relations in abstract but in experience.

A company, from our view, is a very organic aggregate of concrete human relations, which are not easily translatable into numbers and quantifiable data. Because of this philosophy, we paid great attention to people management and took a long-term perspective.

Our social responsibilities extended to the welfare of our employees. We provided various welfare programs and fringe benefits for them.

In our mind, the organic entity of Nippon Kaisha's corporate world was expanded to include Dai-Nippon industrial group through networks of human relationships. Nippon Kaisha managers and Nippon United managers "belonged" to this prestigious industrial group. Our obligations to the member companies were seriously taken into consideration in our corporate planning. The member firms of our group worked together for the prosperity of the total group, and top management's primary responsibility was to maintain the solidarity of the company employees and of Dai-Nippon industrial group.

To us, the role of the shareholder was not of primary importance. The major shareholder of Nippon Kaisha was Dai-Nippon, which understood and endorsed the long-range view. Our annual shareholders' meeting was often a mere formality where no difficult questions would be asked. We had no outside directors on the board. Our banks were interested in long-term business relationships with the firm, and we could be counted on to be cooperative as long as we made sufficient profits. This was another reason why our management could afford to take a long-term view in corporate strategy planning.

We applied this concept to the operation of the joint-venture company, wanting Nippon United to grow first before harvesting the profit.

Our managers, like many other Japanese managers, were proud of Japan's economic development, which they believed was partly due to our managerial competence. We did not believe that Western management techniques were superior to ours, although we were willing to utilize and modify them, if necessary, for our specific needs.

COMPARISON OF CORPORATE IDEOLOGIES

A comparison of these two positions illustrates in a general way how far apart the prospective partners of a joint-venture company could be in their thinking. Because of the different ways they regarded and responded to organizational phenomena, their strategies and decisions differed considerably. The main differences can be summarized as follows:

1. *Rationale for Joint Ventures and Ultimate Goals.* While Americans considered a joint venture as a means for further expansion in the Japanese market, Japanese often wanted only foreign technology. Americans sought to exchance technology for market access; Japanese wanted only technology, which they felt they could improve to be the best in the world.

2. *Profit Motivation.* American businessmen put greater emphasis on immediate profitability, while Japanese tended to hold a longer-term perspective.

3. *Technology and Quality.* Nippon Kaisha managers and engineers believed that they could introduce a particular technology from a foreign country and could sustain a program of continuous, incremental improvements on the product.

   Nippon Kaisha's companywide attention to quality production was developed during the 1960s, when the Japanese management philosophy was profoundly influenced by the quality circle (QC) movement, in which quality was defined as "customer satisfaction." From this viewpoint, product appearance was considered as an item of legitimate priority in quality management.

   United America management was also committed to quality, but they believed in striking a balance between quality and cost/profit. While the Japanese proposed further work on the product's aesthetics to satisfy the customer, the Americans with their perception of (American) customer satisfaction believed it to be totally unnecessary. From their viewpoint, the function of the product, not the appearance, was of primary importance.

4. *The Responsibility of the Manager.* Americans put emphasis on individual responsibility and the right to dismiss incompetent personnel. Japanese emphasized teamwork and group responsibility. They did not like to dismiss personnel.

American approaches to human resource management were individual case-oriented, explicitly explained, and backed by "logical" and "objective" data. They dealt with manpower issues when a need occurred. There was little corporatewide personnel policy making for years ahead.

In contrast, human relationships were the key to Japanese corporate strategies. Japanese approaches to manpower were more implicit, systematic, and holistic.

5. *The Managerial Role and Performance.* American managers were supposed to be independent, pragmatic, goal-oriented, and professionally competent. Americanized behavior such as assertiveness and straightforwardness as well as competence in the English language were often evaluated as positive; characteristics such as civility, quietness, and maturity were de-emphasized.

On the other hand, an effective Japanese manager was supposed to be mature, intelligent, hardworking, humane, and loyal to the group he represents.

6. *Interpersonal Relationship.* Japanese put greater emphasis on stable interpersonal relationships. The employment contract was seen less as a kind of bilateral bargain but as an act of admission to a community wherein good will and sincerity were expected to temper the pursuit of self-interest.

Japanese viewed a company as an organic entity of interactive relationships. The Japanese archetype of a self was one who can feel human in the company of others. A Japanese person was invariably identified as acting in some kind of human relationship.[1]

7. *Intercorporate Relationship.* The Japanese company belonged to a particular industrial group whose members co-

operated with one another for the benefit of the total group. They formed a powerful cross-industrial network of business transactions.

8. *The Social Responsibility of the Company.* Corporate social responsibility in terms of the welfare of the worker was more seriously taken into consideration in Japan. In their corporate mythology, the whole (company) and the unit (individual) were ideologically united for attaining the mutually beneficial goal of economic prosperity.

9. *The Parent Company and the Joint Venture.* The American company justified the right to formally monitor the policy making of the joint-venture company. The Japanese used more personal and informal channels and preferred indirect influence on their decision-making policy. United America tended to consider control in terms of legal contracts, equity ownership, and representation on the board.

※　※　※

The narratives portray two opposite management doctrines. Although the two corporate cultures of Nippon Kaisha and United America were actually entangled in the joint-venture operation, an ideological boundary of the two was retained to repudiate the ongoing acculturation process within the joint-venture corporate culture.

In spite of the "objective" fact that the joint-venture operation was a composite process of environmental requirements, organizational processes, technology, allocation of resources, and macroeconomic characteristics, what mattered most in their decision making was the American and Japanese managers' subjective signification of these variables: The important thing was not what and how they really were, but what the managers saw as being real and how.

As we suspect, the American and Japanese "traditions" are not of scientific neutrality but rather of an ideological nature. The imaginary "homogeneity" of their respective tradition denies the fact that each tradition internally possesses contending voices in its multilayered historicity. It also de-emphasizes any similarities between the two systems.

This study has shown that American managers exhibit a certain degree of cultural insensitivity and arrogance, ignoring the fact that the process of understanding other cultures is so difficult that it must be approached openly and respectfully. At the national level, this cultural insensitivity may derive from several decades of American economic and technological supremacy over the rest of the world, their historical dependence upon the large domestic market, and the relative insignificance of the overseas market. Unlike many European businesses that constantly face multilingual and multicultural competition, American businesses could afford to be inward directed toward the mostly monolingual market. As a consequence, American managers might be inclined to consider their managerial ideology as rational and universally applicable.

At the same time, we have also noticed that the Japanese system exhibits a high degree of insularity and ethnocentrism. At the national level, this insular mentality may derive from Japan's geographical isolation and its prolonged process of cultural and racial homogenization during the Tokugawa period (1603–1868). State Shintoism enforced since the Meiji period (1868–1912) until the end of the Second World War (1945) also encouraged the superiority complex of the Japanese race over other races. Many Japanese still believe in the uniqueness (pure blood) of the Japanese in the world.

The Japanese with this concept of Self in mind tend to look at their relationship with foreigners as that of "we versus they" or "insider versus outsider." The famous term *gaijin* (outsider/foreigner) applied to all non-Japanese. Unlike the United States where citizenship can be obtained, the only way to win complete acceptance by Japanese is to be born into this race. The Japanese identity is an ascribed status, not an achieved status.

This exclusivity spills over to corporate customs as well. It takes an extraordinary amount of time and effort for a foreign firm to move into the inside of the Japanese system of reciprocal relations.

Though Japanese rarely admit it, this study shows that their system is an exclusive one. Becoming an insider of the system is very difficult and time-consuming because the system is composed of close human relationships that have evolved internally over years with a clear psychological boundary of membership.

THE THIRD LAYER OF TRADITION: NIPPON UNITED

While United American and Nippon Kaisha cultures became mutually entangled, there began to emerge a temporary interplay between denial and recognition, at least in the minds of some individuals, where memories which were denied at one level were readmitted at another level, and where dominant memories at one level were dropped into oblivion at another level.

In the mid-1980s, after the corporate reorganization, the Japanese side began to cite some "positive" aspects of the joint venture. At the same time, United America managers began to admit that the extremely high quality of the product, which included the aesthetic issue, was indeed the major reason for the corporate success.

The two sides, after more than fifteen years of operation started to "understand" each other. Patriotic exclusivity within memberships as formally conceived began to be replaced by reflexive dialogues.

For example, Mr. Kawamura, a Nippon Kaisha sales manager who became the joint venture's marketing manager, stated in the mid-1980s: "Fortunately, United America shares a long-term view with Nippon Kaisha in terms of future production and marketing strategies." Nippon Kaisha's past memories about the "short-term view" of United America disappeared from the narrative, replaced by a new (and rather contradictory) view of reality. Similarities between the two systems were emphasized, and coexistence, not rivalry was discussed.

Mr. Kawamura needed to maneuver his career in between the two systems partly because of his role as Nippon United marketing manager. Figuratively speaking, Mr. Kawamura had to serve two contending "gods" and had to internalize their dialogical relationship for his own survival.

The long years of cultural contacts also affected United American executives. In the mid-1980s, Mr. O'Leary began to talk about the high quality of the Nippon United product. He stated that "the success of the joint-venture company has been due to the extremely high quality of the product, the strong distribution and sales network due to the company's affiliation with the Dai-

Nippon Group, various support from the parent companies to the joint-venture company, and the improvement and changes in the management of the company." His narratives were devoid of the memory of past battles regarding the product aesthetics issue, the *keiretsu* domination, and the joint-venture independence.

Individual recollections in dialogical relationships were swayed and influenced by interpenetrating alien memory sources. These people started to talk half in their language and half in the others' language as their words became "double voiced" (Mumford 1989:22). The focused mind eroded, imaginary boundaries of the self and the other began to crumble, and stories of "betweenness" started to unfold.

According to Mumford, this is like the beginning act of reflexive awareness. The result should be the emergence of a third narrative on Nippon United whose organization culture should be perceived as an entity created for polyphonic coexistence rather than for binary opposition.

Unfortunately for this joint venture, it was the time when many key actors left the scene, and cultural contacts between the two decreased to a bare minimum. When Mr. Gilbert resigned from the Tokyo office of United America for another foreign subsidiary in Japan, Mr. O'Leary did not replace him. United America decided to keep only a small liaison office in Tokyo, and its physical presence in Japan was reduced considerably.

CULTURE AND CONTROL

Culture not only dictates what is desirable but how one should reach the desirable end. It affects how one exerts control. In this joint venture, the Americans tended to consider control in terms of legal contracts, equity ownership, and representation on the board. United America did not consider much of manpower as means of control. The American side did not control people in order to filter information on the local market, Japanese management know-how, and Japanese production methods back to the American side.

Those Japanese who could have become the bridge between

United America and the joint venture (i.e. Mr. Ōbayashi and Mr. Ōta) left the company, and those Americans (i.e. Mr. Hart, Mr. Franklin, Mr. Martin, and Mr. Gilbert) who could have continued reflexive dialogues moved elsewhere.

On the other hand, the Japanese used the joint-venture firm as a reservoir of jobs for managers and employees of the Japanese parent firm. Nippon United worked for disseminating American technological know-how among Japanese employees who were loyal to the Japanese partner.

Over the years, Nippon Kaisha mastered the American technology and improved it. Nippon Kaisha still controlled the joint-venture operation and its access to the market. Although United America did not accept the offer of the joint venture takeover by the Japanese side, United America's presence in Japan lessened significantly when they did not replace Mr. Gilbert.

In fact the Japan office representative was no longer meaningful because the American side by then had little control over the joint venture, had lost its technical advantages, and had become like a silent partner.

This pattern has been repeated over and over again in U.S.-Japanese joint ventures in Japan, indicating the crucial strategic shortcomings of the American approach, which tends to neglect human strategy.

American firms, with some notable exceptions, underestimate the critical role of human relationships in the long-term viability of the cooperative venture in Japan.

CULTURE AND BUSINESS

We have learned that corporate culture is not born in a vacuum but is deeply embedded in wider cultures. Nippon Kaisha manager's views on manpower utilization are a result of the organizational response to a wider Japanese business culture and Japanese primary culture concerning human relationships. Likewise, United America management views on individual manager's accountability are often shared by businessmen in American society whose culture justifies individualism and individual responsibility.

This study has also shown that, in developing a certain corporate culture within professional and primary cultures, there are distinct internal organizational processes of creative activities, signification, and communication among individual actors. Corporate culture is a product of collective human "praxis," not a passive result of environmental contingencies or a reaction to downward pressure. Corporate culture is not created simply as a result of influence by primary and professional cultures. It is created through interconnected rubrics of micro and macro dynamics of human reflexive and mental activities.

Managers reflect and act upon events, phenomena, and relationships relying upon their meanings, metaphors, and affective consciousness, and upon their cognitive re-creation of past experiences. Such meanings help managers define, interpret, and comprehend reality, and these meanings are continuously re-created through a constantly shifting cosmos of relationships, communications, and managerial involvements and actions.

Corporate culture is multivocal. People who have been primarily and professionally socialized bring their cultural heritage to organizational life. They rely upon their layers and nests of symbolic memories, which are constantly modified in their responses to a new situation. Because people share their knowledge, emotion, and creativity, they create kaleidoscopic conscience and an emotional amalgam beyond individual idiosyncracies. Corporate culture is born as a result of such supersubjective activities of the human mind.

This study has illustrated that many of the problems encountered in the joint venture are embedded in ideological differences in the way the two partners approach various relationships and phenomena. The study has demonstrated the polysemous nature of phenomena: The same phenomenon, event, and/or object has different meanings to different people. In business, the same economic term, issue, and action may have multiple meanings.

This study dismisses the notion that managerial decision making is univocal guided by "rational" thinking. It challenges the validity of currently rampant economic reductionism of human (economic) activities: Reduction of any human resource to a unit or a commodity governed by capitalistic principle in abstract must necessarily be incomplete and fictitious.

In behavioral sciences, there has been an increasing number of studies on corporate culture.[2] While America faces intense international competition and transnational business activities, there rose a growing frustration with past management research and its inadequacy in dealing with human behavior and organizational behavior across cultures.

In the mid-1980s the so-called orthodox model based on Max Weber's organization theory was attacked as an inadequate classical paradigm to explain multicausal, multilinear and nonrational organizations.[3] An organization, according to the Weberian orthodox school, was basically a rational, goal-oriented and bureaucratic model: An organization was viewed in terms of goal-reaching behavior, cause-effect sequence, rational decision-making behavior, functional division of labor, and power hierarchy. In Weber's rational-legal system, the means were explicitly designed to achieve certain specific goals. The organization was like a well-designed machine with a certain function to perform, and every part of the machine contributed to the attainment of maximum performance of that function. It was called legal because authority was exercised by means of a system of rules and procedures through the office, which an individual occupied at a particular time.[4]

"Nonorthodox" theorists are challenging the usefulness of this paradigm. Pfeffer, for example, suggested that rationality of human action is considered important not because humans act in a rational fashion but because they (Westerners) think they act in a rational fashion, and they (Westerners) think that rationality provides legitimacy to action.[5] By stating it, he acknowledges the cultural origin of Western management thinking.

Management scientists have begun to see that the formation and development of organizational behavior theories has been conditioned by basic Western cultural premise. Lincoln and Guba proposed a "naturalistic" rather than "rationalistic" method of inquiry.[6]

Anthropologists have learned that culture is itself not rational or irrational. It is nonrational. Culture is something that is learned, shared, and transmitted by members of a social group, which in turn governs what is perceived to be rational or irrational.

Anthropologists have also learned that we tend to project onto the other our cultural rationality as truth. We tend to forget that many "objective" realities are in fact socially enacted realities, reflecting ideologies of our time. Unfortunately, like fish in the water that cannot see the color of the water, we often fail to see the texture of our culture from within. This study attempts to show how one "feels" when one puts on clothes of a different cultural texture.

Today, we are constantly facing other cultures in our existence. We realize more than ever that no culture is completely isolated or self-contained. Cultural and ideological meanings within a nation, a group, or a person, become visible and significant in their relationships to alternatives presented by others. Social phenomena, which include economic arrangements, become "real" to the organizational members only through such cultural signification.

In summary, this study characterizes corporate culture as a multimeaning entity placed in a wider culture, which is in a constant flux. There is no universally applicable logical chart to guide managerial behavior because management is culture-bound with its shifting relations and communications. I hope that this ethnographic document has successfully exemplified that those domains most taken for granted as universal in our time and space, such as economic behavior, may be peculiar and unique in another historical time and geographical space.

We need to diversify our approach against economic reductionism if we want to learn the multiplicity of capitalistic forms and human adaptation in this field. Culture is how humans whose lives are influenced by institutionally developed capitalist principles recreate them in their everyday life and experience. Ethnography is a tool to define the nature and texture of capitalism in human form.

The anthropological concept of culture and of ethnographic field methods in organizational theory and business management analysis promises a new insight into the study of economic behavior and business institutions. I hope that this study has effectively demonstrated that we are all historically situated and that "meaning" is always related to value, valuation, and validation at a particular historical moment.

THE HISTORICAL CONTEXT

INTRODUCTION

Since Henderson's book (1973), there has not been an update on the history of foreign enterprise in Japan, although Abegglen and Stalk (1985) briefly touched on the topic, R. Christopher (1987) talked about some successful cases of foreign companies in Japan, and C. V. Prestowitz, Jr. (1988) bitterly complained about the closeness of the Japanese market.

A more comprehensive and systematic historical view of foreign direct investment will give a solid understanding of the past legal and regulatory restrictions on foreign investment in Japan. I will discuss how the legal climate of foreign enterprises changed throughout modern Japanese history so that the reader will have a good knowledge of historical factors affecting American business operations in Japan.

Let us begin with the Tokugawa era (1600 – 1867) and discuss the development of foreign enterprises in modern Japan up to the 1980s.

THE CLOSING AND OPENING OF JAPAN

During the history of foreign direct investment in Japan, perhaps the most important historical factor was Japan's two centuries of isolation from the western world during the Tokugawa period. This period of almost total isolation helped create distinctly Japanese, rather introverted, homogeneous, national characters.

In 1616, the Tokugawa government, in order to strengthen its domination over feudal lords and to stamp out Western influences, specifically that of Christianity, ordered all European ships confined to the two ports of Nagasaki and Hirado.

In 1623 the English gave up Japan trade as unprofitable. In the next year the Spanish were expelled, and in 1635 all Japanese were prohibited from going abroad or from returning home if already overseas. In 1639 the Portuguese were expelled, and in 1641 the representatives of the Dutch, who were the only remaining European traders, were moved from Hirado to a tiny island called Deshima in Nagasaki harbor. Thus Japan closed her door to the world and slipped into a peaceful isolation in the mid-seventeenth century.

The Tokugawa government might not have been able to maintain a stable system of rule if they had not isolated Japan from the upsetting foreign influences that had poured in East Asia during the sixteenth century. In Japan's two centuries of isolation, however, technological, political, and social changes slowed, at a time when the West was accelerating such changes. This lag later caused the Japanese to make frenetic efforts to catch up with the West in the late nineteenth and early twentieth centuries.

The Tokugawa era was a period of great cultural and economic prosperity. By turning inward, the Japanese developed their own cultural identity. Their extraordinary cultural homogeneity was also the product of the whole Tokugawa system of control, particularly the institution of "alternate residence" of the lords. The Tokugawa government sought to control feudal lords through the holding of hostages and periodic attendance and service of the vassal at the lord's court. The government asked feudal lords to send their wives and heirs to Edo (the capital city of the Tokugawa regime, later the city of Tokyo) in 1633. In addition, attendance at the Edo castle was made into a rigid compulsory system after 1635. Both the hostage and the "alternate attendance" systems forced each feudal lord to travel back and forth between his residence in Edo and his home province every other year. The constant flow of a large proportion of the ruling class between Edo and the provinces created a high degree of cultural, intellectual, and ideological unity in Japan.

In July 1853, Commodore Matthew C. Perry, leading a quarter of the American navy (three steam frigates and five other ships) proceeded from Norfolk, Virginia by way of the Indian Ocean to Edo (Tokyo) Bay. The arrival of the "black ships" terrified the Japanese. Commodore Perry, showing an obvious American superiority in technology and military strength, forced the Japanese to accept a letter from President Millard Filmore, which asked Japan to open her ports for international trade.

The term "black ship syndrome" was born. Later in the 1970s, the term came up again for common use in the Japanese mass media to describe the Japan's fear of possible economic domination by giant American multinationals.

On July 29, 1858, the Tokugawa Shogun's Regent Ii reluctantly agreed to sign a trade and commerce treaty with the United States, presented by American Consul Townsend Harris. During that summer, the Dutch, Russian and British representatives made similar arrangements. The French envoy arrived in September and completed a treaty early in October.

These treaties specified that foreigners in Japan were to remain under their country's law (the privilege known as extraterritoriality); they could establish commercial and residential premises in designated foreign settlements in Japan; and trade was to be entirely free of official intervention and subject to low tariffs. In a snowy morning of March 24, 1860, a group of samurai attacked and assassinated Regent Ii for "dishonoring our divine land" by dragging Japan into a humiliating position under "Free Trade Imperialism" (Beasley 1990:34).

In 1868, fifteen years after the arrival of the "black ships," the feudal Tokugawa government collapsed and the sovereign power was passed to the then fourteen-year-old Emperor Mutsuhito, later known as the Meiji Emperor. The Meiji Restoration (1868) marked the beginning of Japan's modern era, and especially Japan's industrialization process.

The new leaders of the Meiji government realized that the only way for Japan to ensure national security was through economic development and military strength. Thus, we observe a complete change of the Japanese attitude towards Western nations, from *sonnō-jōi*, or the "Revere the Emperor, expel the barbarian" mentality of the late Tokugawa period to *wakon-yōsai*, or "Japanese Ethics and Western Skills" of the early Meiji.

Home Minister Ōkubo Toshimichi, one of the most important members of the Meiji leadership argued that Japan's industrialization could be attained by direct patronage and encouragement of the government. The imperial government provided an infrastructure and financial mechanism to channel capital into appropriate directions to fund the initial stage of industrial growth. Japan did not receive heavy capital inputs from foreign countries and had no considerable foreign debt before the Russo-Japanese War (1904–1905).

Meiji Japan began to build strategic industries on which modern military power depended. The Meiji government inherited from the Tokugawa government two shipyards, one at Yokosuka and another at Nagasaki, and added yet another at Hyogo (as Kobe was called). It also operated large ammunition and weapons factories in Tokyo and Osaka, and three gunpowder plants.

The government adopted an open-door policy for international trade, and after victory in the Sino-Japanese War (1894–95), Japan began to accept foreign direct investment through joint ventures.

Early U.S.-Japanese joint ventures founded during that time included Nippon Electric Company (NEC), International Petroleum, and Osaka Gas. Nippon Electric was the brainchild of Western Electric, the manufacturer of the telephone equipment and systems. Western Electric took advantage of an 1899 revision in the Japanese Commerce Law, which permitted foreign firms to invest in Japanese companies, to set up Nippon Electric with a 54 percent capital participation. Several directors of the board were from Western Electric, and they gained management control almost immediately (Onozawa 1982).

After the Russo-Japanese War (1904 – 1905), Japanese industries began to depend heavily on foreign technology and capital for expansion. This was the time when General Electric Company (GE) invested in Tokyo Electric Company. Tokyo Electric, then a major electric lamp maker, was having difficulty in competing with imports. They decided to set up a joint venture with GE in 1905 to overcome a financial crisis. The newly beefed up Tokyo Electric Company became the largest electric company of its kind in Japan and quickly monopolized the electric lamp market. The company later merged with Shibaura Works, a telegraph equipment maker, to form what is today known as Toshiba Corporation.

Lagging behind international standards in technological progress, key industries for Japan's economic future, such as the steel
and electrical industries, took the initiative in seeking foreign
technology and capital.

It is a well-known fact that the Japanese government provided
a favorable environment for Japan's industrialization by removing many feudalistic barriers to private enterprise. The government also initiated key strategic industries, such as shipbuilding,
communication, iron mills, and textiles. In contrast to Western-
style industrialization, Japan's industrialization was, at the beginning, driven by the state.

But by the 1880s, many state-owned industries were operating
in the red. The government sold them to entrepreneurs who gave
promise of building up the economy, just before industrialization
started to pay off. For example, the Tomioka silk-reeling mill was
sold to Mitsui; the Nagasaki shipyard to Mitsubishi; cement and
brick factories to Furukawa; and various mines to Asano and Kuhara. The firms established in the late nineteenth century grew
faster than the economy as a whole and by the 1920s controlled a
large part of the nation's industries. Around the turn of the century and the beginning of the twentieth century, such cliques of
firms began to emerge as *zaibatsu*. The term, *zaibatsu*, a strongly
pejorative term, came into common use for these business giants.
Well-known *zaibatsu* included Mitsui, Mitsubishi, Sumitomo, Yasuda, Furukawa, Kōnoike, Kuhara, and Kawasaki.

The establishment of industrial capital under *zaibatsu* ownership provided a more favorable environment for potential foreign
investors, who had been cautious in investing in the country,
which suffered from a low level of technology and lack of private
capital. Some joint ventures born in this period have survived to
today, including Mitsubishi Electric Corporation, Fuji Electric
Company, Mitsubishi Oil Company, Tōyō Otis Elevator Company, Yokohama Rubber Company, and Nippon Sheet Glass
Company.

Foreign capital helped *zaibatsu* secure funds and technology to
expand. Understandably, areas where foreign technological advantages were greater, such as electrical machinery, saw a larger
number of tie-ups and joint ventures. For example, Fuji Electric
Company was established as a joint venture between Siemens
A. G. (Germany) and the Furukawa Electric Company in 1921. Al-

though Siemens' share was only 30 percent, all the machinery installed there was of German make and performed according to German specifications.

Mitsubishi Electric and Westinghouse also concluded a tie-up in 1923, which enabled many Mitsubishi employees to visit the United States and study advanced management methods first-hand at Westinghouse.

There was a nationwide effort to absorb foreign management skills and technology, in which the role of American firms in Japan should not be overlooked. One example of such grassroots dissemination of information from the West is found in the case of National Cash Register Company (NCR). The rise and fall of foreign investment in prewar Japan could be better understood with a concrete case of one American company.

NCR is one of America's older corporations, founded as the National Cash Register Company in Dayton, Ohio in 1884. National Cash Register Company started selling cash registers in Japan in 1897.[1] In 1919 as part of the firm's strategy for professionalizing its sales force, NCR opened the first sales training school in Japan.

The founder of NCR in the United States, John H. Patterson, invented many innovative management practices, sales training, and contingent compensation for the sales force.

At this school, all sales approaches, developed originally by Patterson and other NCR men, tested, and improved in the American soil, were systematically and scientifically taught to eager Japanese sales staff. For the Japanese, it was an eye-opening experience that scientific methods should and could be applied to sales and marketing.

The company kept the founder's philosophy of keeping close relations with customers. According to that philosophy, NCR sales people should not sell cash registers only but also efficient management methods at the point of sales. Thus NCR enabled Japan's sales force to become trained professionally to provide customers with the latest management methods and sales strategies, disseminating American management methods among a wide Japanese audience.

NCR introduced the installment payment and brought new American advertising methods into Japan. At a show window of the American Trading Company in the Ginza, the most prestigious and busy downtown district of Tokyo, NCR exhibited a large-scale original display, emphasizing supreme technology and sophistication. The display was changed every week, attracting much publicity and public attention.

NCR's cash register was virtually the first modern control device available to many Japanese businesses. NCR, with its technological lead, dominated the Japanese market in no time. By 1923 NCR had opened branches in eight Japanese cities in addition to its original two offices in Tokyo and Kobe. Their sales expanded rapidly.

In 1933, NCR cancelled its agency agreement with American Trading Company and founded a new company of its own, taking on those employees previously engaged in NCR cash register sales. Mr. R. Berman, who was a European NCR manager, became the first president. He decided to import half-finished products and parts and to have them assembled in Japan. By having a final assembly line close to the market, NCR was able to avoid high tariffs on imports, to reduce costs, and to secure dependable delivery and maintenance service of cash registers.

Moving in the direction towards local manufacturing, the company merged with Japan Cash Register, privately owned by the Fujiwara family in 1935. In this new form of the organization Japan Cash Register took charge of machine production while Japan National Cash Register concentrated on sales. The United States parent company sent American engineers to Japan Cash Register's factory in Shizuoka to train and supervise Japanese workers.

⁂ ⁂ ⁂

The introduction of foreign capital and technology helped grow Japanese capitalism. In order to strengthen their economic positions, Japanese firms were eager to receive foreign capital, technology, and management know-how.

Because of the way Japanese capitalism developed, initially through governmental industries and then through *zaibatsu*, the prewar Japanese industrial structure showed a dual structure, composed of giant *zaibatsu* firms at the top, and numerous small mom-and-pop workshops at the bottom. Some argue that this capital intensive-monopolistic system was efficient and "was almost inevitable" for a country like Japan, where capital, skilled labor, and technological know-how had to be brought in together in a concentrated form to ensure rapid growth.[2] *Zaibatsu* were indeed formidable. During the 1920s and 1930s, Mitsui and Mitsubishi were perhaps the two largest private economic empires in the world. American capital in prewar Japan, closely tied in with *zaibatsu*, provided much needed technology and capital to the nation.

The *zaibatsu*'s positive attitudes toward direct foreign investment, however, would soon find opposition from another powerful institution, which voiced strong anti-Western, anti-American sentiments in the 1930s — the Japanese imperial army.

The catastrophe of the 1929 Great Depression hit Japan in early 1930. The value of Japanese exports dropped 50 percent from 1929 to 1931. Unemployment rose to about 3 million. It hit rural Japan the hardest. To make the matter worse, northern Japan experienced an unprecedented crop failure in 1931. Peasants sold their daughters to brothels. Children died of starvation.

The blame for the depression fell on the civilian government and political party leaders. Party leaders, in the public mind, were intimately associated with the *zaibatsu*, the bureaucracy, the landlords, and the urban white-collar class. The economic depression called into question the utility of this coalition.

As the inability of the parliamentary system to solve the immediate economic crisis became widely perceived, an alternative force emerged as a dark wave of future — the imperial army. Certain leaders argued that military expansion abroad could create an autonomous empire, which would ensure economic prosperity for Japanese. "Japan will free Asians from Western colonial domination!" became a common theme of propaganda campaigns in the 1930s.

While the civilian government took Japan to a financial recovery by 1936, it came too late. In the 1930s, the ascent of militarism became increasingly apparent as Japan was looking to a more authoritarian and dictatorial form of government to guide the nation.

Zaibatsu, although monopolistic and nondemocratic in nature, did not fit in well with the rising tide of the military, which manifested strong nationalism and anti-Westernism. The higher education and overseas experience of *zaibatsu* executives, together with an awareness of the importance of global trade, tended to give *zaibatsu* an international outlook.

On the other hand, the Japanese army, with its strong rural background, considered the *zaibatsu* as pro-Western, urban, and corrupt. The Japanese Kwantung Army in Manchuria, for example, shut *zaibatsu* out of the early phase of Manchurian development after 1931.[3]

While *zaibatsu* sought to maintain tie-ups with foreign companies, the military initiated action to order foreign capital eliminated from Japanese firms. As Japan slipped deeper into militarism cum ultranationalism, Japanese-American business ties grew increasingly precarious.

By the early 1930s, it became practically impossible to import parts. Rigid restrictions were placed on any product. Later the Japanese government froze all United States capital in Japan in retaliation for the seizure of Japanese Americans' property by the United States Government. The outburst of the Pacific War on December 7, 1941 put the final and complete hold on all U.S.-Japanese business activities.

The rise of Japanese militarism and the eventual outbreak of World War II created a crisis situation to foreign investors in Japan. Many left Japan, but some showed amazing tenacity under extremely harsh conditions. The previously mentioned Japan National Cash Register was one of them. In the early 1930s, it became impossible for Japan National Cash Register to import iron and parts for the local cash register manufacturing. The production had to be halted. As the war was declared, Japan National Cash Register was placed under the management of the Finance Ministry. By then the American managers had left the scene, but Japan National Cash Register's fifty some years of work was continued by its Japanese staff, even during the war years.

In 1942 Mr. Fujiwara, owner of Japan Cash Register, managed to buy the entire company. The Fujiwara family continued to provide services to customers throughout the 1940s. In 1949, four years after the defeat of Japan, the machine production line in Japan Cash Register reopened when NCR's engineers returned to Japan and started providing the company with NCR's main company support.

From 1868 to 1941, throughout the period from the Meiji Restoration to the Second World War, there were less than 100 foreign-affiliated companies in existence at any one time. About thirty foreign-affiliated enterprises survived the war to reemerge in the postwar period.[4]

IMMEDIATE POSTWAR PERIOD

In the scorching August of 1945, Japan lay in ruins. The country was hopelessly crippled for lack of capital, the wartime destruction of key industries, and outmoded technology. One of the first major postwar joint economic policies of the Supreme Commander for the Allied Powers (SCAP) and the Japanese government was to designate several key industries such as steel, coal, electric power generation, and chemical fertilizer as top priorities for industrial restoration.[5]

The American Occupation Force began to provide food, medicine, fertilizer, petroleum, and other essential commodities in order to assist Japan's economic recovery. Total American direct aid was terminated in 1951, but the outbreak of the Korean War at that time put Japan in the midst of the first postwar economic boom. American economic aid and United States military expenditures were the two major income sources in Japan's immediate postwar recovery.

Foreign capital entry in the petroleum industry started during the occupation. Five major oil companies — Shell, Caltex, Tidewater, Union, and Stanback — organized the Japan Oil Storage Company (JOSCO) in order to supply fuel to the Allied Powers in Japan. The petroleum section of SCAP controlled the oil supply of all Japan. In June 1946, the Petroleum Distribution Public Corporation was established, and in August, Standard Oil, Rising Sun Oil (Shell), and Caltex were allowed to sell oil to residents of the member countries of the Allied Powers.

From 1948 to 1949, SCAP started to encourage the recovery of the oil industry in Japan. Most of the Japanese oil companies except three — Maruzen, Nihon-kōgyō, and Daikyō Oil — made capital investment agreements with large world oil companies. Shōwa-Shell, Nisseki-Caltex, Tōa-Stanback, Koa-Caltex, and Mitsubishi-Tidewater were among them. Because of the unique setup of foreign-related oil companies in Japan, which were originally protected and encouraged by SCAP, their oligopoly in the market is still evident. The petroleum industry today is still largely in foreign hands, rather exceptional for Japan.

MITI, or the Ministry of International Trade and Industry, which has been regarded as one of the most important ministries to foreigners seeking entry into the Japanese market, came into existence on May 25, 1949, as the body succeeding the prewar Ministry of Commerce and Industry.

In December of the same year, the Foreign Exchange and Foreign Trade Control Law (Law No. 288, December 1, 1949) was enacted to control foreign exchange. The law was also used "as an important tool for Japan's industrial rationalization, industrial protection and the promotion of exports."[6]

The Foreign Investment Law (Law No. 193, May, 1950) was established to encourage foreign investment without hurting Japan's interests, following the SCAP's policies announced in 1949. The law provided that any earnings or patent royalties could be taken out of Japan without reference to foreign exchange control, once it was approved by the Ministry of Finance.

While the Foreign Investment Law provided control over the introduction of technology and foreign capital to the Japanese market, the Foreign Exchange and Foreign Trade Control Law provided rules for ordinary exchange. The Foreign Investment Law controlled technological agreements with royalty payment terms of one year or more (Type A), and the Foreign Exchange and Foreign Trade Control Law handled those shorter than a year (Type B). After the enactment of the two laws, the introduction of foreign technology started to raise the Japanese technological level. Type A agreements accounted for more than 100 cases a year in 1951, 1952, and 1953. Type B agreements numbered forty-nine cases in 1950, eighty-seven in 1951, 110 in 1952, and more than 130 in 1953 and 1954, respectively.

In the initial postwar period, Japanese industrial development was comparable to that of the late 1920s and early 1930s. Japanese companies were desperate to get advanced foreign technology, and the government encouraged and sometimes even welcomed direct foreign investment. The weakness of the economy and the technological backwardness of Japan, however, discouraged foreign firms.

Toyo Rayon Company, predecessor of Toray Industries, now Japan's leading synthetic fiber and resin maker, for example, was a traditional textile manufacturer in the immediate postwar period. Before the war, in 1936, Toyo Rayon learned that nylon had been invented by DuPont, and in 1951 it bought a patent from DuPont. At that time, the total equity of Toyo Rayon was 0.75 billion yen. Shigeki Tashiro, chairman of the board, decided to pay the royalty of 1.08 billion yen to DuPont, making installment payments. Toyo Rayon's importation of nylon technology was a celebrated instance of advanced technology imports from abroad by risk-taking Japanese companies. The pioneering manufacturing and market development by Toyo Rayon enabled this company to leap ahead in the textile industry, which eventually expanded into other synthetic fibers and to fiber optics.

DuPont, back in 1951, did not enter the Japanese market by way of capital investment primarily because of its perception of the poor Japanese market and its technological backwardness. One had to wait until 1960 for DuPont to start joint-venturing with Japanese partners, and 1964 with Toray Industries in particular.

The postwar conditions of the automobile industry in Japan were weak and confused. The Occupation Forces limited the production of vehicles and rationed those available. The Japanese government recommended the revitalization of the industry using foreign passenger car technology and governmental financial assistance. The Restoration Loan Corporation, established in 1947, financed new production facilities.

In 1949, however, SCAP adopted a politically unpopular austerity policy to curve the inflation and spur foreign trade (the Dodge plan). The policy forced price reduction of major items. The 1949 deflationary policy severely hurt the automobile industry. Toyota and Nissan had to cut back expansion and lay off thousands of employees. The American authorities had restricted car production to merely a few hundred units until 1950 because they did not consider cars essential.

Shintaro Kamiya, president of Toyota Auto Sales, flew to the United States on June 23, 1950 with the hope of overcoming the financial difficulties of the company by introducing Ford capital. Two days later the Korean War broke out, and the negotiations between Toyota and Ford had to be halted. The war saved Japanese car manufacturers as orders from the American army for $23 million worth of vehicles restored them to profitability (Cusmano 1985:19).

In October 1952, MITI issued the "Basic Policy for the Technological Licensing and Assembly Agreements in the Passenger Car Industry." MITI's new policy sought to make technological agreements more attractive to licensors by guaranteeing the remittance of royalties from Japan while retaining quotas and tariffs on auto parts to protect the domestic manufacturers. Nissan made an agreement with Austin (1952), Isuzu with Roots (1953), Hino with Renault (1953), and Mitsubishi with Willys (1954). The big American auto manufacturers did not, however, enter the Japanese market due to their reluctance to invest in the still small and fragile market and also because the size of the American car was not suitable to Japanese conditions. Toyota and Prince, two of the three major passenger car producers in Japan at that time, did not form technical agreements with foreign licensors and used domestic know-how exclusively.

It is reasonable to assume that the Japanese government might have permitted, even welcomed, foreign auto manufacturers' capital participation at that time, but foreign auto firms were reluctant to do so, considering the weak Japanese auto industry with its low level of technology and an annual car production of a mere twenty thousand units in 1955.

MITI combined low-interest loans with several tax privileges to help passenger car development. Starting in 1956, MITI also exempted auto companies from import duties on machinery and tools purchased abroad and permitted companies to deduct as income any revenues obtained from export sales. Japan abandoned this latter practice only when it joined the General Agreement on Tariffs and Trade (GATT) in 1964 (Cusmano, ibid).

After the signing of the San Francisco Peace Treaty (1951) and the end of the Occupation (1952), Japanese officials, under the Foreign Investment Law, started to wield a greater deal of discretion, deciding into which fields and industries foreigners could invest. Certain industries such as banking, transportation, insurance, and public utilities were designated as "restricted," and tighter rules were applied to these.

Governmental priority was given to those industries that would most speedily and effectively contribute to the improvement of Japan's balance of payments.

JAPAN'S OFFICIAL POLICIES

In the postwar history of foreign direct investment in Japan, there have been basically three distinct phases: (1) Pre-liberalization period 1945–1963; (2) The period of capital liberalization 1964–1973; and (3) Post-capital liberalization 1974–present.

During the first period, Japan needed advanced technology desperately, and Japanese firms aggressively sought foreign technology and capital. The Japanese market was, however, not attractive to many foreign investors because the economy had not recovered from the wartime destruction, the nation's technological level was equivalent to that of the 1920s and 1930s, consumer spending was low, and capital was scarce.

In the late 1950s and 1960s, the Japanese economy expanded dramatically, recording two-digit GNP growth rates annually. The second phase of the governmental policy started when Japan joined the Organization for Economic Cooperation and Development (OECD) and began her program of capital liberalization in 1964. The government liberalization policies, however, turned out to be more restrictive than before.

The initial reason for control over foreign investment was that the economy was still small and fragile, low in capital inputs and technology, requiring protection in the national interest. Secondly, many important Japanese companies were undercapitalized and might be attractive as acquisition candidates for foreign firms. The government regulated tightly the acquisition of shares in existing Japanese companies.

The Japanese have a keen sense of national identity and have greatly feared possible foreign economic domination. They also feared that the entry of foreign capital might disrupt the system of "economic concertee" because a foreign investor's basic economic interest and commitment was not the development of Japan's economy.[7] This was Japan's official stance in the 1960s and early 1970s. Let us examine the Japanese government's protectionist policies in more detail.

THE 1950S AND EARLY 1960S

The Japanese government in the 1950s and early 1960s was unlikely to validate the purchase of more than 50 percent of the shares of companies, except in some special cases where Japan's need for certain technology from foreign firms exceeded her reluctance for foreign direct investment in Japan. It has been said that "the biggest area of U.S. investment in Japan has been in the licensing of patents and technology."[8] The OECD report of 1968 estimated that roughly 30 percent of all Japanese manufacturing was based to a greater or lesser extent on imported technology.[9]

IBM was one of a few exceptions where the Japanese government allowed 100 percent direct investment in Japan during that period. If the government refused its entry, IBM could have refused to license its patents to all interested Japanese producers. The Japanese government faced the dilemma between its need to gain access to advanced foreign technology and its wish to develop the domestic computer industry. During the 1950s the Japanese were far behind the Americans in developing computer technology.

In 1957 the first legislation in the computer field was enacted (The Electronic Industry Development Act), which, prepared by MITI's Heavy Industry Bureau, established the outlines of governmental assistance programs and fund allocation. The Electronic Industry Deliberation Council was formed within MITI and was later renamed as the Electronic and Machinery Industries Deliberation Council in 1971. The council consisted of bureaucrats of MITI and the Ministry of Finance, presidents of major electronic and machinery companies, representatives of the industry's trade associations, and scholars. The act authorized direct governmental loans to assist manufacturers in commercializing electronic products. Although the governmental assistance did not cover a major portion of manufacturers' research and development and production costs (the total subsidy during 1957–61 did not exceed $1 million), it provided favorable conditions for them, one of which was MITI's authority to selectively exempt any portion of the electronics industry from the Anti-Monopoly Law.

MITI's aim was to strengthen the Japanese computer industry, which promised future export markets and relative freedom from fluctuation in values of raw materials.

As Japanese computer producers began to expand their capacity, they sought basic electronic data processing equipment patents held by American computer companies. IBM, which held many basic patents, had a relative advantage over others to negotiate the establishment of a 100 percent Japanese subsidiary with the Japanese government. IBM offered, in exchange for the establishment of a 100 percent subsidiary, the supply of some basic patents, but not know-how, to Japanese producers.

In 1959 Japan IBM, a 100 percent subsidiary of IBM, was established. Japanese manufacturers, who did not get know-how and technical assistance from IBM, turned to its major competitors and made licensing agreements: Nippon Electric with Honeywell in 1962, Toshiba with General Electric in 1964, Mitsubishi Electric with TRW in 1962 and Oki Electric with Sperry Rand in 1963. Sperry Rand formed Oki-Univac with Oki Electric with 43 percent ownership in 1953. While the Japanese government "gave in" to the IBM request for a 100 percent subsidiary, it turned down Texas Instrument's similar request in the mid 1960s, which will be discussed later.

YEN-BASED COMPANIES

Prior to 1963, there were few ways by which foreign firms could establish a 100 percent subsidiary in Japan. One of them was to found a "yen-base" company. Between October 1956 and June 1963, nonresidents from sixteen countries, including the United States, were allowed to make certain direct investments on the understanding that neither income nor liquidation proceeds would be transferred abroad.

The yen-base companies were often the result of foreigners' strong wish to control their own local operations. They would rather forego the privilege of income repatriation than accept all the official restrictions that came with such a privilege. The yen-base companies were abolished in 1963, at the beginning of capital liberalization. At that time, there were 289 yen-base companies and 273 yen-base branches. Their total nominal capital was $140 million. Out of thirty wholly owned foreign manufacturing companies of any scope at that time, twenty-nine were originally yen-based. Yen-base investments were chiefly in the machinery and equipment, cosmetics, entertainment, food, import and export, and machinery.

CAPITAL LIBERALIZATION 1964-1973

The First Liberalization (1964)

In 1963, Prime Minister Hayato Ikeda announced in Paris Japan's wish to join OECD. Japan signed the Memorandum of Un-

derstanding Between the Organization for Economic Cooperation and Development (OECD) and the Government of Japan
Concerning the Assumption by the Government of Japan of the
Obligations of Membership of the Organization in July 1963.
OECD membership meant that Japan had to accept the OECD liberalization code. Japan, however, made reservations to eighteen
items of the OECD liberalization code, including her reservation
against inward direct investment. Among major nations of
twenty-three OECD members, Japan's reservations were the
most numerous. Among the six leading nations, only Japan
lodged a reservation against direct investment.

In the agreement with OECD, the Japanese government said:

> The Japanese government will, in future, deal with all applications for in-
> ward and outward direct investments in the spirit of the item in question and
> would disapprove applications only in exceptional cases where serious det-
> rimental effects to the economy are to be feared.[10]

From 1964 to 1967, the expected "liberalization" proved to be
an increase of restrictions and a decrease in foreign capital entries
into Japan, temporarily at least. It was ironic that purely foreign
companies were forbidden due to the abolishment of the yen-
base companies in 1963. The foreigner was required to seek governmental authorization for direct capital investment.

Validation of some applications took years after they were
handed to the Foreign Investment Council. The council, composed of the representatives of so-called economic ministries,
had the right to advise on applicant revisions. The members of
the council were representatives from MITI, the Ministries of Finance, of Agriculture and Forestry, of Transportation, of Health
and Welfare, of Construction, of Posts, and of Foreign Affairs, the
Science and Technology Agency, the Anti-Monopoly Committee,
the Economic Planning Agency, and the Bank of Japan.

The advice for revision by the Foreign Investment Deliberation
Council was *orally* given by the section in charge of the ministry
having jurisdiction over the business concerned to the Japanese
firm, which was the opposite party to the agreement in principle.
Then negotiations for revision in terms of the agreement were
carried on between the parties along the lines of the advice. In order to "avoid misunderstanding between the government and the
applicants," it was necessary for the Japanese applicant to pre-

pare the draft of a letter or telegram to be forwarded to the foreign investor.[11] See Figure 14.

Then the Japanese applicant would submit the draft to the sections in charge of the Ministry of Finance and the ministry having jurisdiction over the business concerned for confirmation before contacting the foreign investor on revision. If the proposal of the Japanese applicant was accepted by the foreign investor, negotiations were concluded. However, if the proposal was not accepted by the foreigner, the reply was examined by the council, and, if necessary, renegotiations took place.

> Validation of some applications took years. Some were turned down after waiting for years. MITI officials drove hard bargains with foreign company officials. They would not hesitate to ask for ridiculously low initial payment or royalties, using the most favorable (to the Japanese side) past agreements with other foreign firms as levers to pry loose the best arrangements they could get from new foreign applicants. They would refer to past low initial payments, ignoring intentionally associated high royalties, or to past low royalties, ignoring associated high initial payments.[12]

Foreign businessmen severely criticized such governmental policies. Carl H. Boehringer, the then head of the American Chamber of Commerce in Japan, wrote to a United States representative for the Japan-U.S. Economic Meeting in Washington in July 1965, complaining that American firms could not establish manufacturing plants, nor obtain majority ownership of an established company, that the Japanese government enforced a very strict control over direct investment while they eagerly sought indirect private investment or technical agreements, and that the Japanese government, not always, but very often, asked for modifications of the conditions of joint-venture contracts in favor of the Japanese side.

OECD also criticized Japan's slow progress on capital liberalization, stating that:

> Rejection of the original application—unless there were substantial modification of the proposed terms—can rarely be ascribed to 'exceptional cases' which might have 'serious detrimental effects' for Japan. So far the impression is that refusals of what has been asked for, or failure to approve, are general rather than exceptional.[13]

In January 1964 Texas Instruments applied to MITI to establish a 100 percent subsidiary. The Japanese electronics industry then

FIGURE 14: THE DRAFT OF A LETTER REGARDING THE JOINT-VENTURE AGREEMENT

From: Mr. _____ , _____ , _____ Company, Japan.
To: Mr. _____ , _____ . Company, U.S.A.
Date: _____ .

Re: Joint-Venture Agreement Concerning _____

Concerning the captioned matter for which an application was filed with the Japanese Government under the date of _____ , we have been advised that the Japanese Government is, as the result of deliberation at the Japanese Government's Foreign Investment Council, prepared to grant formal validation if you agree to alternation of the following clauses in the agreement concerned. We beg you will kindly sympathize with our situation and give us a prompt reply so that the agreement may be concluded amicably.

(1) _____
(2) _____
(3) _____

Yours truly,

_____

was still at the height of the transistor age, and integrated circuit (IC) production was just starting. MITI set aside Texas Instruments' application for a long time in fear of its dominance over the future Japanese IC market if it was allowed to enter the Japanese market before the Japanese IC industry itself had even started. The delaying tactic of the Japanese government was strategically motivated.

When the Japanese government turned down Texas Instruments' request for a 100 percent subsidiary, John Connolly, the U.S. Secretary of Commerce, claimed that Japan's refusal of Texas Instruments' entry was a violation of the U.S.-Japan Treaty of Friendship, Commerce and Navigation. The allegation by Connolly that Japan had violated the treaty was successively renewed by American participants at the annual joint U.S.-Japan Meetings on Trade and Economic Affairs. The Business and Industrial Advisory Committee of OECD also supported this view.

Such foreign statements were perceived by the Japanese as another aggressive United States move to penetrate the still "fragile" Japanese market. There were also arguments regarding Japan's legal commitments under the treaty, which was a kind of gentlemen's agreement between the two countries.

The U.S. Secretary of Commerce who succeeded Connolly saw that the United States' treaty violation argument had little problem-solving potential and that the problem would more likely be solved by effective United States' reactions to the Japanese governmental policies in trading off restrictions. The American official considered it politically wise not to continue referring to the treaty.

The case of Texas Instruments indicated that the difficulties of foreign entry derived mainly from the close relationships between MITI and the Japanese business world, where aggressive power politics might not produce favorable results for a foreign investor. Consequently, Texas Instruments changed their strategies and opted for a joint venture. In May 1968 Texas Instruments received permission to establish a 50–50 joint venture with Sony.

Texas Instruments had, however, made an internal agreement with Sony, that Sony would withdraw its investment after three years of the joint corporation's establishment, and that Texas Instruments would convert the company into a 100 percent subsidiary.

Texas Instruments, after four years took a foothold in Japan. An important early strategy of Texas Instruments was the establishment of production facilities in Japan from the beginning. In 1968, Texas Instruments started its production in Hatogaya, Saitama Prefecture.[14]

＊　＊　＊

The Japanese government in the 1960s preferred joint ventures to a majority foreign ownership and the direct foreign capital entry to existing Japanese companies because "allowing foreign managerial participation in existing Japanese companies may cause many problems."[15] On the eve of capital liberalization, the biggest concern of MITI was how to improve the comparative strength of domestic industries while keeping foreigners out, or at least at the arm's length. The time was running out.

The Late 1960s

MITI, knowing the inevitability of capital liberalization in the near future, conducted an extensive survey of 104 key industries in Japan to evaluate their relative strength vis-a-vis foreign capital. Based on this study report, the Foreign Investment Deliberation Council and the Industrial Structure Council held meetings in 1967.

The government, in order to implement the 1968 liberalization decisions, made four industrial categories: the first category of industries in public and security-related fields were excluded from liberalization (nineteen industries). The second category encompassed all industries where foreign investors could enter only after a case-by-case screening. The industries of this category included: electronic computers and computer peripheral equipment, data processing, oil refining and sales, retail chains of more than eleven stores, agriculture, forestry, fishery, real estate, and leather products. The definition of industries was so broad that one industry actually meant several industries.

The third and fourth categories were to be liberalized industries: in the third category, 100 percent foreign ownership was automatically approved (seventeen industries). They included ordinary steel, bicycle, cement, cotton, and piano and organ manufacturing. Some industries in this category meant only one product, in contrast to those in the second category. In the fourth category, the government preferred joint ventures to 100 percent foreign ownership because the industries needed further development to compete with foreigners. Up to 50 percent foreign ownership were automatically approved in this category, which included electric appliances, radio, television, cameras, watches, synthetic fibers, records, ammonia fertilizer, and the glass plate industries (thirty-three in total).

The intention of the Japanese government was to conduct a "controlled" liberalization by stages utilizing bureaucratic procedures rather than amendment of laws, so that each relaxation coincided with the counterbalancing competitiveness of Japanese firms. The real policy of the government on direct capital investment and the attitudes of the bureaucrats towards the issue can be best illustrated by the informal announcement of the Ministry of Finance in September 1967, named "Ten Commandments for Foreign Investors." The foreign investor should:

1. Invest in industries where a 50 percent equity is automatically approved rather than in industries where a 100 percent is possible;
2. Avoid industries in which goods are produced mainly by medium to small factories;
3. Avoid restrictive arrangements with overseas parent companies or affiliates;
4. Cooperate with Japanese producers in the same industry in order to avoid "excessive competition";
5. Contribute to the development of Japanese technology;
6. Help promote Japanese exports;
7. Ensure that in a joint venture the number of Japanese directors reflects the Japanese equity percentage;
8. Avoid layoffs and plant closures that might disrupt the Japanese labor market;
9. Cooperate in maintaining Japan's industrial harmony and help in the achievement of her economic goals; and
10. Avoid concentrating their investments in any particular industry or industries.[16]

The official requirements for governmental approval on foreign capital investments were never clearly stated. Foreign investors had to learn the real intention of the government the hard way through bargaining and negotiations with MITI and other ministries.

The Second Liberalization (1969)

On March 1, 1969, the second step for liberalization was taken by the Foreign Investment Deliberation Council: 100 percent foreign ownership was automatically approved in forty-four industries; twenty industries were newly added to the list. They included steel, electric bulbs, electric appliances, fluorescent lights, boilers, textile machinery, fish meal processing, etc.

In the 50 percent category, 135 industries were newly added (160 industries in total), which included automobile tires, ceramics, detergents, medical equipment, toys, wholesale (including exporting), and specialized retail shops. The characteristic of the second liberalization was to include some industries that were attractive to foreign investors, such as wholesale and specialized retail industries, in the 50 percent category.

The Third Liberalization (1970), and the Fourth Liberalization (1971)

The Japanese government moved slowly but steadily towards capital liberalization. To some foreign investors and observers, the move was too slow with many countermeasures placed against the effective entry of foreign firms, but the government with a strong pro-Japan attitude moved at its own pace.

Such major industries as computers, automobiles, and petrochemical industries were excluded in the second round of liberalization, which invited severe foreign criticism of governmental protectionism. Having balanced the mounting foreign pressure and the self-interests of Japan, the government announced in September 1970, the third liberalization, and also the schedule for the fourth liberalization, which would be half a year earlier than originally planned.

As of September 1970, foreign portfolio investments of up to 25 percent of the shares of an existing Japanese company were automatically approved, although in the special industries the upper limit remained as 15 percent. During the third liberalization, industries in the 50 percent category increased to 447 (315 industries were newly added), and those in the 100 percent category numbered seventy-seven, including eight newly added ones.

In the 50 percent category, cosmetics, special steel, female and children clothes, furniture, printing machines, banking, and security industries were newly added. Exporting, newspapers, department stores, and supermarket industries were added to the 100 percent liberalization category.

The American automobile industry's representatives had been pressing the Japanese government for capital entry to Japan. The government, in an attempt to meet their demands, announced that automobile manufacturing and auto parts manufacturing industries as well as auto sales industries would be liberalized in April 1971.

The fourth round of liberalization was initially scheduled for March 1972. Due to the rapid growth of domestic industries in terms of international competitiveness, and the unstable international currency situation, the government announced the fourth liberalization in August 1971. The reasons for the shift of the governmental policies were:

1. The fact that foreign entries by automatic approval had been fewer than expected. Automatic approvals were eighteen cases between 1967 and 1975, thirty-five in 1971, and seventy-five in 1972.
2. The initial fear of foreign takeover was weakened by the fact that foreign-related companies kept a low posture in the Japanese market. Total sales of foreign-related firms were around 1 percent of the sales of domestic firms.
3. The Japanese government had realized the importance of liberalization of the Japanese market, which in turn justified free trade and Japan's overseas investments. Japanese overseas investment had been growing rapidly ($10 billion up to 1973), and the government considered it necessary to demonstrate to other countries its liberal policies regarding direct capital investment in order to avoid possible rise of protectionism in other countries. After the "Nixon Shock" of August 1971, the Japanese government came to realize that it could no longer expect to increase exports without importing in return from foreign markets.

In the fourth round of liberalization, the government changed the list from a positive one (listing liberalized items) to a negative one (listing unliberalized items). The principle of 50 percent liberalization in all industries, except special ones such as agriculture, fishery, mining, film, nonferrous metal, industrial machinery, and electric machinery, was announced in 1971. In the 100 percent approval category, 151 new industries were added, totaling 228, which included advertising, air conditioners, electric audio equipment, paper and pulp, and prefabricated housing material industries. The government announced that 57 percent of manufacturing industries were at least 50 percent liberalized, and 30 percent were completely liberalized in the fourth round of liberalization. The nonliberalized industries were, however, the areas of major interest to the foreign investor, which was why they were not liberalized.

The Fifth Liberalization (1973)

Foreign capital entry in Japan, which reached a peak of 255 million dollars in 1972, dropped to 160 million in 1973, reflecting the value change of the yen. Japanese overseas investment, on the other hand, jumped up to 3.5 billion dollars in 1973 alone. Mr. Hideaki Yamashita, director of the Enterprise Bureau of MITI, said in a press conference:

> The time has changed. When we announced the fourth liberalization in 1971, there was a concern that foreign capital might swallow up the Japanese economy. We, however, proceeded to liberalize an increasing number of industries, and can now proudly present our liberalization policies to OECD.
> The most important contributing factor which enabled rapid and satisfactory liberalization in the past year and a half was the rising value of the yen.[17]

Japan announced the principle of 100 percent liberalization in May 1973. The governmental acceptance of the 100 percent principle reflected its growing confidence in the strength of domestic industries vis-a-vis foreign capital. The Cabinet Statement Concerning Liberalization of Inward Direct Investment (April 27, 1973) reads:

> In line with the marked improvement of Japan's economic position in recent years, the role that the Japanese economy plays internationally has been strengthened. Japan's overseas business activities have been rapidly expanding. Under these circumstances, it is deemed necessary for Japan to demonstrate to the world its determination and posture aiming at promoting

in a most positive manner the internationalization of its economy in the belief that this type of action will help avoid possible surges of protectionism in the world economy, and thus prove instrumental to the maintenance of world peace and prosperity, which depends on the spirit of international cooperation.

By this liberalization policy, 100 percent automatic approval of foreign direct investment was granted to all industries except agriculture, fishery, oil, mining, and leather manufacturing (five exceptional industries), and seventeen industries that were to be liberalized in the mid-1970s. The seventeen industries included integrated circuits, meat processing, apparel manufacturing and wholesale, pharmaceuticals and medicine for animals, medical and electric measuring instruments, hydraulic machinery, phonograph records, and fruit juice.

The computer industry was 100 percent liberalized in the mid-1970s. The import of computers was liberalized on December 23, 1975, and the software field was liberalized in April 1976.

DISCUSSION

We have seen that Japan steadfastly protected her market by enforcing tight control over foreign direct investment up until the mid-1970s. We have also observed that Japan's capital liberalization movement (1963–1973) very slowly unfolded, partly because of *gaiatsu* or foreign pressures.

Japan's move was very political, beyond a mere economic calculation. The liberalization movement was in part her new political drive for international economic status. Throughout the carefully planned and implemented liberalization, governmental policies were set between the need for achieving the status of an advanced industrialized state with an open capital market and the need to protect and develop domestic industry.

The same dualism existed between Japan's need for advanced Western technology and the need for technological innovation at home, and between the need for a Western-styled industrial structure and the survival of the small traditional crafts. Many requests for foreign capital entry were turned down as the government carefully balanced these two conflicting needs for Japan's economic prosperity.

When Japan started liberalizing its economy, many intellectuals and bureaucrats originally feared that United States multinationals would dominate the Japanese market, as was the case in some areas of the European market. In order to avoid this problem, the Japanese government attempted and often succeeded in strengthening the domestic economy and expanding exports while using the best foreign technology.

In the mid-1970s, the Japanese government seemed to realize that an overemphasis on economic nationalism could hurt Japan more than benefit her. This apparent shift in governmental policy coincided with the increasing confidence of the Japanese people in their economic strength, the shift of industrial structure towards information and service-oriented industries, the end of Japan's phenomenal economic expansion, and the beginning of a slow and steady economic growth.

The Japanese government's protectionist policies were conducted less and less frequently in the late 1970s. The role of the state in the economy, however, remained the same in principle: the government served as a guardian of Japanese industries, attempting to provide a favorable environment for target industries.

The problems of "foreign firms in Japan" in the 1980s were similar in nature as far as the government was concerned. The government continued its efforts to preserve national autonomy and economic independence, and to cope with the growing internationalization of production and distribution by private corporations with multinational stances.

Multinationals are fundamentally motivated by the economic rationality of production and exchange, not by political considerations of preserving local jobs, small industries, defense, or other national interests. The interests of the state and the multinational are not always compatible. In a strategic-oriented industrial state, however, the economic well-being of the people is an important security issue.

The Japanese government is very conscious of its role as the initiator of Japan's industrial policies. While it must protect local interests, the government and its bureaucrats are aware of the fact that the Japanese economy must depend upon the global economy. Japanese officials realize the critical dependence of the Japanese economy on free worldwide markets and the danger of foreign protectionism toward Japanese exports or capital investments. What they face is the problem of balancing these often conflicting goals: protecting local interests and encouraging free international trade at the same time.

THE GOVERNMENT AND FOREIGN ENTERPRISES IN THE 1980S

In 1980, The Foreign Exchange Control Law (FECL) changed the basic premise of the law and allowed foreign investment in principle. Under the new law, foreign investment was limited only in agriculture, forestry and fishing, mining, petroleum, and leather and leather products. The first three areas paralleled restrictions permitted under the OECD agreements.

The last, leather, was tied to Japan's unique domestic problem concerning *burakumin,* who are ethnically Japanese, engaged in works of leather, an occupation considered polluted according to Buddhist tenets in the feudal Tokugawa era. In feudal Japan, the people were classified into four social classes of the samurai, the peasant, the artisans, and the merchants. Below these "human" classes was the class of untouchables. After the Meiji Restoration (1868), the class system was abolished, but *burakumin* still form a Japanese minority group, subject to varying degrees of social injustice. In the 1980s the Japanese government considered it politically unwise to touch upon the leather and leather good industry, which was still controlled by *burakumin,* thus a politically sensitive area.

In addition, the FECL-limited foreign ownership of eleven companies, mentioned by name, which were related to national security, public order, or welfare. They were Sankyo Co., Ltd. (narcotics), 25 percent; Katakura Industries Co., Ltd. (silk), 25 percent; Arabian Oil Co., Ltd. (oil), 25 percent; Fuji Electric Co., Ltd. (defense/electronics), 26 percent; Hitachi, Ltd. (defense/electronics), 30 percent; Tokyo Keiki Co. Ltd. (defense/aircraft), 32 percent; General Sekiyu, K.K. (oil), 49 percent; Showa Oil Co. (oil), 50 percent; Mitsubishi Oil Co., Ltd. (oil), 50 percent; Toa Nenryo Kogyo K.K. (oil), 50 percent; and Koa Oil Co., Ltd. (oil), 50 percent.[4]

In all other areas, the government changed the prior case-by-case approach to foreign ownership greater than 25 percent to the prior notification system of foreign ownership greater than 25 percent. The government restricted areas where foreign ownership over 25 percent might harm national security, public order or welfare, or the national economy.

In 1984, Prime Minister Nakasone stated the government's intention of welcoming foreign capital investment in Japan. In April of the same year, MITI set up within the ministry a special section to promote foreign capital investment in Japan. The government changed the regulation again so that prior notification was required only where a single foreign investor would acquire 10 percent or more of a listed company's share.

Concerning technology transfer, in twelve designated technology areas, most of which were closely related to national security issues such as nuclear power, aerospace, and weaponry, governmental investigation and approval were still required. The rest were to be automatically approved in principle.

As the Japanese economy continued to internationalize, the Japanese government's official stand changed dramatically. In the 1980s there was little "official" protectionism against foreign direct investment.

In 1982 BOC acquired a 43 percent share position in Osaka Oxygen, the third largest industrial gas producer in Japan. The Ministry of Finance and MITI posed no obstacles to the acquisition, which was promptly approved. As a matter of fact, in the BOC Group Annual Report, the chairman of BOC thanked the two ministries for their advice in this transaction. A similar governmental reaction was observed in 1983 when Merck acquired a majority equity position in Banyu Pharmaceuticals, one of the top Japanese pharmaceutical companies. Merck at the same time acquired a majority interest in Torii Pharmaceuticals and integrated the two companies with Merck's existing joint venture with Manyuu, Nippon Merck Manyuu.

Despite the complexity of financial arrangements involving this acquisition/reorganization, the approval by the Ministry of Finance and the Ministry of Health and Welfare came without trouble.

In the 1980s, Japan's official position was for liberalism. Because of the huge trade surplus, of rapidly growing overseas investment by Japanese firms, the government encouraged reciprocal direct investment by foreign firms in Japan. The legal climate of foreign firms in Japan changed drastically during the past decade.

The overview of Japanese governmental policies has shown that Japanese industrial policies were always strategic, serving the purpose of providing a dynamic basic environment to Japanese enterprise, and at the same time of encouraging fierce competition among them. The Japanese government fully recognized the importance of competition in the marketplace and the initiative of the individual entrepreneur. The purpose of industrial planning in the past was to "guide" them towards the agreed national goal of economic prosperity.

NOTES

CHAPTER ONE: CULTURAL ENCOUNTERS

1. See for example, Martin Tolchin and Susan Tolchin, *Buying into America: How Foreign Money is Changing the Face of Our Nation* (New York: Times Books 1988).

2. Robert Green and T. L. Larsen, Only Retaliation Will Open Up Japan. *Harvard Business Review.* (November-December) 1987.

3. For more discussion on Japanese economic structure, see Yamamura and Yasuba (1987), and Okimoto and Rohlen (1988).

4. The historical meaning of the *kokusaika* debate is given by Kumon (1987).

5. There are several books on the subject of foreign direct investment in Japan, but they tend to discuss the issue at a national level. A classical study on foreign direct investment is found in Henderson (1973). Abegglen and Stalk (1985) briefly discussed foreign enterprise in Japan. R. Christopher (1987) also reported success stories of selective American firms in Japan.

6. For general discussion on approaches to organization culture in management sciences, see Frost, et al (1985), Ott (1989), and the entire issue of *Administrative Science Quarterly* (1983 Vol. 28). For the history of organization culture studies from an anthropological viewpoint, see Baba (1986), Gamst (1990), and Hamada and Jordan (1990). I am also grateful to Dr. Stan R. Mumford for clarifying some of the ideas presented here.

7. For a good example of the invention of Japanese tradition, see Bester (1989).

8. Adler (1983) reviewed past cross-cultural management research to reach this conclusion.

9. Bouchner and Ōsako (1977), Bouchner and Perks (1971), and Mishler (1965).

CHAPTER TWO: WORKING IN JAPAN

1. Nippon Kaisha is a pseudonym. It means the Japanese Company.

2. *Meishi* or Japanese name card indicates the company name, the title of his position within the firm, the person's name and his address, telephone/telex/fax numbers.

3. It is a Japanese custom to pour drink into the cups/glasses of other people. Guests are not supposed to pour drinks into their own glasses because it is the host's responsibility to make sure their glasses are always full. In return, guests should fill the glass of the host. Pouring drinks by oneself or *tejaku* is considered as a poor manner because it points out the inattentiveness of the host.

4. See Neustupny (1987).

5. Large Japanese companies provide their employees with semi-annual bonuses. The amount depends upon the performance of the firm and industry, and fluctuates from year to year. It is a form of profit sharing. Because a large amount of salary is paid twice a year, it actually encourages saving by employees.

CHAPTER THREE: FOREIGN ENTERPRISES AND JAPANESE CORPORATE ENVIRONMENT

1. A recent surge of activities in the financial sector should be noted. During the 1980s many countries clamored demanding a wide open admissions policy for membership in the Tokyo Stock Exchange. Despite the crash of the stock market in 1987, the number of financial institutions that wished to participate in the Tokyo market increased: By February 1988, forty-four foreign stock brokerage houses had a license to operate in Japan, which included nineteen American firms. At the same time, sixteen foreign stock brokerage houses, including six Americans were members of the Tokyo Stock Market.

   The significant impact of new direct investment by financial institutions is understated in these statistics because the major direct investments in banking and securities are very frequently in the form of establishing a branch. These statistics, however, capture only new investment in locally incorporated companies, and branches are not included. In the 1980s, financial services were a major area of new entry by foreign companies. If comparable statistics on branches were available, the trend to wholly owned entities would be more dramatic.

Also in the late 1980s, an increasing number of investment consulting companies, including many Americans, were granted permission to set up operations in Japan. Concerning liberalization measures to diminish financial barriers in the 1980s, see Nihon bōeki shinkō-kai (1988a). Yoichi Shinkai also discussed, "The Internationalization of Finance," in *The Political Economy of Japan*, Vol. 2, edited by Takashi Inoguchi and Daniel I. Okimoto. Pp. 249–274. (Stanford, Calif.: Stanford University Press 1988).

2. The Japanese government statistics are based on announcements by foreign companies of their intention to invest in Japan. Not all of these intended investments are actually realized, and thus the Japanese statistics overstate the actual totals of new equity investments.

   Secondly these statistics cover direct investment only, which includes investment in existing companies in which the investor has more than a 10 percent ownership share. The statistics do not include investment flows for purely financial purposes and are therefore not distorted by these types of investments.

3. Japanese Government, *Tsūshō-sangyō-shō* (Ministry of International Trade and Industry or MITI) 1987.

   The government definition of a foreign-affiliated firm was changed in the 1980s: Prior to 1975, enterprises with 20 percent or more foreign capital were defined as "foreign," no matter how little foreign investors actually participated in their management. Between 1975 and 1985, those with 25 percent or more foreign ownership were defined as foreign capital-affiliated enterprises. In 1984, MITI modified the definition of foreign related firms in Japan in its report: Only those with 50 percent or more foreign ownership are now considered foreign-related. These changes symbolically reflected the changes in governmental attitudes toward foreign affiliates in Japan.

4. Nihon bōeki shinkō-kai, or Japan External Trade Relations Organization (JETRO) 1988a. P. 42. Foreign chemical firms have increased their investment at a 15.5 percent rate since 1981. See The American Chamber of Commerce in Japan (ACCJ) and the Council of the European Business Community (EBC) 1987.

5. 42.8 percent of foreign manufacturers in Japan in 1987 were 50–50 joint ventures, while more than a half of foreign firms in service and commerce sectors were 100 percent subsidiaries (57 percent in the service sector and 53.4 percent in the commercial sector).

6. In 1985, 10.2 percent of the Japanese population was sixty-five years or older. According to the Institute of Population Problems, a committee of the Ministry of Health and Welfare, those who will be sixty-five years old or older will increase to 14.1 percent by 1995, to 16.1 percent by 2000, and to 23.5 percent by 2020. These figures will lead those of other nations.

   Although persons of sixty-five years or older accounted for only 10.2 percent of the population in 1985, they constituted 30 percent of those needing medical treatment of some kind, not including dental treatment.

7. According to *Tokyo Business Today,* "Top 300 Japanese Corporations" (The Oriental Economist Vol 55. No. 932. June 1988). Tokyo: Tōyō keizai shinpō-sha.

8. Ken'ichi Imai and Hiroyuki Itami (1988) Pp. 112–7.

9. The Japanese household saving ratio (= household saving / household disposable income) was more than 17 percent in 1985. In contrast, the American household saving ratio was less than 6 percent. (Japan Institute for Social and Economic Affairs 1988:86)

10. The Japanese manufactures' rate of capital to capital and liability [{capital / (capital + liability)} × 100] rose rapidly during the 1980s, but it still lagged behind that of American manufacturers. The Japanese firms' capital to capital and liabilities ratio was 29.58 compared to 45.05 of the American firms, and the Japanese manufacturing enterprises' liabilities to capital ratio was 238.10 in contrast to the United States' 121.97 in 1985. (Nihon bōeki shikō-kai, ibid., 1988).

    Large firms are defined as those capitalized at more than one billion yen.

11. *The Economist,* December 7, 1985.

12. Tōkyō Keizai, *Kigyō keiretsu sōran* (1990) P. 58. Tokyo: Tōyō keizai shinpō-sha.

13. Flaherty and Imai (1984). P. 151.

14. Fair Trade Commission Report. "Long-term Relationships Among Japanese Companies: Report by the Study Group on Trade Frictions and Market Structure." April 1987. Tokyo: Kōsei torihiki kyōkai.

    See also, Kenichi Imai, "Kigyō gurūpu," *In* Ken'ichi Imai and Ryūtarō Komiya eds. *Nihon no kigyō.* Tokyo: University of Tokyo Press. 1989.

15. Clark (1979) P. 204.

16. For discussion on environmental issues of Japanese industrialization, see Norie Huddle and Michael Reich, *Island of Dreams: Environmental Crisis in Japan* (Cambridge Mass.: Schenkman Books, 1987). A famous case of industrial pollution is discussed in Masazumi Harada, *Minamata-byō* (Minamata Disease), (Tokyo: Iwanami-shoten, 1972).

17. Unlike some Chinese and Korean corporate groups, Japanese *keiretsu* arrangements today do not show a strong influence of kinship. The Japanese corporate alliance is more sociological and economic, and so are many institutional arrangements in contemporary Japan.

     The Japanese household (the very heart of kinship), for example, extends its membership to nonkinsmen, and the adoption of a nonkin, adult man to become the heir and to carry the descent line is a commonly observed practice in Japan. The Japanese practice of adopting a "stranger" would be considered as objectionable and contaminating in Korea and China, where the lineage must be based upon the blood line, and the heir must come from its own family or its closest kin.

18. Hamada (1980) Pp. 397–406.

CHAPTER FOUR: NIPPON KAISHA

1. Although there are equivalents of English personal pronouns such as *kare* (he) or *kanojo* (she) in the Japanese language, terms of address and reference that derive from words of physical locations/directions are commonly used in Japanese conversation. For example, a Japanese term *anata* literally means "over there," which is a common polite form of "you." Likewise, *omae* means "in front," which indicates a casual or intimate form of "you," and *anokata* or *achira* means "that direction," which translates as "that person."

2. In Nippon Kaisha, like many large Japanese firms, the managerial hierarchy consists, from bottom to top, of *kachō* (section chief), *buchō* (department head: director), *jōmu* (board director without executive power), *senmu* (senior board director with executive power), and *shachō* (president) or sometimes *kaichō* (chairman). There are assistant and deputy positions below each managerial position to create finer distinctions of power, status and authority.

3. United America is a pseudonym for the American joint-venture partner of Nippon Kaisha.

4. Although the Western-style calendar is common, the Japanese use a calendar based on the era of the emperor. The year 1989 marked the change in the era from *showa* to *heisei*, due to the Emperor Showa (Hirohito)'s death. *Heisei* means the achievement of universal peace.

5. See Iwata, *Gendai nihon no keiei fūdo* (1978).

6. *Nenkō-joretsu* or seniority rule literally means the order according to age and experience (*toshi no kō*). It refers to the practice of the Japanese firm where salary and promotion are directly linked with the age and years of service of the individual.

7. See for example, Plath (1983).

8. In Confucianism, the most important relationships are those of father-son, elder brother-younger brother, husband-wife, lord-servant, and friend-friend.

9. See Dore (1987).

10. Dore (ibid.).

11. One example is found in Toyota's *kanban*, or just-in-time delivery/inventory control system.

CHAPTER FIVE: THE JOINT VENTURE COMPANY: NIPPON UNITED

1. See, for example, Hofstede (1980), and Olie (1990).

2. Terpstra and David (1985).

3. Pascale and Athos in their comparison of American and Japanese firms concluded that the two systems are very similar in terms of "hardball" S's — strategy, structure, and systems. Major differences are observed in "softball" S's — skills, style, staff, and superordinate goals. This study confirms their findings. See Pascale and Athos (1981) Pp. 204 – 6.

4. Japanese manufacturers such as Toyota developed inventory control systems, which lessen or eliminate stockpiling at their assembly plants. Based upon finely tuned ordering systems where cooperation of vendors/subcontractors is essential, necessary parts and raw materials are delivered "just in time" to the manufacturing line.

5. *Sōgō shōsha* played an important role in Japan's foreign trade be-tween the 1960s and 1980s. Recently, however, their role in inter-national trade has been declining, as large Japanese manufacturers have moved directly into the international market. For the analysis of *sōgō shōsha*, see M. Y. Yoshino and Thomas B. Lifson (1986).

6. Tung (1984) P. 22.

7. Ojile (1986) P. 38.

8. Abegglen and Stalk (1985) P. 188.

CHAPTER SIX: ORGANIZATIONAL CULTURE

1. Robert Smith (1983).

2. See for example, Deal and Kennedy (1982), Smircich (1983), Ouchi (1981), Ott (1989), Pacale and Athos (1981), and Wilkins and Ouchi (1983).

3. See for example, Clark (1985), Jordan (1988), Lincoln (1985), Walck (1990).

4. Max Weber (1947).

5. Pfeffer (1981).

6. Lincoln and Guba (1985).

APPENDIX: THE HISTORICAL CONTEXT

1. Later American NCR gradually increased capital participation in Ja-pan Cash Register and acquired total control by 1955.

2. Fairbank, Reischauer, and Craig (1978). P. 657.

3. After Japan entered the war, the *zaibatsu* capital inevitably became the core capital for Japan's military expansion.

4. The American Chamber of Commerce 1987.

5. In theory, the Occupation was international, and its guiding bodies were supposedly a thirteen-nation Far Eastern Commission in Washington, and a four-power Allied Council in Tokyo. But in prac-tice the Occupation was American throughout. Under the iron com-

mand of General MacArthur, the whole Occupation administration came to be known as SCAP.

6. Japanese Government, *Tsūshō-sangyō-shō* (Ministry of Trade and Industry) 1969. P. 32.

7. Johnson (1982).

8. Louis B. Lundborg (1964).

9. OECD (1968) P. 30.

10. Japanese Government, *Tsūshō-sangyō-shō* (Ministry of Trade and Industry) ibid., P. 206.

11. Japan Industry Series (1965) P. 6.

12. Glazer (1968) P. 34.

13. OECD (1968) P. 62.

14. It built another factory in November 1973 in Hiji, Oita Prefecture in Kyushu, and expanded that factory in 1975. Because of its presence, Kyushu, the southern island of Japan has developed into a Japanese equivalent of the Silicone Valley. Though many other semiconductor makers followed the lead of Texas Instruments and came to Japan, such as AMI (in 1971), Fairchild (1972), Motorola (1973) and AMD (1974), starting local IC production in Japan as early as 1968 brought Texas Instruments several great advantages.

   Texas Instruments' full commitment to Japan seems to have been paid off by now. Its Japanese operation has become a significant corporate success story. Texas Instruments was one of the few nonmembers of the American Semiconductor Industry Association, an organization which engaged in campaign against Japanese "dumping" of computer chips in the 1980s.

15. Japanese Government, *Tsūshō-sangyō-shō* (Ministry of International Trade and Industry), ibid. P. 209.

16. Kobayashi (1967) Pp. 239–40.

17. Yamashita (1973).

BIBLIOGRAPHY

Abegglen, James C. 1971. *Business Strategies for Japan*. Tokyo: Sophia University Press.

————. 1958. *The Japanese Factory: Aspects of Its Social Organization*. Glencoe: Free Press.

Abegglen, James, and George Stalk, Jr. 1985. *Kaisha: The Japanese Corporation*. New York: Basic Books.

American Chamber of Commerce in Japan (ACCJ) and Council of the European Business Community (EBC), eds. 1987. *Direct Foreign Investment in Japan: The Challenge For Foreign Firms*. A study prepared by Booz, Allen & Hamilton Inc. Tokyo: ACCJ.

Adler, Nancy J. 1983. Cross-cultural Management Research: The Ostrich and the Trend. *Academy of Management Review* 8(2):226–32.

Adler, Nancy J., Robert Docktor, and S. Gordon Redding. 1986. From the Atlantic to the Pacific Century: Cross-cultural Management Reviewed. *Journal of Management* 12(2):295–318.

Aiken, M., and S. B. Bacharach. 1979. Culture and Organizational Structure and Process: A Comparative Study of Local Government Administrative Bureaucracies in the Wallooon and Flemish Regions of Belgium. In *Organizations Alike and Unlike*. C. J. Lammers and D. J. Hickson, eds., Pp. 215–250. London: Routledge & Kegan Paul.

Azumi, Koya, et al. 1978. Japanese Organization: Are They Really So Different? Paper presented at the Colloquium, Center for Japanese and Korean Studies, University of California, Berkeley.

Azumi, Koya, and Charles J. McMillan. 1976. Worker Sentiment in the Japanese Factory: Its Organizational Determinants. In *Japan: The Paradox of Progress*. L. Austin, ed. New Haven: Yale University Press.

Baba, Marietta L. 1986. Business and Industrial Anthropology: an Overview. *NAPA Bulletin* 2. Washington, D.C.: American Anthropological Association.

Ballon, Robert J., ed. 1985. *The Business Contract in Japan*. Sophia University Institute of Comparative Culture, Business Series No. 105. Tokyo: Sophia University Press.

———. 1971. *Japanese Market and Foreign Business*. Tokyo: Sophia University Press.

———. 1969. *Joint Ventures and Japan*. Tokyo: Sophia University Press.

———. 1966. *The Japanese Employee*. Tokyo: Sophia University Press.

Ballon, Robert, and Eugene H. Lee, eds. 1972. *Foreign Investment in Japan*. Tokyo: Sophia University Press.

Bateson, Gregory. 1979. *Mind and Nature: A Necessary Unity.* New York: Bantam Books.

———. 1974. *Steps to an Ecology of Mind*. New York: Ballantine Books.

Beck, Brenda E. F., and Larry F. Moore. 1985. Linking the Host Culture to Organizational Variables. In *Organizational Culture*. Frost et al., eds., Pp. 335–54.

Beasley, W. G. 1990. *The Rise of Modern Japan*. New York: St. Martin's Press.

Bester, Theodore. 1989. *Neighborhood Tokyo*. Stanford, Calif.: Stanford University Press.

Bergsten, C. Fred, and William R. Cline. 1985. The United States-Japan Economic Problem. *Policy Analysis in International Economics* No. 13. Washington: Institute for International Economics.

Bouchner, S., and T. Ōsako. 1977. Ethnic Role Salience in Racially Homogeneous and Heterogenous Societies. *Journal of Cross-cultural Psychology* 8:455–92.

Bouchner, S., and R. W. Perks. 1971. National Role Evocation As a Function of Cross-cultural Interaction. *Journal of Cross-cultural Psychology* 2:157–64.

Briody, Elizabeth, and Marietta L. Baba. 1987. The Repatriation Process From GM Overseas Assignments. Paper delivered at the 86th American Anthropological Association annual meeting, Boston, November 18–22.

Child, J. 1981. Culture, Contingency and Capitalism in the Cross-national Organizational Research. In *Research in Organizational Behavior* Cummings, L. L., and B. M. Staw, eds., Pp. 303–56. Greenwich, Conn.: JAI Press.

———. 1973. *Man and Organization*. N.Y.: Halsted Press.

Christopher, Robert. 1987. *Second to None: American Companies in Japan*. New York: Crown.

Clark, D. L. 1985. Emerging Paradigms in Organizational Theory and Research. In *Organizational Theory and Inquiry*. Lincoln, Yvonna. S., ed., Pp. 43–78. Beverly Hills: Sage Publications.

Clark, Rodney. 1979. *The Japanese Company.* New Haven: Yale University Press.

Cole, Robert. 1979. *Work, Mobility, and Participation: A Comparative Study of American and Japanese Industry.* Berkeley, Calif.: University of California Press.

————. 1976. Changing Labor Force Characteristics and Their Impact on Japanese Industrial Relations. In *Japan, the Paradox of Progress.* L. Austin, ed., Pp. 165–214. New Haven: Yale University Press.

————. 1972. Permanent Employment and Tradition in Japan. *Industrial and Labor Relations Review.* 26:47–70.

————. 1971. *Japanese Blue Collar: The Changing Tradition.* Berkeley: University of California Press.

Cusmano, Michael A. 1985. *The Japanese Automobile Industry.* Harvard East Asian Monographs 122. Cambridge, Mass.: Harvard University Press.

Curtis, Gerald L. 1975. Big Business and Political Influence. In *Modern Japanese Organization and Decision Making.* E. Vogel, ed., Pp. 33–70. Berkeley: University of California Press.

Daiamondo, ed. 1978. *Shachō-nenkan: Zen-jojo 1699sha shachō no sugao* (President Almanac: Personal Profiles of Presidents of 1,699 Firms on the Stock Exchanges) Tokyo: Diamondo-sha.

Daft, Richard L. 1986. *Organization Theory and Design.* New York: West.

Davis, Stanley M. 1984. *Managing Corporate Culture.* Cambridge, Mass.: Ballinger.

Davis, Allison, Burleigh B. Gardner, and Mary R. Gardner. 1941. *Deep South: A Socal-Anthropological Study of Caste and Class.* Chicago: University of Chicago Press.

Deal, Terrence E., and Allan A. Kennedy. 1982. *Corporate Cultures: The Rites and Rituals of Corporate Life*. Reading: Addison-Wesley.

Dore, Ronald. 1987. *Taking Japan Seriously: A Confucian Perspective on Leading Economic Issues*. Stanford, Calif.: Stanford University Press.

———. 1985. *Flexible Rigidities: Industrial Policy and Structural Adjustment in Japan 1970–1980*. New York: Athlone Press.

———. 1973. *British Factory – Japanese Factory: The Origins of National Diversity in Industrial Relations*. Berkeley: University of California Press.

Drake, H. Max, Roger D. Karlish and Ann M. Drake. 1985. Directory of Practicing Anthropologists. *NAPA Bulletin* 1. Washington, D.C.: American Anthropological Association.

Fairbank, John K., Edwin O. Reischauer, and Albert M. Craig. 1978. *East Asia: Tradition and Transformation*. Boston: Houghton Mifflin.

Fair Trade Commission. 1987. *Long-Term Relationships Among Japanese Companies: Report by the Study Group on Trade Frictions and Market Structure (April)*. Tokyo: Kosei-torihiki iinkai.

Flaherty, M. Therese, and Hiroyuki Itami. 1984. Finance. In *Competitive Edge: The Semiconductor Industry in the United States and Japan*. Daniel I. Okimoto et al., eds. Palo Alto: Stanford University Press.

Form, W. 1979. Comparative Industrial Sociology and the Convergence Hypothesis. *Annual Review of Sociology* 5:1–25.

Frost, Peter J., Larry F. Moore, Meryl Reis Louis, Craig C. Lundberg, and Joanne Martin, eds. 1985. *Organizational Culture*. Beverly Hills: Sage Publications.

Galbraith, Jay R. 1973. *Designing Complex Organizations.* Reading: Addison-Wesley.

Gamst, Frederick C. 1990. Industrial Ethnological Perspectives on the Development and Characteristics of the Study of Organizational Cultures. In *Cross-cultural Management and Organizational Culture,* Hamada, Tomoko and Ann Jordan, eds., Pp. 13 – 48. Williamsburg: College of William and Mary.

Geertz, Clifford. 1973. *The Interpretation of Cultures.* New York: Basic Books.

Glazer, Herbert. 1968. *The International Businessmen in Japan.* Tokyo: Sophia University Press.

Graham, John L., and Yoshihiro Sano. 1984. *Smart Bargaining: Doing Business with the Japanese.* Cambridge, Mass.: Ballinger.

Green, Robert T., and Trina L. Larsen. 1987. Only Retaliation Will Open Up Japan. *Harvard Business Review.* November-December 1987, 6:22 – 8.

Guba, Egon G. 1985. The Context of Emergent Paradigm Research. In *Organizational Theory and Inquiry.* Lincoln, Yvonna S., ed., Pp. 79 – 104. Beverly Hills: Sage Publications.

Gudykunst, William B., Lea P. Stewart, and Stella Ting-Toomey, eds. 1985. *Communication, Culture and Organizational Processes.* Beverly Hills: Sage Publications.

Halloran, Richard. 1973. *Japan: Images and Realities.* Tokyo: Charles E. Tuttle.

Hamada, Tomoko. 1989a. Anthropology and Business. In *Social Sciences and International Education.* Zamora, Mario, and Tomoko Hamada, et al. eds. Dubuque: Kendall/Hunt Publishing.

———. 1989b. Institutional Barrier to Foreign Investment in Japan. *Pacific Review* 2 (3):189–197.

———. 1988. Working with Japanese: U.S.-Japanese Joint Venture Contract. *Practicing Anthropology* 10(1):4–6.

———. 1985. Corporation, Culture and Environment: The Japanese Model. *Asian Survey* XXV 12:1214–28.

———. 1980. Winds of Change: Economic Realism and Japanese Labor Management. *Asian Survey* XX 4:397–406.

Hamada, Tomoko, and Ann Jordan. 1990. *Cross-cultural Management and Organizational Culture.* Publication Number 42, Studies in Third World Societies. Williamsburg: College of William and Mary.

Hamaguchi, Eshun. 1977. *Nihon rashisa no sai-hakken* (Rediscovery of Japaneseness). Tokyo: Nihonkeizai Shinbun-sha.

Handler, Richard. 1988. *Nationalism and the Politics of Culture in Quebec.* Madison: University of Wisconsin Press.

Harris, Philip R., and Robert T. Moran. 1987. *Managing Cultural Differences.* Houston: Gulf Publishing.

Hayes, Richard D. 1970. Behavioral Aspects of U.S. Expatriate Manager, Working Paper. Tulane: Tulane University, Graduate School of Business Administration.

Hayes, Robert H., and Steven C. Wheelwright. 1984. *Restoring Our Competitive Edge: Competing through Manufacturing.* New York: Wiley.

Hazama, Hiroshi. 1974. *Nihon-teki Keiei: Shudan-shugi no Kozai* (Japanese Style of Management: Merits and Demerits of Groupism). Tokyo: Nihon Keizai Shinbun-sha.

———. 1964. *Nihon rōmu Kanri-shi kenkyū* (Study of the History of Japanese Labor Management). Tokyo: Daiamondo-sha.

———. 1963. *Nihon-teki keiei no keifu* (Genealogy of Japanese Style of Management). Tokyo: Nihon Nooritsu Kyookai.

Henderson, Dan Fenno. 1973. *Foreign Enterprise in Japan.* Tokyo: Tuttle.

———. 1964. Contract Problems in U.S.-Japanese Joint Venture. *Washington Law Review* 39:479–83.

Hickson, D. J., C. R. Hinnings, C. J. M. McMillan, and J. P. Schwitter. 1974. The Culture-free Context of Organization Structure: A Tri-national Comparison. *Sociology* 8:59–80.

Hirschmeier, Johannes, and Tsunehiko Yui. 1981. *The Development of Japanese Business 1600–1980.* London: George Allen & Urwin.

Hofstede, Geert. 1980. *Culture's Consequences: International Differences in Work-Related Values.* Beverly Hills: Sage Publications.

Imai, Ken'ichi, and Hiroyuki Itami. 1988. Allocation of Labor and Capital in Japan and the United States. In *Inside the Japanese System.* Okimoto, Daniel and T. Rohlen, eds., Pp. 112–7. Stanford, Calif.: Stanford University Press.

Imai, Ken'ichi, and Ryūtarō Komiya, eds. 1989. *Nihon no Kigyō.* (Japanese Enterprise). Tokyo: University of Tokyo Press.

Inoguchi, Takashi, and Daniel I. Okimoto, eds. 1988. *The Political Economy of Japan, Volume 2: The Changing International Context.* Stanford, Calif.: Stanford University.

Institute for International Business Communication. 1987. *Foreign Affiliates in Japan: The Search for Professional Manpower.* Tokyo: Institute for International Business Communication (IIBC).

Iwata, Ryushi. 1978. *Gendai nihon no keiei fudo* (The Climate of Management in Contemporary Japan) Tokyo: Nihon keizai shinbun-sha.

————. 1971. *Nihonteki keiei no hensei genri* (The Organizational Principles of the Japanese Management). Tokyo: Bunshindo.

Japan Economic Journal. 1977. Japanese Managerial Practices Have Arrived At Turning Point. February 8.

————. 1968. CBS Sony Joint Venture Wins Approval. February 10.

Japan Economic Institute. 1990. Keiretsu and Other Large Corporate Groups in Japan. In *JEI Report* 2a January 12.

————. 1986a. Maekawa Commission Report Unveiled. In *JEI Report* 14b April 11. Washington, D.C.: Japan Economic Institute.

————. 1986b. Japan's Role In World Financial Markets. In *JEI Report* 42a November 14, Washington, D.C.: Japan Economic Institute.

Japan Institute for Social and Economic Affairs. 1988. *Japan 1988: An International Comparison*. Tokyo: Keizai kōhō center (Japan Institute for Social and Economic Affairs).

Japan Industrial Series. 1965. *Foreign Direct Investment*. Tokyo: Japan Industrial Series.

Japanese Government, Keizai kikaku-chō, kokumin seikatsu-kyoku (Economic Planning Agency, National Lifestyle-Bureau) ed. 1987. *Kokusai-ka to kokumin-ishiki* (Internationalization and Public Attitudes). Tokyo: Ōkura-sho Insatsu-kyoku.

Japanese Government, Rōdō-shoo (Ministry of Labor). 1978–84. *Gaishi-kei kigyo no rōmu-kanri* (Labor Management of Foreign-affiliated Companies). Tokyo: Ōkura-sho Insatsu-kyoku.

Japanese Government, Sōri-fu (Prime Minister's Office). 1977a. Gekkan yoron-chosa (Monthly Public Opinion Survey) February. 2–19. Tokyo: Sori-fu Koho-shitsu.

―――. 1977b. Seishōnen mondai chōsa hokoku-sho (Survey Report on the Problems of the Youth) Tokyo: Sori-fu Kōhō-shitsu.

Japanese Government, Tsūshō-sangyō-shō (Ministry of International Trade and Industry), ed. 1969a. Tsūsan-shō 20nen-shi (Twenty-year History of MITI). Tokyo: Ōkura-sho Insatsu-kyoku.

―――. 1969b. Tsūshō Sangyō gyōsei 4seiki han no ayumi. Tokyo: Tsūshō sangyō-shō.

Japanese Government, Tsūshō-sangyō-shō, sangyō seisaku-kyoku, kokusai kigyō-ka (Ministry of International Trade and Industry, Industrial Policy Bureau, International Enterprise Section) ed. 1977–87. Gaishikei kigyō no dōkō chosa (Survey of Foreign-affiliated Firms) Tokyo: Keibun Shuppan.

Johnson, Chalmers. 1982. MITI and the Japanese Miracle: The Growth of Industrial Policy 1925–1975. Stanford, Calif.: Stanford University Press.

―――. 1975. Japan, Who Governs? An Essay on Official Bureaucracy. Memeograph. Berkeley: University of California, Berkeley, Center for Japanese and Korean Studies.

Johnson, Chalmers, Laura D'Andrea Tyson, and John Zysman, eds. 1989. Politics and Productivity: The Real Story of Why Japan Works. Cambridge, Mass.: Ballinger.

Johnson, Richard T. 1977. Are the Japanese Managers Really Better? The Journal of the American Chamber of Commerce. February:55–7.

Johnson, Richard T., and Ouchi, William G. 1974. Made in America Under Japanese Management. Harvard Business Review 52 (5):61–9.

Jordan, Ann. 1988. The Noise in the System: The Study of Organizational Culture. Paper presented at the 87th American Anthropological Association's Annual Meeting, Phoenix, November 16–20.

Kagano, Tadao, Ikujiro Nonaka, Kiyonori Sakakibara, and Akihiro Okumura. 1984. Mechanistic Vs. Organic Management Systems: A Comparative Study of Adaptive Patterns of American and Japanese Firms. In *The Anatomy of Japanese Business*. Kozo Sato and Yasuo Hoshino, eds., Pp. 27–69. Armonk, N.Y.: M. E. Sharpe.

––––––. 1983. *Nichi-bei kigyō no keiei hikaku* (Comparison of Management between Japanese and American Enterprises). Tokyo: Nihonkeizai Shinbun-sha.

Kamata, Satoshi. 1982. *Japan in the Passing Lane: An Insider's Account of Life in a Japanese Auto Factory*. Translated and edited by Tatsuru Akimoto. New York: Pantheon Books.

Kawashima, Takeyoshi. 1971. *Ideorogi to shiteno kazoku-seido* (The Family System as an Ideology). Tokyo: Iwanami-shoten.

––––––. 1950. *Nihon shakai no kazoku-teki kōsei* (The Familistic Construction of Japanese Society). Tokyo: Nihon hyōron-sha.

Kerr, C. J., T. Dunlop, F. Harbison, and C. A. Myers. 1952. *Industrialism and Industrial Man*. Cambridge, Mass.: Harvard University Press.

Keys, J. B., and T. R. Miller. 1984. The Japanese Management Theory Jungle. *Academy of Management Review* 9:342–353.

Kobayashi, Noritake. 1967. *Nihon no gōben-gaisha* (The Joint-venture Company in Japan). Tokyo: Toyo keizai shinpo.

Koike, Kazuo. 1988. *Understanding Industrial Relations in Modern Japan*. Translated by Mary Saso. New York: St. Martin's Press.

————. 1987. Human Resource Development and Labor Management Relations. In *The Political Economy of Japan: Domestic Transformation.* Kozo Yamamura and Yasukichi Yasuba, eds., Pp. 289–330. Stanford, Calif.: Stanford University Press.

————. 1981. *Nihon no jukuren* (Skill Formation Systems in Japan). Tokyo: Yuhikaku.

Kono, Toyohiro. 1984. *Strategy and Structure of Japanese Enterprises.* Armonk, N.Y.: M. E. Sharpe.

Kroeber, A. L., and C. Kluckhohn. 1952. *Culture: A Critical Review of Concepts and Definitions.* Cambridge, Mass.: Harvard University Press.

Kumon, Shumpei. 1987. Dilemma of a New Phase: Can Japan Meet the Challenge? In *The Trade Crisis: How Will Japan Respond?* Kenneth B. Pyle, ed., Pp. 229–40. Seattle, Wash.: Society for Japanese Studies, University of Washington.

Lawrence, P. R., and J. W. Lorsch. 1967. *Organization and Environment.* Boston: Harvard University Press.

Lett, James. 1987. *The Human Enterprise: A Critical Introduction to Anthropological Theory.* Boulder: Westview Press.

Levin, Solomon, Kazuo Okochi, and Bernard Karsh, eds. 1973. *Workers and Employers in Japan: The Japanese Employment Relations System.* Princeton: Princeton University Press.

Levitt, T. 1983. The Globalization of Markets. *Harvard Business Review* 83. (3):92–102.

Likert, Rensis. 1967. *The Human Organization.* New York: McGraw Hill.

————. 1961. *New Pattern of Management.* New York: McGraw Hill.

Lincoln, James R., John Olson, and Mitsuyo Hanada. 1978. Cultural Effect on Organizational Structure: The Case of Japanese Firms in the United States. *American Sociological Review* 43:829–47.

Lincoln, Yvonna S., ed. 1985. *Organizational Theory and Inquiry: The Paradigm Revolution.* Beverly Hills: Sage Publications.

Lincoln, Yvonna and Egon G. Guba. 1985. *Naturalistic Inquiry.* Beverly Hills: Sage Publications.

Lundborg, Louis B. 1964. Direct Investment in Japan. Paper presented at the Third Japan-U.S. Businessmen's Conference in Japan. March 18–23.

Marsh, Robert M. 1988. *The Japanese Negotiator: Subtlety and Strategy Beyond Western Logic.* Tokyo: Kodansha International.

Marsh, Robert M., and Hiroshi Mannari. 1976. *Modernization and the Japanese Factory.* Princeton: Princeton University Press.

———. 1971. Lifetime Commitment in Japan: Roles, Norms and Values. *American Journal of Sociology* 76:795–812.

Marunouchi Research Center. 1977. *Nihon ni okeru gaikoku shihon no jittai* (The Real Situation of Foreign Capital in Japan). 7th edition. Tokyo: Marunouchi Research Center.

———. 1975. *Nihon ni okeru gaikoku shihon no jittai* (The Real Situation of Foreign Capital in Japan). 5th edition. Tokyo: Marunouchi Research Center.

———. 1972. *Nihon ni okeru gaikoku shihon no jittai* (The Real Situation of Foreign Capital in Japan). 3rd edition. Tokyo: Marunouchi Research Center.

Maruyama, M. 1984. Alternative Concepts of Management: Insights from Asia and Africa. *Asia Pacific Journal of Management* 1 (1):100–111.

———. 1982. New Mindscapes for Future Business Policy and Management. *Technology Forecasting and Social Change* 21:53–76.

———. 1980. Mindscapes and Science Theories. *Current Anthropology* 21, (5):389–400.

Mayo, Elton. 1945. *The Social Problem of an Industrial Civilization*. Andover, Mass.: Andover Press.

————. 1933. *The Human Problems of an Industrial Civilization*. Cambridge: Murray.

McLendon, James. 1982. The Office: Way Station or Blind Alley? In *Work and Lifecourse in Japan*. Plath, David W., ed., Pp. 156–82. Albany: State University of New York Press.

Mishler, A. L. 1965. Personal Contact in International Exchanges. In *International Behavior: A Social-psychological Analysis*. Kelman, H. C., ed., Pp. 555–561. New York: Holt, Rinehart, and Wilson.

Morgan, Gareth. 1986. *Images of Organization*. Newbury Park, Calif.: Sage Publications.

Mouer, R., and Sugimoto, Y. 1981. *Japanese Society: Reappraisals and New Directions*. Bedford Park: University of Adelaide.

Mumford, Stan Royal. 1989. *Himalayan Dialogue: Tibetan Lamas and Gurung Shamans in Nepal*. Madison: University of Wisconsin Press.

Nader, Laura. 1972. Up the Anthropologist: Perspectives from Studying Up. In *Reinventing Anthropology*. Hymes, Dell, ed., Pp. 284–309. New York: Random House.

Nakane, Chie. 1978. *Tate-shakai no riki-gaku* (Dynamics of the Vertical Society). Tokyo: Nihon keizai shinbun-sha.

————. 1971. *Japanese Society*. Berkeley: University of California Press.

Needham, Rodney. 1983. *Against the Tranquility of Axioms*. Berkeley: University of California Press.

Negandhi, A. R. 1985. Management in the Third World. In *Managing in Different Cultures*. Joynt, P. & M. Warner, eds. Pp. 69–97. Oslo, Norway: Universitetsforlaget.

————. 1979. Convergence in Organizational Practices: An Empirical Study of Industrial Enterprise in Developing Countries. In *Organizations Alike and Unlike.* Lammers, C. J., and D. J. Hickson, eds., Pp. 323–345. London: Routledge & Kegan Paul.

Neustupny, Jiri. 1987. *Communicating with the Japanese.* Tokyo: Japan Times.

Nihon bōeki shinkō-kai (Japan External Trade Relations Organization: JETRO).

————. 1988a. *Jetro-hakusho: Tōshi-hen: Sekai to nihon no kaigai chokusetsu tōshi* (JETRO White Paper: Volume on Investment: Overseas Direct Investment, the World, and Japan). Tokyo: Nihon Boeki Shinkō-kai (JETRO).

————. 1988b. *Nippon 1988: Business Facts and Figures.* Tokyo: JETRO.

Nihon keizai chōsa kyōgi-kai (Japan Economic Research Council). 1978. *Gaishi-kei kigyō jittai chōsa hokoku-sho* (Survey Report on Foreign-affiliated Firms) Tokyo: Nihon Keizai Chōsa Kyōgi-kai.

Nihon keizai shinbun (Japan Economic Journal). 1967. *Shihon-jiyū-ka to nihon keizai* (The Capital Liberalization and Japanese Economy) Tokyo: Nihon Keizai Shinbun-sha.

Nikkei bijinesu (Nikkei Business). 1976a. *Zainichi gashi: shippai no kenkyū* (Foreign Capital in Japan: Study of Failures) August 30:28–35.

————. 1976b. *Keiei dai-toku-shū* (Special Issue on Management) September 27. Special issue.

Nishiyama, Tadanori. 1984. The Structure of Managerial Control: Who Owns and Controls Japanese Businesses? In *The Anatomy of Japanese Business.* Sato, Kazuo and Yasuo Hoshino, eds., Pp. 123–63. New York: M. E. Sharpe.

———. 1980. *Shihai kōzō ron* (A Study of the Structure of Managerial Control). Tokyo: Bunshi-do.

Noda, Kazuo. 1975. Big Business Organization. In *Modern Japanese Organization and Decision Making*. Vogel, Ezra, ed., Pp. 115–45. Berkeley: University of California Press.

———. 1973. Traditionalism in Japanese Management. *Ōyō shakaigaku hyōron* 6:127–70.

Noguchi, Paul. 1982. Shiranai Station: Not a Destination But a Journey. In *Work and Lifecourse in Japan*. Plath, David, ed., Pp. 74–96. Albany: State University of New York Press.

OECD (Organization for Economic Cooperation and Development). 1971. *Japan: OECD Economic Survey*. Paris: OECD.

———. 1968. *Liberalization of International Capital Movements: Japan*. Paris: OECD.

Ojile, Constance S. 1986. Intercultural Training: An Overview of the Benefits for Business and the Anthropologist's Emerging Role. In *Anthropology and International Business*. Serrie, Hendrick, ed., Pp. 35–52. Williamsburg: College of William and Mary.

Okimoto, Daniel I. 1989. *Between MITI and the Market: Japanese Industrial Policy for High Technology*. Stanford, Calif.: Stanford University Press.

Okimoto, Daniel I., and Thomas P. Rohlen, eds. 1988. *Inside the Japanese System: Readings on Contemporary Society and Political Economy*. Stanford, Calif.: Stanford University Press.

Okimoto, Daniel I., Takuo Sugano and Franklin B. Weinstein, eds. 1984. *Competitive Edge: The Semiconductor Industry in the US and Japan*. Stanford, Calif.: Stanford University Press.

Okimoto, Daniel I., ed. 1982. *Japan's Economy: Coping with Change in the International Environment*. Boulder, Colo.: Westview Press.

Okumura, Hiroshi. 1983. The Closed Nature of Japanese Inter-corporate Relations. *Japan Echo* 9(3):59–61.

———. 1981a. *Mitsubishi: Nihon o ugokasu kigyō-shūdan* (Mitsubishi: An Enterprise Group That Moves Japan). Tokyo: Diamond Publishing.

———. 1981b. Interfirm Relations in an Enterprise Group: The Case of Mitsubishi. In *The Anatomy of Japanese Business*. Sato, Kazuo, and Yasuo Hoshino, eds., Pp. 164–193. Armonk, N.Y.: M. E. Sharpe.

———. 1969. *Gaikoku-shihon* (Foreign Capital) Tokyo: Tōyō Keizai-sha.

Olie, Rene. 1990. Cultural Factors and the Success or Failure of Transnational Business Ventures: the Case of German-Dutch Cooperation. In *Cross-cultural Management and Organizational Culture*. Tomoko Hamada and Ann Jordan, eds., Pp. 145–72. Williamsburg: College of William and Mary.

Onozawa, Jun. 1982. Past, Present and Future of Foreign Companies in Japan. In *Breaking the Barriers: True Accounts of Overseas Companies in Japan*. Sadamoto Kuni, ed. Tokyo: Survey Japan.

Ott, J. Steven. 1989. *The Organizational Culture Perspective*. Chicago: Richard Irwin.

Otterbeck, Lars. 1985. Joint International Business Ventures: Their Motives and Their Management. In *Japan's Emerging Multinationals: An International Comparison of Policies and Practices*. Takamiya, Susumu and Keith Thurley, eds., Pp. 49–57. Tokyo: University of Tokyo Press.

Ouchi, William. 1981. *Theory Z*. New York: Addison Wesly.

Pascale, Richard T., and A. G. Athos. 1981. *The Art of Japanese Management*. New York: Simon and Schuster.

Perrow, Charles. 1982. Disintegrating Social Sciences. *Phi Delta Kappan* 63:684–88.

———. 1970. *Organizational Analysis: A Sociological View.* Roberts, B. C., ed. Belmot, Calif.: Wadsworth.

———. 1968. The Effect of Technological Change on the Structures of Business Firms. In *Industrial Relations: Contemporary Issue.*

Peters, Thomas J., and Robert H. Waterman. 1983. *In Search of Excellence.* New York: Warner Books.

Pfeffer, Jeffrey. 1981. *Power in Organizations.* Marshfield, Mass.: Pitman Press.

Plath, David, ed. 1983. *Work and Lifecourse in Japan.* Albany: State University of New York Press.

Pondy, L., P. Frost, G. Morgan, and T. Dandridge, eds. 1983. *Organizational Symbolism.* Greenwich, Conn.: JAI Press.

Pucik, Vladimir. 1988. Strategic Alliances with the Japanese: Implications for Human Resource Management. In *Cooperative Strategies in International Business.* Contractor, F. J., and P. Lorange, eds. Lexington, Mass.: Lexington Books.

———. 1987. Joint Ventures as a Strategy for Competition. In *The Japanese Competition: Phase 2*, Pp. 47–55. Ann Arbor: University of Michigan, Center for Japanese Studies.

Putnam, L., and M. Pacanowsky, eds. 1983. *Communication and Organizations: An Interpretive Approach.* Beverly Hills: Sage Publications.

Pyle, Kenneth B., ed. 1987. *The Trade Crisis: How Will Japan Respond?* Seattle, Wash.: Society for Japanese Studies, University of Washington.

Rabinow, Paul and William M. Sullivan, eds. 1987. *Interpretive Social Science: A Second Look.* Berkeley: University of California Press.

Richardson, F. L. W. 1979. Social Interaction and Industrial Productivity. In *The Uses of Anthropology. A Special Publication of the American Anthropological Association 11.* Goldschmidt, Walter, ed., Pp. 79–99. Washington, D.C.: American Anthropological Association.

Roethlisberger, F. J. and William J. Dickson. 1939. *Management and the Worker.* Cambridge, Mass.: Harvard University Press.

Rohlen, Thomas. 1974. *For Harmony and Strength: Japanese White-Collar Organization in Anthropological Perspective.* Berkeley: University of California Press.

Sadamoto, Kuni, ed. 1982. *Breaking the Barriers: True Accounts of Overseas Companies in Japan.* Tokyo: Survey Japan.

Sanwa Sōgō Kenkyū-sho. 1988. *Nihon-kigyō wa gaishi-kigyō o dō miteiruka* (How Japanese Enterprises View Foreign-affiliated Enterprises). In the 1987 MITI Investigation Program: Study on International Cooperation by Japanese Economy and Society: Investigation on Current Situation for Promoting Foreign Direct Investments in Japan. Tokyo: Sanwa Sōgō kenkyū-sho.

Sathe, Vijay. 1985. *Culture and Related Corporate Realities.* Homewood, Ill.: Richard D. Irwin.

Sato, Kazuo and Yasuo Hoshino, eds. 1984. *The Anatomy of Japanese Business.* Armonk, N.Y.: M. E. Sharpe.

Schein, Edgar H. 1987. *Organizational Culture and Leadership.* San Francisco: Jossy-Bass.

Schon, Donald A. 1987. The Art of Managing: Reflection-in-Action within an Organizational Learning System. In *Interpretative Social Science: A Second Look.* Rabinow, Paul and W. Sullivan, eds., 302–326. Berkeley: University of California Press.

———. 1983. *The Reflective Practitioner: How Professionals Think in Action.* New York: Basic Books.

Servan-Schreiber, Jean-Jacques. 1969. *The American Challenge.* New York: Atheneum.

Seward, Jack and Howard Van Zandt. 1985. *Japan: The Hungry Guest: Japanese Business Ethics vs. Those of the U.S.* Tokyo: Yohan Publishing Co.

Shishido, Zenichi. 1986. *Kokusai-teki jointo-bencha no sho-mondai* (Various Problems of International Joint Ventures). NIRA Series 15. Tokyo: National Institute for Research Advancement.

Smircich, Linda. 1983. Concepts of Culture and Organizational Analysis. *Administrative Science Quarterly,* 28:339–58.

———. 1983a. Studying Organizations as Cultures. In *Beyond Method: Strategies for Social Research.* G. Morgan, ed., Pp. 160–72. Beverly Hills: Sage Publications.

Smith, Robert. 1983. Japanese Society: Tradition, Self, and the Social Order. New York: Cambridge University Press.

Swedenborg, Emmanuel. 1955. "Correspondences and Representations." *Psychological Transactions* 13:215–61.

Taira, Koji. 1970. *Economic Development and the Labor Market in Japan.* New York: Columbia University Press.

Takamiya, Susumu, and Keith Thurley, eds. 1985. *Japan's Emerging Multinationals: An International Comparison of Policies and Practices.* Tokyo: University of Tokyo Press.

Terpstra, Vern, and Kenneth David. 1985. *The Cultural Environment of International Business.* Cincinnati: South-western.

Thian, Helene. 1988. *Setting Up and Operating a Business in Japan.* Tokyo: Charles E. Tuttle.

Tolchin, Martin, and Susan Tolchin. 1988. *Buying into America: How Foreign Money is Changing the Face of Our Nation.* New York: Times Books.

Tōyō keizai. 1990. Kigyō keiretsu sōran (Overview of Enterprise Affiliation). Tokyo: Tōyō Keizai Shinpō-sha.

Trevor, Malcom. 1985. *Japanese Industrial Knowledge: Can It Help British Industry?* Aldershot, Hamshire, England: Gower.

————. 1983. *Japan's Reluctant Multinationals: Japanese Management at Home and Abroad.* New York: St. Martin's Press.

Tsudo, Masumi. 1977. *Nihon-teki keiei no ronri* (Principles of the Japanese-Style Management). Tokyo: Chuo keizai-sha.

————. 1973. *Shudan-shugi keiei no koso* (Designing of Management Based on Groupism). Tokyo: Toyo keizai shinpo-sha.

Tsurumi, Yoshi. 1976. *The Japanese Are Coming.* Cambridge, Mass.: Ballinger.

Tung, Rosalie. 1984. *Business Negotiations with the Japanese.* Lexington, Mass.: D. C. Heath.

Upham, Frank K. 1981. Law in Japan. In *Business and Society in Japan.* Richardson, Bradley and Taizo Ueda, eds., Pp. 141–68. New York: Praeger.

Van Maanen, John. 1979. The Fact of Fiction in Organizational Ethnography. *Administrative Science Quarterly* 24:539–50.

Van Maanen, John, and Barley, Stephan. 1985. Cultural Organization: Fragments of a Theory. In *Organizational Culture.* Frost, Peter et al., eds., Pp. 143–89. Beverly Hills: Sage Publications.

Van Willigen, John. 1987. *Becoming a Practicing Anthropologist: A Guide to Careers and Training Programs in Applied Anthropology.* Napa Bulletin 3. Washington, D.C.: American Anthropological Association.

Vogel, Ezra, ed. 1975. *Modern Japanese Organization and Decision Making.* Berkeley: University of California Press.

———. 1963. *Japan's New Middle Class: The Salary Man and His Family in a Tokyo Suburb*. Berkeley: University of California Press.

Walck, Christa L. 1990. A Call for Collaboration Between Business and Anthropology. In *Cross-cultural Management and Organizational Culture*. Hamada, Tomoko and Ann Jordan, eds.,Pp. 49 – 76. Williamsburg: College of William and Mary.

Warner, W. L. 1941 – 1949. *Yankee City Series*. New Haven: Yale University Press.

Weber, Max. 1968. *Economy and Society: An Outline of Interpretive Sociology*. New York: Bedminster.

———. 1961. *General Economic History*. New York: Collier.

———. 1958. *The Protestant Ethic and the Spirit of Capitalism*. New York: Scribners.

———. 1947a. *The Theory of Social and Economic Organization*. London: Oxford University Press.

———. 1947b. *The Methodology of the Social Sciences*. New York: Free Press.

Wilkins, Alan. 1983. The Culture Audit: A Tool for Understanding Organizations. *Organizational Dynamics* 12:24–38.

Wilkins, Alan, and William G. Ouchi. 1983. Efficient Cultures: Exploring the Relationship Between Culture and Organizational Performance. *Administrative Science Quarterly* 28:468–81.

Woodward, Joan. 1965. *Industrial Organization: Theory and Practice*. London: Oxford University Press.

Yamada, Makiko. 1976. *Amerika no bijinesu elīto* (The American Business Elite). Tokyo: Nihon keizai shinbun-sha.

Yamashita, H. 1973. *Jiyūka ni mukete* (Towards Liberalization). *Asahi Shimbun* April 15.

Yamamura, Kozo, and Yasukichi Yasuba, eds. 1987. *The Political Economy of Japan Volume One: The Domestic Transformation.* Stanford, Calif.: Stanford University Press.

Yoshino, Michael Y. 1976. *Japan's Multinational Enterprises.* Cambridge: Harvard University Press.

————. 1968. *Japan's Managerial System, Tradition and Innovation.* Cambridge: M.I.T. Press.

Yoshino, Michael Y., and Thomas B. Lifson. 1986. *The Invisible Link: Japan's Sogo Shosha and the Organization of Trade.* Cambridge, Mass.: MIT Press.

Zimmerman, Mark. 1985. *How to Do Business with the Japanese.* New York: Random House.

MAJOR PLAYERS IN THE JOINT VENTURE, NIPPON UNITED

Americans

Franklin—President of United Asia. Franklin later became President of United Europe, while O'Leary became President of United Asia. Franklin finally succeeded Murray and became President of United America International.

Gilbert — Head of the Philippine Operation of United America International, who succeeded Martin and became General Manager and President of the Japan Office (United Japan) of United America International. He later resigned from the company.

Hart—the first General Manager and President of United Japan. Hart was replaced by Martin. He resigned from the company.

Herb—Corporate Vice President of United America under President Lang. Herb succeeded Lang and became President of United America.

Lang—President of United America, who encouraged corporate expansion into Asia. Lang was succeeded by Herb.

Martin — He succeeded Hart and became General Manager and President of United Japan, Vice President of United Asia, and Vice President of Nippon United. Martin was succeeded by Gilbert.

Murray — President of United America International, later Corporate Vice President, and Corporate Vice Chairman. Murray retired at the same time Lang retired. Murray was succeeded by Franklin.

Nicholson—President of the Chemical Division (United Chemical), who headed the Hammond Plant, U.S.A.

O'Leary — President of United Europe. O'Leary became President of United Asia while Franklin became President of United Europe.

Weaver — Technical Manager of United Chemical at Hammond, U.S.A. He visited Kamiyama for solving technology problems.

Saymour—Marketing Manager of United America International. Saymour moved to United Europe when Franklin became President of United Europe. Saymour resigned from the company.

Japanese Managers of United America

Ōbayashi — Manager of Kakubeni Trading Company, who later became the first representative of United America in Japan. After Hart opened the Japan office, Ōbayashi became Vice President of United Japan. Ōbayashi resigned from the company.

Ōta — Japanese Controller of United Japan, hired by Martin. Ōta became Board Director of Nippon United. He resigned from the company.

Japanese Managers of Nippon Kaisha/Nippon United

Aono—engineer of Nippon Kaisha, who later became Chief Engineer of the Kamiyama plant of Nippon United and Section Chief of Nippon United. Aono worked with Mochida in solving quality problems.

Higashi—Personnel Manager of the Kamiyama plant of Nippon Kaisha. Higashi succeeded Yamashita and became Director of Personnel of Nippon Kaisha.

Hosono — Director of the Chemical Division of Nippon Kaisha, and Board Director of Nippon United.

Imai—Section Chief of the Overseas Division of Nippon Kaisha, who served as an interpreter for meetings.

Kaji — Salesman of Nippon Kaisha, who later became salesman of Nippon United.

Kawamura—Sales Manager of Nippon Kaisha, who later became Marketing Manager of Nippon United.

Kihara — Manager of the Kamiyama Plant, who became the first Plant Manager of the Kamiyama Plant of Nippon United. Kihara was replaced by Mochida.

Kitazawa — Senior Manager of Nippon Kaisha. Kitazawa succeeded Mochida and became President of Nippon United.

Kubo — President of Nippon Kaisha.

Mochida — Plant Manager of a subsidiary of Nippon Kaisha, who succeeded Kihara and became Plant Manager of the Kamiyama Plant of Nippon United. Mochida became General Manager and President of Nippon United after having solved technical problems. Mochida was replaced by Kitazawa.

Shimada — Senior Director of Nippon Kaisha, who became the first (part-time) President of Nippon United.

Yamagi — Senior Director of Nippon Kaisha, and Board Director of Nippon United.

Yamashita — Director of the Personnel Division of Nippon Kaisha. Yamashita retired and was succeeded by Higashi.

INDEX